The Swahili Novel

The Swahili Novel
Challenging the Idea of 'Minor Literature'

Xavier Garnier

JAMES CURREY

James Currey
is an imprint of Boydell & Brewer Ltd
PO Box 9, Woodbridge,
Suffolk IP12 3DF (GB)
www.jamescurrey.com

and of Boydell & Brewer Inc.
668 Mt Hope Avenue
Rochester, NY 14620-2731 (US)
www.boydellandbrewer.com

The right of Xavier Garnier to be identified as
the author of this work has been asserted in accordance with
sections 77 and 78 of the Copyright, Designs and Patents Act 1988

Copyright © Xavier Garnier 2013
1 2 3 4 5 17 16 15 14 13

All rights reserved. Except as permitted under current legislation no part of this work may be photocopied, stored in a retrieval system, published, performed in public, adapted, broadcast, transmitted, recorded or reproduced in any form or by any means, without the prior permission of the copyright owner.

Translated by Rémi Tchokothe Armand and Frances Kennett from the French edition. First published as *Le roman swahili: la notion de 'littérature mineure' à l'épreuve* (Éditions Karthala: Paris, 2006)

British Library Cataloguing in Publication Data
A catalogue record for this book is available
on request from the British Library

ISBN 978-1-84701-079-7 James Currey (Cloth)

The publisher has no responsibility for the continued existence or accuracy of URLs for external or third-party internet websites referred to in this book, and does not guarantee that any content on such websites is, or will remain, accurate or appropriate.

Contents

	Introduction	1
1	Narrating Values *Describing a World*	19
2	Shaaban Robert *The Optimism of Writing*	47
3	The Crisis of the Bildungsroman	63
4	Euphrase Kezilahabi *An Initiatory Realism*	78
5	The Political Novel	95
6	Mohamed Suleiman Mohamed *Narrating a Dual Reality*	115
7	The Criminals & the Corrupted	127
8	Investigations & Enigmas	142
9	Said Ahmed Mohamed *The Dark Side of Images*	163
	Conclusion	178
	Bibliography *Index*	182 193

Introduction

The emergence of prose fiction in the age-old Swahili literature provided the opportunity for a new evaluation of literature's political function. The experimentation with novel forms is closely tied to the political adventure in which East Africa and particularly Tanzania was involved in the mid-twentieth century. In this book, I would like to draw attention to the nature of this link between literature and politics in the making of Swahili literature with an emphasis on the novel.

A characteristic of the substantial amount of work on the Swahili novel is that it focuses on political questions, exclusively the socio-cultural dimension. The novel has often been analysed as a means of interrogating the cultural conditioning of classical Swahili literature. In 1973, many relevant articles were published in the journal *Kiswahili*. They stressed the need to take a new critical approach to Swahili literature which, until then, had been regarded as no more than the cultural embodiment of an hypothetical vision of the Swahili world. The aim of these articles was to respond to an ethnographic tradition inspired by colonization and to propose a socio-historical reading of literature, notably classical poetry.

All these young critics had taken note of the need to alter the perception of modern Swahili literature as one confined to the coastal cultures that are presented as the cradle of Swahili civilization. This enquiry will emphasize the historical and social nature of the literature, not merely its cultural aspect. Works of the early Swahili novelists will be studied from this new critical perspective. Arnold (1973) and Kezilahabi (1976) suggest a socio-political reading of Shaaban Robert's novels. Ohly (1981) made a synthesis of the evolution of the novel in the 1970s through the socio-historical context of Tanzanian society. The title of his essay, *Aggressive Prose*, embodied the idea of a literature of agency in a precise historical context.

Madumulla studied the growth of novels in relation to social growth through the decades. The novel will be considered as the literary form *par excellence*, revealing both its social and historical contexts. In particular the novel can be a powerful tool for revealing the progress of politics. The exclusion from the histories of Swahili literature of the first Swahili novel *Uhuru wa watumwa* [1934] (*The freeing of slaves*) by James Mbotela is due to its explicit support for the colonialist project.

While a political reading may have been imposed at times on Swahili poetry, its application to the novel was instantly recognized, although cultural questions were not completely forgotten. Rather, they were examined from the perspective of their social and historical conditioning. In this alternative critique between a literature that would be the expression of a Swahili culture and a literature that would express the historical and social conditions, the link between literature and politics is anyway indirect. From the 'classical' perspective, what is political is linked to literature given that both politics and literature are a manifestation of Swahili culture. From the 'modernist' perspective, the novel serves politics. The novel is used for political purposes, which is not to say that the novel is necessarily of a political nature.

I will attempt a new political reading of the development of the Swahili novel over more than half a century by building on the propositions of 'minor literature' that Gilles Deleuze and Félix Guattari (1975) used in their critiques of Franz Kafka's works. There is a link between certain uses of language that characterize 'minor' writers and that reveal the political nature of their writing. Given that Kafka 'makes a minor usage of a major language', according to Deleuze and Guattari, he is involved in a literary practice that is at the heart of literary creativity. Thus the essence of this minor literature is its politics. It is important to understand that to a 'minor literature', what is political has to be redefined on the one hand in relation to the language and the culture and on the other hand in relation to the historical and the social situation. In a way Deleuze and Guattari make comparisons between three constraints of 'minor literature', namely deterritorialization, the collective dimension and the political one.

The concept of deterritorialization will be useful for reevaluating the linkage between literature and language/culture. Similarly, the concept of the collective may be interrogated through a social awareness; a connection to people's lives is essential for the creation of a political literature. Language, society and life correspond to these three levels of the definition of literature given by Swahili critics, with the image of the mirror (*kioo*) implicit in each level of definition.

A word from Arabic (*fasihi*) was chosen to refer to literature, taking into account its original sense of elegance and formal beauty, which gives priority to the link to language. The literary journal of Dar es Salaam University students in the 1970s was called *Kioo cha lugha* (*The language mirror*). This name worked as the first level of definition of literature. As previously noted, novel writing is not primarily concerned with this definition of literature that was implicitly the conception of German and Anglo-Saxon scholars who worked on ancient manuscripts and made classical Swahili literature known in Europe. Linguists and anthropologists searched these texts for knowledge about Swahili language and civilization. Their culturalist approach has in a marginal sense contributed to a perspective from which one can read modern literature.

A second definition of literature is that of the mirror of the society (*Kioo cha jamii*). Beginning with the 1960s this definition will generally apply to creative fiction:

> To writers, the desire to shape a new society cannot be separated from displaying [the] problems faced by their societies. Because literature is like a mirror, the novel is like our reflection or our image in that mirror. (Mlacha, 1984: 4)[1]

Here, one recognizes the socio-critical approach to the study of the novel that has been largely dominant in East Africa. Literature is considered as inscribed in a social project. Literature exists at a macropolitical level.

Finally, a third level of definition widens the metaphor of the mirror to the mirror of life (*Kioo cha maisha*):

---

[1] *Hamu ya waandishi ni kuiumba jamii mpya, kufuatana na jinsi wanavyoyaona matatizo ambayo yanazikabili jamii zao. Kwa vile fasihi ni kama kioo na riwaya kama vivuli au picha yetu kwenye kioo kicho* [...]

Literature studies mankind. It throws lights on human life. This is why some people call it the mirror of life: a mirror that human beings can use to watch their progress in daily life and maybe to improve themselves [...]. Literature is not simply a language ornament, it is an important tool used by a human being to speak to another human being. (Ramadhani, 1972:7)[2]

Such a definition is not a plain extension of the former definition. It requires an important qualitative leap that brings about a complete reassessment of literature. Literature will then be found at a micropolitical level.

Despite their wide divergences, all these parallel definitions of literature make use of the central metaphor of the mirror (*kioo*). It seems to me that there is a misunderstanding in interpreting the image of the mirror as a requirement for realism. I have not found the expression 'mirror of reality' (*kioo cha uhalisi*) anywhere, in the sense of a mere 'representation of reality'. All these definitions of literature have no bearing on representation. I will attempt to show that the mirror is not used for representing but for *revealing*. The goal of literature is to reveal a language, a society or to reveal life. Revealing is completely different from representing. At no point in its development has the Swahili novel given up the ambition to reveal a truth to the world. This demanding quest for a truth is the best recommendation of this literature which is of a deeply political nature.

Developing the language: '*Kioo cha lugha*'

Writing in Kiswahili did not happen by chance. Modern Swahili literature emerged and developed in the context of a great project on language normalization. Classical poets used to write in a dialect that reflected their attachment to either Lamu, Mombasa or Tanga. Writers of the modern period are writing from a base of standardized Swahili – the Zanzibar

---

[2] *Fasihi ni somo juu ya ubinadamu kwa darubini binadamu katika maisha. Hii ndiyo sababu wengine wameiita fasihi kioo cha maisha. Kioo ambacho binadamu anaweza kukitumia kwa kujitazama katika maisha ya kila siku na labda akajirekebisha [...]. Fasihi si jambo la lugha tu, bali ni chombo muhimu kinachotumiwa na binadamu mmoja kusema na binadamu mwingine.*

dialect that was chosen during colonial times as the vehicle for a '"modern" language'. The work undertaken by the East African Swahili Committee since its creation in 1930 is impressive (Whiteley, 1969). It is noteworthy that Africans were admitted to this committee only in 1959, that is, on the eve of independence. The standardization of Kiswahili was a colonial issue. The link between written Kiswahili and the British presence in East Africa has been evident since 1923 with the launch of the monthly periodical *Mambo Leo* that was clearly tinged by colonialism. Kiswahili is undeniably an African language but its development owes much to the colonial adventure. At the risk of offending some readers, one may even say that Kiswahili is a bit English at least as far as its standard version is concerned. Noor Shariff puts it quite sharply in the following statement:

> In the area of language and literary study, it would be accurate to say that the European colonial administrators and educators *invented* a new language and a literature, for what came to be taught in the colonial classroom was neither the traditional literature of the Swahili people nor the literature *written* by the Swahili themselves outside the narrow social perimeters of the missionary educators. (Shariff 1991, 40)

The Swahili novel is specific in that it is written in a language whose status as a major one was not quite confirmed at the time of its birth. The 'Standard Kiswahili' that was shaped during the colonial period was still a very formal material that did not have the cultural weight of the German language in the time of Kafka. Deterritorialising Kiswahili would become a natural trend to Kiswahili writers composing in a language that state institutions had not yet had the time to set in stone. From the end of the nineteenth century until the middle of the twentieth, a major concern for people promoting Kiswahili was to build a corpus of prose works. In this regard, many anthologies were compiled relying on texts illustrating and embodying Kiswahili as a described language ready for use. This production of these anthologies was undertaken by European linguists and ethnographers.

In an article on 'the development of the Swahili language' published in the journal *Africa* in 1930 (the year in which the

East African Swahili Committee was launched), Gerald W. Broomfield first insisted on the need for European assistance in developing Kiswahili. Later on, he concluded that

> In the course of time the part of the European will be complete. Africans will have reached a far higher standard of education than is possible at present. They will become conscious of their own creative gifts, and will realize that their own language, developed and enriched concurrently with their intellectual advance, is the one medium of expression of the special genius of their race. (Broomfield 1930: 522)

Such rhetoric was usual during those years that witnessed the birth of modern Swahili literature. The committee came up with a language that a brilliant African intellectual called Shaaban Robert would later bring home. Literature is grounded on strong linguistic foundations. Literature implies a great talent, and optimism is mandatory to literature. This is how Jay Kitsao comments on Shaaban Robert's fictional works that he regards as the real starting point of Swahili fiction writing:

> It is to be noted that Shaaban Robert, unequivocally the pioneer of modern 20th century Swahili literary *riwaya* texts, invariably concerns himself with teaching and developing the language as well as preaching what he considers to be the ideal human qualities. (Kitsao, 1982: 106-7)

A language to praise goodness, a balanced language to express the longing for a harmonious society. This was to Kitsao the optimistic ideal that preceded the birth of the Swahili novel. As mentioned above, the word *fasihi* means 'speaking well' and verbal elegance. What characterizes a literary work is the beauty of a language whose proper use has been determined by linguists. Associating elegance with factual issues is thus the agenda of this modern literature that dreams of imposing itself as a major literature.

With independence, things moved on as writers from the interior like Mhina, Kezilahabi and Ruhumbika started publishing. Leaving fixed ideas behind, they got hold of the Kiswahili that had meticulously been prepared for them. Testimony to this open attitude to Kiswahili is the confrontation between the then young writer George Mhina and the British scholar Lyndon Harries in the 1960s. In 1966, Mhina published a short narration with the title 'Safari ya Ndoa Saba' (The journey of seven weddings) in the journal *Swahili*. The introduction strongly indicates the linguistic consciousness of Swahili writers: 'I had decided to attempt writing something in Kiswahili. I was asking myself what I could in fact write about' (Mhina, 1966: 15).

The will to point up a language and to give it a literary corpus was the major concern of the first Swahili writers of the modern period. A year after the publication of Mhina's narrative, a very harsh article by Lyndon Harries was published in the same journal. Lyndon Harries accused Mhina of damaging Kiswahili and of not respecting the purity of the language nor the rules of a beautiful style. Harries immediately called for a body to control Kiswahili as had existed during colonial times: 'There is a great need in East Africa today for some authoritative body, amply financed, to direct the development of Swahili usage especially with reference to the use of good style' (Harries 1967: 48).

Harries was worried about a stylistic drift in Kiswahili. Syntactic norms are however, clearly set. Lexical creation is well controlled but nothing stops writers from mistreating the language in their works. Quoting some sentences from Mhina's narrative, Harries shows how things could have been said in an easier and 'purer' manner. The Kiswahili stylistic ideal is one of simplicity. Shaaban Robert is considered a great Swahili writer by members of the East African Swahili Committee essentially because of stylistic criteria : his expression is direct and economical.

George Mhina is neither impressed by the scientific authority nor by the dogmatic attitude of Lyndon Harries. He answered Harries in the same year in the second issue of the journal:

> Languages are not static, and the people engaged in working in the language today are more interested in exploring new fields which were neglected in the past by the few who considered themselves skilled in linguistic oversight. (Mhina, 1967: 189)

Mhina's primary statement on the non-static nature of language repeats a point of view long present in the debate on Kiswahili, especially since independence. Kiswahili's instability cannot be separated from the modernity that is claimed for it. Harries himself opens the debate on this basis:

> With the present fluidity of Swahili, some African writers experiment with it even though it is a second language for them. They strive to use the language in what they believe to be a true Swahili style, even though they may have no direct or in-depth experience of coastal Swahili. (Harries, 1967: 47)

The initial ambition of the East African Swahili Committee to establish a 'major' language had to face a social reality that had made this language the common good of a people. What Kafka said about Yiddish can hold for Kiswahili: 'It has no grammar. Non-professionals try to write a grammar of the language but Yiddish is constantly spoken: it does not rest. People do not abandon it to grammarians.'

While linguists and grammarians tried to forge a new language and to stabilize it, while taking into account the regional geo-political project, the language went its own way in the social world, especially via borrowings from all over the place. There is a permanent rivalry between the Swahili recognized as the official language, (*kiswahili safi*) and the everyday language that is still recognized as deviant. 'Correct' Swahili is standard form which is ignored in practice. Peoples and writers do not allow Swahili to be left to the grammarians. The awesome propensity of Kiswahili to borrow words from wherever it can is a feature of all languages that have spread world-wide. Kiswahili is predatory. It has words from all parts of the world: Persian, Arabic, western languages and of course from the many Bantu languages it has come in contact with. Once more, what Kafka said of Yiddish fits perfectly with Kiswahili: 'It is made only of foreign words but these words are not static at the heart of it. They hold on to the vivacity and speed with which they were taken up. Yiddish is shot through from top to bottom with the migrations of many peoples [1912].' For Deleuze and Guattari, these are the characteristics of a de-territorialized language: its vocabulary is not from within but from outside, and thus filled with intensity. Swahili words are unruly. As paradoxical as it may seem, Swahili seems to have been unstable, in constant evolution, ever since its standardization. This image of a fluid and shifting language will direct the course that modern Swahili literature takes. This is why stylistic questions will become crucial; and why such questions reveal the political issues behind the constitution of a national language, even of a sub-continental language. A dissertation in French (Kanyarugika 1975) addressed Kezilahabi's works entirely from the perspective of language politics. The instability of Kiswahili is connected to the sociopolitical instability of Eastern Africa. Shaaban Robert, writing between the 1940s and 50s, could still dissociate style from politics. His ambition was to establish a style of prose writing that could serve as the matrix for future literature. His concern was literary in nature, although this did not stop him from dealing with political issues in his texts. However, these issues were subordinated to his literary concerns.

Harries' reaction to Mhina's first text reveals that this sudden appearance of writers from the interior did not occur without some hard feelings. The idea that one could do whatever one fancied with the language that the committee had refined during more than thirty years was intolerable. Style had to be controlled to keep the brand-new integrity of Kiswahili and to ensure its effective diffusion in the sociopolitical sphere. In the 1960s there was a surge in associations for the promotion and control of Kiswahili.[3] Without doubt the most active was surely the *Baraza la Kiswahili la Taifa* (BAKITA/ The National Swahili Council) that launched the journal *Lugha yetu*. The mission of this state organization was 'to encourage the achievement of high standards in the use of Swahili language and to discourage its misuse' (Mbatiah, 1999a: 61). At that period, it was evident that literary issues were connected to political issues via the language question. Thus, style found itself at the crossroads of where literary, linguistic and political issues meet.

---

[3] Besides *Taasisi ya Uchunguzi wa Kiswahili* (Institute of Kiswahili Research), the new name for the East African Swahili Committee, one can mention the *Jumuiya ya Kustawisha Kiswahili* (The Association for the Advancement of Swahili) founded in 1963; and the *Chama cha Usanifu waKiswahili na Ushairi Tanzania* (The Tanzanian Association for Swahili Art and Poetry) led by the poet Mathias Mnyampala.

Taking the wraps off the society: 'Kioo cha jamii'

The sudden appearance of prose fiction in Swahili brought a literature that led to a new reading assessment of the notion of *fasihi*. The question of its relationship to the society became the literary issue *par excellence*. The debate on language then plays a secondary role, and will be overtaken by an explicitly political debate on the relationship between the novel and the society: will the novel say what the situation is, or what it should be? Between the 1960s and the 1980s writers seemed to be more interested in political issues than in stylistic considerations. Literature was widely perceived as the mirror of the society; which is understandable at a period when Marxist criticism largely dominated the African continent.

In 1973, several articles on the role of the literary critic were published in the Swahili student review journal at the University of Dar es Salaam: *Kioo cha lugha*. The following remark typifies the general tone in these articles: 'the literary critic teaches the society how to look at writers' works and how to benefit from them' (Senkoro 1973: 5). The main goal of criticism is to explain the necessary link between a literary work and the social field. In 1978 a revealing article by A. G. Gibbe on the role of the literary critic was published in the journal *Mulika*. It takes note of the essential relationship between the writer and the society from which he/she originates and about which he/she writes. The critic's role lies somewhere else: as the ideological guardian of literature. The critic must assess writers and estimate their value following ideological criteria that determine what is useful for the society: 'The literary critic ought to unmask writers who spread bad ideas in order to stop them from contaminating the society. The critic must unmask and make public any dangerous ideas that a writer has spread, intentionally or not' (Gibbe, 1978: 4).

This critical activity provides a sociopolitical reading of fiction. The critic's job is to indicate what is good and what should be improved in each novel. Thus, works by Mhina, Kezilahabi, Mung'ong'o, Said Ahmed Mohamed could not ignore the *Ujamaa* project of restructuring the society, and they have brought many debates to the literature on the role of women, education, solidarity in urban or rural settings, and so on. The publication of every novel is followed by a refreshing of the social debate. One could define the genre of fiction according to its success in contributing to social debate. Thus, writers from the Islands, such as Shafi Adam Shafi, Said Ahmed Mohamed or Mohamed Suleiman from Zanzibar wrote in the wake spirit of the violent revolution of 1964, and were obsessed by the possibility of a radical overthrow of social hierarchies (Njogu 1997). These are some social issues that take us away from the linguistic considerations that were our starting point. The critic pays attention to formal and stylistic aspects only in the sense that they can help convey the ideological message.

In the 1990s the journal *Kiswahili* featured a discussion on a famous novel by Said Ahmed Mohamed entitled *Dunia Mti Mkavu*. This novel touched on the General Strike in Zanzibar of 1948. After the publication of the novel in 1984, A. M. Mazrui relied on purely ideological criteria to review this text in glowing terms. Thirteen years later, Mwenda Mbatiah reconsidered this review to make both a criticism of Said Ahmed's novel and Mazrui's criticism of the perspective from which Mazrui had reviewed it. Mbatiah made his two-pronged attack in support of literature. He demanded that works should be judged on the basis of literary criteria, not on the basis of ideological ones. Thus, his judgement was unequivocal: Said Ahmed's novel is a literary failure. This iconoclastic position left its mark on the history of Swahili literature, provoking intense reactions. Said Ahmed Mohamed also took a stand in defence of his text. Mbatiah used two principal arguments to attack Said Ahmed Mohamed's novel: (1) the characters are caricatures without development; and (2) there are too many ideological intrusions from the author. Mbatiah's comment targeted literary creativity as being in the thrall of ideology. It is Wamitila who brought an end to that argument by denouncing Mbatiah for substituting literary dogmatism for the ideological dogmatism he was decrying. Wamitila called on the literary critic to give up any political or literary prejudices before reading a work. The debate about Said Ahmed Mohamed's work was not futile. It created the space for a deeply serious interrogation of the value of dogmatic critique of literature; both at the ideological level, and at the stylistic or formal level.

This debate raised the crucial question of the role of politics in literature. Is it the business of a writer to make up his/her idea about society or to focus on the experience of that society? A long-lasting, realist and anti-ideological trend has been maintained by Swahili writers even when called into question for the very nature of the 'thesis novel'. The writer is involved in the society. He/she should report on its most profound changes. One of the first Swahili novelists wrote in an article with the title, 'The writer and the society': 'Writing about the daily problems encountered by the average Tanzanian is much more important than writing about culture, politics or economics' (Omari, 1972:5). A much-quoted article by Kezilahabi to which reference has often been made is 'The Swahili novel and the common man in East Africa' (1988). Kezilahabi represented both the political and anti-ideological evolution of Swahili literature during the period of Nyerere's government in Tanzania.

Whenever Kezilahabi acted as a critic, it was always to sharply condemn wholesale non-political trends in fiction. He disapproved of the detective novel that was and is still very popular in Tanzania by defending authentic literature, whose roots would be at the heart of the Tanzanian society and not in very commercial or genre writing fields. Kezilahabi criticizes the detective story for being too conventional and not sufficiently political, which means not really anchored in the real world around it. To Kezilahabi, this lack of commitment to society has important formal consequences: detective novels use contrived procedures because they have no social roots. Kezilahabi's criticism of the detective novel stands with Mbatiah's criticism of the formulaic thesis novel; they both emphasize the need to create fiction anchored in social reality. This criticism posits literature as linked to the social experience. The issue at stake in these criticisms is the danger that the concern with stylistic issues may become too involved with the political dimension of literature. Literature cannot be political without a process of stylistic invention. Ultimately,

Kezilahabi's works would become one of the first works to be studied from its stylistic aspects, which is certainly his greatest political victory.

The concern to ground the novel in a social experience rather than a social exigency to any political agenda was in itself the very political response that writers gave to ideological demands from state institutions. Kezilahabi argues that this combination is the only way to enable literature to find its style. To vary the wording in a text means to juxtapose discourses. To adjust the sense of things means to situate one's writing at the precise point where these discourses interact, in order to create a unique singular style on which language may rely:

> The role of African writers writing in African languages is therefore to try recapture inner movements of the discourses of consciousness which take place in the daily life, to reshape these discourses into collective articulations. (Kezilahabi, 1988: 136)

In the same vein, Deleuze and Guattari's concept of *agencement collectif d'énonciation* (collective construction of enunciation) has to do with giving a form to discourses by articulating them collectively. This concept cannot be separated from the possibility of a creative use of language. The collective dimension is the means for the literary statement to escape from the hold of enunciation and its ideological conditioning. The 'internal shifts' of discourses that Kezilahabi tries to capture attest to the existence of a collective dynamic that is the vibrant nerve of every society. Social concerns lead Swahili writers to raise social questions and to discover at play in social issues collective dynamics that go beyond macropolitical issues, and take them on into the field of a micropolitics of life.

Revealing life: '*kioo cha maisha*'

Kezilahabi, who condemned the authors of detective novels for being apolitical, was also accused of not being ideologically committed. He defended himself by insisting on the fact that life is actually the message of literature:

> In works which are politically oriented the content is often over-determined by the dominant ideology, and absolute clarity seems to be the measure of good art. But as long as literature is 'life' there can never be such a thing as absolute clarity in literature, for it is not absolute clarity that makes life worth living. What is blurred is what makes the contours of life worth pursuing – 'the hidden god'. (Kezilahabi, 1988: 135)

What critics of ideology reproach Kezilahabi for is his pessimistic view of society. The title of his third novel says it all: *The world is an arena of chaos*. With such an assessment it is difficult to convey a message of progress. The strength of Kezilahabi's novels lies in his emphasis on the problems faced by Tanzanian society that leave him little room to write in order to serve any ideology. In her thesis on 'The politicization of Swahili literature', Patricia Mbughuni (1978a) depicts Kezilahabi as a writer who is radically pessimistic. This thesis occupied a prominent position in Swahili literary criticism. Kezilahabi's pessimism contradicts the ideological necessity for a literature that matches the force of progress, but the problem is that the critics have never been able to catch the writer's conspicuous state of false consciousness. What has been read as pessimism in Kezilahabi's novels has nothing to do with ideology, for it is profoundly political.

Disapproval of Kezilahabi's pessimism is the same as that applied to Kafka's œuvre, including his *Journal*, because it seemed indifferent to the Great War that was tearing Europe apart. The reason for this detachment is that the writer is miles away from the journalist who transforms reality in communicable information.

To Kezilahabi, the fact that literature is subversive explains why it cannot be considered journalistic: 'This kind of literature is often critical and non-journalistic in nature and of a much more far-reaching significance' (Kezilahabi, 1988: 135).

It is impossible to report on the impact of great historical events without couching them in terms of an ideology and social control. Deleuze and Guattari speak of such language use as the '*mot d'ordre*' (political watchword), that is at the opposite extreme from the liberating work of literature.

Taking a closer look at the situation, at least in Tanzania

during *Ujamaa*, one can say that Swahili novelists were indeed far from the social realism they were expected to depict. Support of this view was the *consensus* on 'round' characters (*wahusika duara*) instead of 'flat' characters (*wahusika bapa*) regarded as fixed and unchanging. The disqualification of the positivist hero of the social-realist novel was quickly dismissed on the grounds of the novel's 'trueness' to a complex and shifting reality. One can see behind this impulse the need to free the novel from any ideological constraints that dominate it, for example, in its narrative. The complexity of the character of the novel is a response to the fixedness of the character in a tale, or the hero of an epic in traditional narratives. However, the new aesthetic to delve into character rapidly turned into dogmatic criteria for the evaluation of the novel that authors themselves were soon to reject.

Paradoxically, the 1990s saw the revival of the story and of 'flat' characters because of the ever-present concern with exploring the mysteries of reality. Kezilahabi's two short initiation narratives, *Nagona* and *Mzingile*, opened new perspectives on the novel and allowed a synthesis of the tale and social realism. Thus, the flat character is no longer looked at as acting on 'political watchwords'; rather, such a character is the signal for an immersion in a reality so complex that it has become labyrinthine. The revival of the 'flat character' in the Swahili novel from the 1990s onwards is the result of a quest for a political writing that has never been abandoned. The very lack of depth in a 'flat' character opens the way for a thorough examination of reality, to its fullest extent. Therefore, historical events recur in fiction but are imbricated in one another and mixed with natural disasters, family incidents, and so on. Swahili novelists disseminate a political writing that is both above and beyond the social sphere. Moreover, they no longer recognize the limits of 'society'. Everything in their writing is political. This means both that society is not the only field to which politics applies, and that the novel will graft the social sphere onto the whole of reality.

Kezilahabi calls it the 'Hidden God' – looking for the complexity of reality as if searching for a truffle. This Hidden God took the narrative down a road of initiation that reveals the deeply political nature of all literature. To say that everything is political does not imply that the political must appear in all levels of life. This statement stresses on the contrary that there is no such thing as an independent political sphere because of the lack of a transcending principle that can guarantee the boundaries between different spheres of life. It is in this line of thought that Kezilahabi's appeal in his doctoral thesis is to be understood: for '[T]he non-separation of sociological and political events from the events of literature' (Kezilahabi, 1985). Swahili writers such as Kezilahabi, Said Ahmed Mohamed and many others know that 'the world is an arena of chaos' to be traversed in order to find the pearl that will make it meaningful and true.

In his thesis on Swahili medicine, Beckerleg (1990) shows that Swahili society sees itself in opposition between *taratibu* (connoting order, hierarchy and self-control) and *fitina* (reflecting disorder and chaos). The only form of politics consists in finding the easiest way to stay connected with this world and make it bearable. The result of following the 'watchword' to the last detail while concerning themselves with the life of the people, was that Swahili writers discovered that at every level of society, people cobble together ways and means of putting their politics into practice. The phenomenon of persistent corruption at the heart of many novels is the best symptom of this explosion of the political sphere and its deep penetration into the social body. These little accommodations to life are not confined to the private sphere because they also encompass 'great' world events, not as 'packaged information' but as waves of anxiety, disseminated in broken disturbances that keep on forcing endless adjustments to one's way of life.

From this perspective, it is easy to understand why 'flat characters' are used, in a world in which everyone is trying to negotiate or renegotiate his/her way of life. Here, the character is also overtaken by the shift. With the flat character it is possible to expose the great fluidity of the world and the urgent necessity to have some strategy in place in order not to be taken up by the force of the flood. Everything is political because staying alive is only possible if one is constantly adaptable. One has to choose between a life strategy and preparing oneself for death. There is no alternative upstream… No subject can build himself/herself beyond this alternative.

Round characters can only evolve from flat characters just as a social structure is created from the chaos of life.

During this fifty-year period, the main dichotomy in Swahili political fiction was between didactic works that convey a clearly political message and realist novels that deal with the problems of everyday life without necessarily offering any answers. The border between the political novel and the realist novel genres is not clearly defined because writers of both modes are concerned with the political stakes of writing. Still, there is a section of fiction writing that was long ignored by the critics: namely the popular novel that was considered to be fundamentally apolitical. Rajmund Ohly was the first to reveal the deep attachment of the Swahili novel to the popular genre. Further, Jan Blommaert, through the study of a novel by Akwilombe demonstrated that popular literature is more open to political 'order words' or 'watchwords' than to so-called 'serious' literature written by intellectuals who object to any form of indoctrination.

Mohamed Said Abdulla, a founding father of the Swahili detective novel, and who set his works on the island of Zanzibar, is placed at the cross-roads between political and popular literature. Criticism of his work was based on political or ideological criteria. Mohamed was condemned for not using his talent as a novelist to serve society and for having opened the door to a genre that later proliferated in popular fiction. The readership's taste for crime and strong emotions is regarded as counter to the political education of the masses. No one can see how this kind of novel might help improve society. However recent critiques of the genre have recognized that it corresponds to a change in the definition of the political function of literature.

The 'fantasy' element of society put forward by the crime novel together with its taste for dubious marginal characters (criminals or upholders of the law) does away with any notion of autonomy in the social sphere. The Swahili novel is about a society affected at all levels, leaking out on all sides, thus establishing a connection, in a very dynamic way, from the patriot (*mzalendo*) to the citizen (*raia*), the citizen to the human being (*binadamu*), and the human being to the creature (*kiumbe*). The intrinsic politicization of the Swahili novel, including in its most popular expressions, is related to the strong awareness that nothing is acquired and self-explanatory. Whether the novel sees society as something to be constructed or something threatened by destruction, it is always an external object. The novel is written outside the social even when it is seemingly mostly concerned with the future of that society. The fact that great Swahili novelists turned to describing how the lower classes live enabled these writers to look behind the formal social structure into a swarming anthill of gestures and speeches, which set up a new world. The boundaries of this new world are well beyond the limits set by any society.

1 Narrating Values
Describing a World

In order to understand the background which gave birth to the ethnographic novel, one needs to go back to the first texts produced in the colonial context. The German African scholar Carl Velten published *Desturi za Wasuaheli* (*Customs of the Swahili People*) in 1903. The material for this text was taken from the work of Mtoro bin Mwanyi Bakari who had the aim of studying the customs of the Swahili people in order to make them accessible to a wider audience. More than half a century later, Lyndon Harries and then J.W.T. Allen translated this description of the customs of the Swahili people into English, during the great era of Anglo-Saxon research on the Swahili 'civilization'. Noel Q. King's introduction to J.W.T. Allen's translation speaks for itself:

> The *Desturi za WaSwahili* (*Customs of the Swahili People*) ranks among the world's great but little-known literary achievements. It records something of the life and traditions of a numerically small people, of a culture that has grown up over centuries to give birth to its own literature, philosophy of life, and values. Too many such civilizations – each a unique and irreplaceable gem of human achievement – have disappeared without a trace. Some have left a few place names, a few genes and games, a fell disease or two, while others are brought to mind only by the descriptions of outsiders. Some have managed to survive to the present, be it by sheer refusal to die, by military prowess or non-violent forms of resistance, or by the protection of the unhospitable nature of a xenophobic terrain. In the case of the Swahili we have a people few in number, inhabiting an open land that has no natural borders or defences, who have gone serenely and happily on, while their invaders – various waves of outsider Africans, Arabs, Iranians, Portuguese, Germans, and British – have disappeared, leaving behind their trace in ruins littering the countryside and in vestiges embedded in the Swahili language and culture. (Allen, 1971: VII)

This civilization seems to be Swahili because of its ability to welcome external influences, to absorb and somehow integrate other people's customs even when fossilized in their original place. The dynamic nature of Swahili civilization is related to its capacity for integrating all things foreign. To readers who are familiar with theories of the novel as an open genre, that is, one standing outside a formal code and able to integrate all other literary genres, the kinship between the Swahili world and the novel will seem quite natural.

In the first Appendix to *Desturi za WaSwahili*, James de Vere Allen is perfectly clear on the sensitive question of Swahili identity:

> The Swahili world was, and saw itself as, a cultural unit, not a racial or tribal one. Swahili was the language spoken as a first language by virtually all the inhabitants of the coastal settlements between Barawa in the north and Lindi and Mikindani (near what is now the Mozambique-Tanzania border) in the South. All these people likewise shared, to a remarkable degree, a single, homogeneous culture that gave them a sense of community stronger than that created by any ties of origin or ethnicity which they may have had in common with smaller groups or with outsiders. (Allen, 1971: 211)

These texts reflect the specific perspective that Swahili ethnographic studies adopted. The world of the Swahili is regarded as entirely open, a world without a centre of gravity but nonetheless coherent and consistent. Velten's revealing study was preceded by another anthology, *Safari za Wasuaheli* [1901]. This was a collection of travelogues through Eastern Africa but included a journey to Berlin and Siberia. From the start, prose literature took a particular turn in that detailed descriptions of local customs are combined with travelogues viewing the wider world. The biographies of Amur bin Nasur Homeir [1894] and the merchant Tippu Tip [1902], also published at the turn of the century, take Swahili prose to the outside world. The former depicts Europe while the latter describes Africa's diversity. Swahili travelogues are ethnographic narratives. They describe the culture of other people including those of the West. At the end of the day, there is no major difference between the two anthologies published by Carl Velten: customs are worth describing, whether they are ours or other people's.

The main characteristic of Swahili civilization seems to be its ability to combine an inward view with an outward one, in an integrative perspective. The outsider, the Other, is not enough for the delineation of a vision. Rather, these outsiders are right away a part of ourselves. Both autobiographies and travelogues in which characters can view the world around them belong to the same narrative register. A travelogue is an autobiography in the sense that a journey is a life experience, and an autobiography is a travelogue because a travelogue is inseparable from contact with the outside world.

This bond between the gaze at oneself and the gaze at others is channelled by the notion of 'custom'. The Swahili word for it is *desturi*, which etymologically goes back to writing[1] and semantically to the idea of daily habits. Customs are the ways of life of different peoples and are worthy of attention. Habits are ways of being part of the world and writing keeps them alive. Swahili travelogues are noteworthy for this comparison of one people with another, and putting them on the same level, even if this runs the risk of contamination.

Thus, if one were to talk of a Swahili civilization, it would less be defined by its own cultural capital than by its particular stance to the wider world. The Swahili prose novel reveals this characteristic to a high degree. One would have great difficulty in finding novels aimed at presenting an ethnically pure social world, turned in on itself, even in novels from Ikerewe Island, isolated in the middle Lake Victoria. The inward gaze is inseparable from the presence of the other. Some early Swahili novels celebrated world values but the mere description of customs was part of a much larger and more complex narrative register.

The Swahili novel has raised two interdependent questions: how does a world manage to endure yet deal with the problem of generation change? How does a world survive contact with other worlds? The Swahili novel answers these two questions, related to time and to space: through its lineage on the one hand, and its alliances on the other.

---

[1] To Sacleux (1939), this word of Persian origin signifies a register on which soldiers' names and pay were listed.

Passing on customs through narrative: lineage

The transmission of customs from one generation to the next has so far been poorly studied from the point of view of its impact on the form of the narrative. It seems that early Swahili fiction either implicitly or explicitly falls within the paradigm of transmission. Mbotela's novel *Uhuru wa watumwa* (*The Freeing of Slaves*) deals with a father telling his child the story of his experience as a slave who was freed by British forces:

> 'My son, I see that you are very interested in these issues. Given that you want to know everything, I will explain everything to you from the beginning to the end. If you understand everything, tell your children so that they will also pass it on their own children. It would even be better if you could tell it to the world.' (Mbotela, 1959: 9)[2]

The father's last sentence is related to the nature of Mbotela's own narrative, its starting point being exile from his primary territory, in the sense that he is captured and enslaved. The narrative of his adventure goes well beyond the borders of his people's cultural values, so that this story appeals to the whole world. It remains a fact that transmission is first perceived as intergenerational. The idea of a narrative being translated from one world to the next is subsidiary to the need to have the narrative circulating within one's world. This subsidiary idea clearly has something to do with the birth of the novel.

Another lesson from the father's words in Mbotela's novel is that a tale has to be understood, not just memorized. The words that Mbotela chooses are very clear: to explain (*kueleza*) and to understand (*kufahamu*). A tale is something to be understood. It can only be transmitted if it has been understood. Tales are in no way presented as stories that simply need be memorized. The idea of a narrative heritage is inappropriate: a tale that cannot be understood is already

---

[2] 'Mwanangu, nakuona u mchunguzi mno wa mambo, na kama wataka kujua yote haya, basi mimi nitaanza kukueleza tokea mwanzo hata mwisho. Nawe, uwe na fahamu sawasawa, uje uwaeleze wanao, nao waeleze wana wao baadaye. Na ukiweza kuwaeleza walimwengu ni bora zaidi.'

dead. Comprehension as a necessary criterion of the tale is crucial from the viewpoint of transmission. A tale that lacks any real sense cannot be passed on just for its repetition. Literature is not the sanctuary of ancient texts transmitted for the sake of memory.

Grandparents are major actors in the transmission of social values precisely because they have a perspective on the changes across generations. *Toka kizazi hadi kizazi* (*From one generation to the next*) (Charo, 1976) depicts old people who are fully aware of their social function. 'Grandparents who are storytellers know the impact of one story or the other on people of different age groups.'[3] Bibi Maahira, the storyteller of Suleiman Omar Baalawy's small tales published in the collections *Hadithi za Bibi Maahira* (*Bibi Maahira's Stories*) and *Bibi Maahira tena* (*Bibi Maahira's New Stories*) is also a grandmother who is aware of her role as an intermediary in a society that is going astray:

> Bibi Maahira was a courageous woman who was honoured and respected in the neighbourhood. For this reason she decided not to allow her grandchildren to interact with neighbouring children and told them beautiful stories of the past in order to teach them proper manners. (Baalawy, 1968b: 1)[4]

This concern about passing on rules of life is one of Shaaban Robert's major preoccupation in his short stories that build on oriental tales. The narrative serves to demonstrate the accuracy of a character's behaviour. The readers may pass judgement according to the situation. Each narrative is based on an implicit rule of behaviour that is the key to the narrative. There is a logic to the narrative: it demonstrates a proposition that in most cases takes the form of a proverb. A novel like *Kisa cha Sultani Hatibu* (*The Story of Sultan Hatibu*) (Riwa, 1964) sets out the narrative illustration of a Swahili proverb: 'He who has

---

[3] '*Kina babu wasimulizi walielewa kwamba kisa fulani kina athari gani juu ya watu binafsi wa marika mbalimbali.*'

[4] *Ilivyokuwa Bibi Madhira aikuwa mwanamke hodari mwenye maarifa mazui ya kilimwengu, heshima na adabu pia, aliazimia asuwape nafasi majukuu wake sana ya kuchanganyika na majirani hao na awe anawasimulia hadithi nzuri za mambo yaliyopita zamani. Kwa namna hiyo huenda wale wajukuu wake wakapata msingi mwema wa tabia na maisha.*

patience will eat the ripest fruit.'[5] Each story from Suleiman Omar Said Baalawy's series of small tales illustrates a well-known Swahili proverb. Such tales are closely controlled. The novel produces a realist treatment of the fairy tale. This is very clear in a novel such as *Matatu ya Thamani* (*Three Things of Importance*), the Swahili version of an initiation tale. The hero Sudi foolishly spends his small fortune buying three precepts (or paper statements) sold by crooks. The naive Sudi who should have ended up destitute and crestfallen will become a king thanks to the good use of the precepts. He will forgive his two brothers who had stripped him of most of his heritage. Only the narrative tension of a tale can make readers accept such a reversion.

Novels whose titles are a proverb are countless. Nonetheless, it is necessary to distinguish this type of narrative from the thesis novel that is linked to realism. While the thesis serves as the general frame to the whole novel, the proverb is the main thread for a narrative. A proverb does not determine a societal change. It is a behavioural answer to events. A proverb takes on the role of initiatory teaching because the sense of the proverb can only become obvious to the one who is put to the real test. Once a narrative submits to the law of proverb, it accepts a limit to its depth of reality in order to reorganize itself around the coherence of a certain behaviour. Thus, the anti-hero will be unlucky and the righteous hero will unexpectantly be rewarded by destiny. The proverb forms the narrative tension; in turn the formula determines the narrative. Spirits, magicians, coincidences or supernatural events in the narrative invariably serve the *formula* and mostly come into the narrative to correct the expected law of causality that seemed to be leading to the triumph of the sinful characters and the ill-fate of the righteous.

In line with this argument, such a *formula* is part of the repertoire of proverbs that have survived on the basis of selecting works to be passed on through the generations. One may imagine every proverb as being a survival. Its selection precedes its telling. The formula is laid out in the narrative, but validated elsewhere. The fact that it exists as a proverb is validation enough. Thus, comparing a narrative to a mathe-

[5] '*Mvumilivu hula mbivu.*'

matical demonstration is limited because one cannot find a theorem that has authority via its very demonstration. The proverb subjects its narrative demonstration to its authority, which emanates from the inherent selection that precedes the passing on from one generation to the next. The principle of transmission matters more than the narrative. It is its deepest core. It justifies its telling, which in turn is regulated by transmitted values. It is thus not surprising that the narrative changes in nature as soon as the principle of generational transmission is felt to be weakening. The rise of the novel has to do with this awareness, that an ancient world is threatened. The novel will integrate the problem of generational change in its narrative. Transmission will no longer be a condition for narratives or tales but their object. This attempt to retain a world threatened by disappearance will cause narrative to shift into an altogether different function from mere formulaic explication. Narrative will represent a world, which is altogether different from merely demonstrating a proverb.

Transmitting by describing: the alliance

The Swahili novel from the mainland is more oriented towards this kind of self-representation. A typical example comes from the Ikerewe Islands on Lake Victoria. Aniceti Kitereza's major work, *Bwana Myombekere na Bibi Bugonoka* was written in Kikerewe. It followed a previous work completed in 1942 and published in Kiswahili: *Hadithi na Desturi za Ukerewe*, and the author's new edition of *The History of the Ukerewe Kings* (*Omwanzuro gw'Abakama ba Bu kerewe*). Almas Simard, of the order The White Fathers of Africa, who encouraged Kitereza to write this novel, had a quite predictable agenda: 'I asked him to write a book on habits and customs of his country staging fictional characters that would be acting in every situation and possible circumstances of ordinary life' (Kitereza, 1996:7).[6]

There are many literary texts that emerged in this way

---

[6] Quote from Simon Baguma Mweze and Olivier Barlet in the Preface to their French translation of the Swahili version: *Les Enfants du faiseur de pluie*.

during the colonial era, in European languages as well as in African languages. To East African writers from the mainland, Swahili became an ideal vehicle for putting their own culture into focus. A text like *Mtugeni* from the Kenyan author John Buyu which tells the story of a young boy living in a fishing village near the lake is thematically very close to Kitereza's novel. Termed an ethnographic novel, it is characterized by the fact that it rejects any exceptional adventure. In the preface to such novels, emphasis is laid on daily life.

This kind of novel is explicitly anti-romantic. In discussing a novel by Nkwera, Senkoro touches on the purely literary problem that this type of novel raises:

> First I have to clear up any doubts for those who have read this book and asked themselves whether it was really a story or simply an explanation. The main challenge of such a book is to combine the art of description with truth (namely the description of customs of the Wapangwa). The explanation turns out to be a story precisely because these customs are truthfully disclosed – or perhaps take the form of a story. Those who hold that the lack of a plot inhibits the narrative should take into account the fact that the kind of plot depends on the nature of the story. It is impossible to compare *Mzishi wa Baba ana Radhi*'s plot with for example that of *Simu ya kifo* [a famous Tanzanian detective story]. (Senkoro, 1972)[7]

Senkoro's clarification is necessary due to the fundamental disruption of narrative flow in the ethnographic novel: ethnographic description is perceived as incompatible with narrative dynamism.

Thus, there is no room for adventures but only social events such as births, weddings and burial ceremonies. To treat such events is a social matter that will allow the novelist to emphasize

---

[7] *Kwanza, lazima niondoe mashaka ya wale waliokisoma kitabu hiki na kuuliza swali kama kweli ni cha hadithi au ni maelezetu. Ufundi ulioonekana katika kitabu hiki ni ule wa kuiunganisha sanaa ya maelezo na ukweli wa mambo (yaani maelezo yenyewe juu ya mila hizo ndiyo inayoyafanya maelezo haya yawe ni hadithi — au tuseme yawe na umbo la hadithi. Wale wanaong'ang'ania ' ukosefu wa kipeo il kutizima 'masharti' ya hadithi' inafaa wafahamu kuwa vipeo vya hadithi hufuatana na mazingara na mambo yaongelewayo hadithini. Huwezi kutafuta kipeo cha Mizisho wa Baba ana Radhi kwa kulinganisha na kile cha Simu ya Kifo (kwa mfano).*

the characteristics of the society he/she is describing. At the same time each of these social events embodies a narrative core that is exploited in the novel. The social event prominently featured in Kitereza's novel is the wedding. It is at first about Myombekere's marriage, subsequently debated because his wife is barren. This is followed in the second part of the novel by his son Ntulanalwo's wedding. The theme of marriage as a social institution is typical of this kind of novel. Marriage is a social institution that makes public a private event. The romance underlying marriage is to be found in the intimate event, but the textual expression of marriage is almost entirely public and ceremonial.

Marriage is a key event for displaying custom. The alliance between two people or two families entails taking a risk. Encoding marriage procedures is on a par with the risk that is taken when every new alliance is made. Every marriage prompts social questions. A matrimonial alliance is a dangerous moment, and is thus highly ritualized because it opens the family system to an external site.

Cuthbert Omari's voluminous novel *Mwenda kwao* (*The one who joined the others*) describes the problems in a marriage between a Tanzanian and a black American woman, despite their true love for one another: 'After three months of marriage, they had to face a test that challenged their culture, customs and rules of behaviour' (Omari, 1971: 157).[8] The alliance celebrated through marriage is the risk taken every time by a whole society bringing together families, descendants, ethnicities, countries and even continents (as in Omari's novel):

> You loved me and you agreed to our marriage in pursuit our vision of the world. You took me as I am. You accepted me and all my relatives. You did not marry them but by marrying me you consented to a whole family. We will do everything as Mr and Mrs Kisiwa who are members of the line of Yosefu Kisiwa. We cannot behave as if we were alone and forget all these others. There lies the secret of the vitality of African society. No one acts on on their own account. (Omari, 1971: 157) [9]

---

[8] *Ndoa ya miezi mitatu imeingiliwa na jaribu kubwa. Jaribu ambalo si rahisi kulifumbua kwani linaingilia mambo ya utamaduni, desturei mila na tabia.*

[9] *Uliponipenda na ukakubali kuwa tuoane, kwa kufuata filasifa yetu, ulinikubali mimi na matatizo yangu. Ulinikubali mimi pamoja na watu wa jamaa yangu.*

The paramount role that parents have in the choice of the partner is at the heart of the marriage system. The parents' role is to measure the risk that this or that alliance brings with it to the social body. The title of Agoro Anduru's novel *Kukosa radhi* (*Missing blessing*) gives us the plotline. A young Christian Luo boy falls in love with a young Muslim girl from another ethnic group. The fact that the parents on both sides are against this alliance acts as a curse with damaging consequences. The marriage will turn out badly not so much on account of direct parental interference but because it is impossible to handle disputes between the couple because the marriage has not been inscribed in the social body.

Ndoa ya mzimuni (*Marriage among the spirits*) poses a radical idea: the arranged marriage between a young girl and a spirit (Nurru, 1974). This raises the problem of a possible alliance between two worlds. By chance, the young girl gets in touch with the world of the spirits that is accessible through a gateway in a cave. Then the negotiations for the marriage of the girl to the king's son begin. From this moment onwards the novel describes the movements back and forth between the family's house and the world of the spirits. The fiancée keeps disappearing and reappearing back home; her contact with the other world is marked by her repeated disappearances. The gifts she brings from the other world are quite extraordinary. Whatever the prince's determination the wedding will not take place, the girl must kill the son in order to avoid being killed herself for her rejection of the proposal. The narrative issue of a marriage is to bring about a recomposition of the world by an alliance between families. Nurru's novel shows that it is impossible to have an alliance that reduces marriage to a mere exchange of goods, not a true transaction. Since the two worlds have no point of interpenetration, the idea of such a marriage is obviously against nature.

The central role of marriage in the ethnographic novel is linked to this essential detachment of the self caused by the alliance. In this sense, the marriage is a key moment in the novel

(contd) *Hukuolewa nao, lakini kwa luolewa kwako nami kunakuanya unipokee mimi na watu wa jamaa yangu yote. Na lolote nitakalowatendea ni letu sisi sote kama Bwana na Bibi Kivisa, watu walio sehemu ya ukoo wa mzee Yosefu Kivisa. Hatuwezi hujitendea sisi wenyewe tu na kukasahau watu wengine wa jamaa yetu. Hii ndiyo siri na furaha ya maana ya jamaa ya Kiafrika.*

that serves as the mediator to question one's own values and integrity of identity. At the moment a family, a village, a group or even a society opens up beyond itself, marriage empowers it to recreate the possibility for a new secure space. The ethnographic novel attempts to describe this secure space that each society attempts to find despite the chaos of the world. Marriage is 'custom' *par excellence* because it displays a manner of living in the world. The rituals of birth or death allow for a contact or connection to the 'other world' whereas marriage deals with the risks that arise out of every contact with other people in this world. Through narratives of marriages, the ethnographic novel speaks of the relationship with the Other. This is how different societies negotiate their relationship with the external world. All the narrative fabric of encounters between worlds is hidden beneath these tales of marriage, ready to spring forth.

It is possible to take stock of the state of the social body through the institution of marriage. This is the case in the novel *Harusi* (*Marriages*) which compares those of two brothers. The elder brother challenges his father's authority and has to run away from his family to marry a teenage mother. With a great fanfare and all the splendour of a traditional wedding, the younger brother marries the daughter of a very rich businessman; the latter's father suffers from a venereal disease. The first wedding will be a happy one and will bear offsping. The second couple will succumb to the veneral disease passed on to them.

The traditional marriage ritual conceals the collapse of social and moral values of a Swahili society prey to venality and caught in the grip of ecstatic pleasures. The discreet marriage of the elder brother is an event that is confined to the private sphere. Indeed, it is entirely unknown to the social body. Yet, this marriage is future-oriented. *Harusi* disturbs presupposed conventions of the ethnographic novel by narrowing traditional marriage rituals to simple folkloric signs which are disconnected from any value system.

From alliance to kinship: the healer's narrative function

One of the ever-present dangers that may to occur in the making of an alliance is sterility. This explains why healers are key characters in all these ethnographic novels. Their double role is to find out what might have caused the anger of the world and to intervene to appease it, that is to allow things to go back to their normal state. Solving the problem of barrenness is one of the most frequent tasks of healers. To allow women to bear children is obviously a social function. To consult the healer to solve problems of sterility is an inevitable or predictable episode in all these novels.[10] The novel's centre of gravity is moved to the post-conjugal space. The arrangement of chapters is thus quite predictable: 'Birth of X'; 'Education of X'; 'Marriage of X'; 'X builds a house'; 'X consults the healer'; 'Birth of children'.

Controlling its own reproduction is a central concern of every society. Thus it is self-explanatory that the question of self-reproduction is at the heart of novels that aim to give a literary existence to a society. In *Titi la Mkwe*, Alex Banzi tells the story of how Ena, a woman abandoned by her husband, tries various methods to get pregnant. She finds herself naked in the cave of the ancestors and in the darkness she is surprised by her father-in-law who caresses her breasts without recognizing her. Alex Banzi's novel relates the extraordinary confusion, the complete breakdown of human relationships that leads indirectly to the death of a child, but eventually concludes with the birth of triplets. The healer Dunda is at the heart of all this confusion. By ensuring Ena's fertility and the mending of her marriage, he is the novel's key protagonist and assures its narrative tension.

Once the generational line is guaranteed, cultural transmission can take place. Among the different theories that give some sense to life, there is the notion of cultural force, coming from outside and underlying all cultural structures. This vital impulse, this 'Great Health' is the hidden motif of all novels that take culture as subject:

> As long as grass has not been uprooted it has not yet disappeared. In the same way, human beings experience afflictions of the body or soul. Once the pains stop, human beings rejoice and recover their health. People who share this point of view keep themselves going in hard times by saying: 'bora uzima: health is life' because

---

[10] See Chapter 12 of Kitereza's *Bwana Myombekere*; Chapter 11 of John Buyu's *Mtugeni*; Chapter 5 of Alex Banzi's *Titi la Mkwe*; Chapter 2 of Kinondo Muridhania's *Damu ya Ulimi*; Chapter 1 of Felician V. Nkwera's *Mzishi wa baba ana radhi*.

the healthy person fights off evil and embraces the good. (Buyu, 1971: 92)[11]

This appeal to the Great Health is a powerful source of narrative. All Swahili novels that sound 'culturalist' demonstrate suffering in society. Social disfunction allows cultures to reveal themselves. Of course, without illness it would not be possible to talk of the Great Health.

The narrative plot of *Mzishi wa baba ana radhi* (*The man who buries his father will be blessed by him*), presented by the author as an ethnographic novel,[12] narrates the birth and education of a healer, up to his father's death. The father had passed on all his knowledge to his son before dying and made sure that his son had taken a wife who had given him children. The father's death is sanctioned by this line of descent and at the same time by the possibility of certain values being passed on from one generation to the next.

One finds the same theme in Mung'ong'o's *Mirathi ya hatari* (*A dangerous heritage*) transposed to a modern context. The narrator, Gusto, is a student who inherits his father's secret knowledge and has to take on a lengthy battle against the sorcerer who killed his father. The transmission of this mystical knowledge takes place against the (Gusto) narrator's will. The latter swears by nothing other than Western knowledge as he tells his father's friend,

> 'It is true that we are thirsty for modern knowledge, what you call Western knowledge. This need can be explained on two counts. First, that knowledge is open to all human beings. There is no need to take a secret oath to access that knowledge. Second, that knowledge aims at improving everyone's life whereas our knowledge serves our own interests [...].' (Mung'ong'o, 1977: 25-26)[13]

[11] *Nyasi hazifi ila kuing'oa mizizi yake. Hali khadhalika binadamu pia ana nyakati zake ambapo huteseka sana mwilini au moyoni, baadaye mateso hayo hutoweka na mtu kuanza kuchangamka na kuwa mwenye afya mzuri. Wale watu wanaotambua ukweli huo hujipa moyo wakati wa huzuni kwa kusema 'Bora uzima', yaani mtu akiwa mzima ataondokewa na mabaya na kujiwa mema.*
[12] The novel's subtitle is *Maelezo ya baadhi ya mila ya Wapangwa* which means 'an explanation of some customs of the Wapangwa'.
[13] '*Ni kweli kuwa tunaikimbilia elimu ya kisasa, hiyo uiitayo ya Kizungu. Lakini kuna sababu kuu mbili. Kwanza, elimu hiyo ipo wazi kwa kila mtu. Hamna haja ya mwanafunzi kuchukua kiapo cha usiri wa elimu ajifunzayo. Pili, elimu hiyo ina madhumuni ya kuinua hali ya maisha ya binadamu kwa jumla [...]*'

Gusto argues for a universal knowledge detached from ethnic and cultural conditioning. In the course of the narrative, Gusto comes to terms with his father's secret heritage. The transmission of healers' occult knowledge is only one aspect of the much wider problem of the transmission of knowledge from one generation to the next. The character Gusto is overwhelmed by a social dynamic that goes beyond him as an individual. He finds himself involved in a battle about his lineage and not about him. The whole structure of Mung'ong'o's novel is based on this coexistence of two levels at which to understand the character's actions: the character as an autonomous individual and as the embodiment of a lineage. It is not a question of deciding for one side or the other since both levels are interdependent, as mutual as light and shadow. When the individual's autonomy is foregrounded, the obscure core of the filiation raises the ghost of the ancestor to the surface. When the demands of lineage overwhelm a person's individual space, the youthful spirit kicks over the traces, for the sake of true life.

This dialectical relationship between the individual and the lineage is deeply rooted in the novel. It is one of the tools that the novel uses to question a relationship to the world. A character of a novel is a type of link to the world. A character is not fully developed outside the novel; its sole task is to describe the process of individuation that leads to the full person. In the case of the ethnographic novel, this principle may be described as 'habit' or 'custom' – that is to say, the sum of habitual behaviours that lead us through life. These customs only make sense as a response to the destructive forces of reality, on the one hand, and on the other, the type of individuation that is created. However a character develops, he/she is always pulled back by something external: reality, rumbling on in the background.

The novel as a mechanism for building up ideality

In Kitereza's (1980) novel, Myombekere tries to win back his barren wife who has gone home to her parents because she cannot endure her family-in-law's scorn. The story is thus about saving the marriage. During a visit where Myombekere tries to convince his wife to come back to him, he expresses his distress thus: 'Now, I know a house turns into a dark wood when a man is alone. A house is really only a home only when two people live in it. If one of them leaves for a month or a longer period of time a house becomes a deep, dark wood for the one who lives in it on their own, especially at nights' (Kitereza, 1980: 58-59).[14]

Living as a couple, sanctioned by marriage, is the best protection against the constant pressure of unsociability. The metaphor of the forest is not fortuitous; it is the invisible narrative subplot in Kitereza's whole work. The forest stands for the powerful nature of chaos that can be unleashed when the social body fails. In particular, the marriage-bed deserves to be protected from every contamination:

> Back in the house they found the fire still burning bright and they warmed their legs and feet before it, drying off the dew-wet sand and mud from the rain they had stepped in outside, then wiped their feet clean. Myombekere took off the cow-skin robe he was wearing, gave it to his wife, and she hung it on the screen while he climbed into bed. Bugonoka moved quickly, unfolded the *enkanda*[15] and covered her husband with it. As for herself, she went back to the fire to dry the *obunerere*[16] she was wearing on her calves, brushing her fine wire ornaments clean of dust so that she didn't carry it into their bed and make it dirty. When she finished cleaning and dusting her *obunerere*, she left the fireside but not before pulling out the burning logs and sticking their hot ends into the ground, so that they would not burn on during the night, then fall out of the hearth and burn down the house. The fire well ordered, she undressed and she too hung her clothes on the screen, then rubbed the soles of her feet clean of dust on a wooden step beside the bed.[17] Then she climbed in and lay down on the

[14] 'Nimejiona mwenyewe, kumbe, nyumba, kwa mtu mmoja, inageuka kuwa msitu! Kweli inaweza kuhesabiwa kuwa nyumba kama mnalala ndani yake watu wawili, walakini, mmoja wenu akiondoka akaenda mahala na kukaa huko kama muda wa mwezi mmoja au miezi kadha, hapo mtu atakayebaki nyumbani mle, anafanana kama yumo katika msitu mkubwa, hasa wakati wa usiku.'

[15] Cow-skin which has been treated and turned into very soft material for wear or for a quilt made from pieces of such cow-skins. *Enkanda* is also the name of a women's dance, sometimes called *Iwakalera*, performed at weddings, in which women drum on rolls of rawhide and play maracas to the tune of traditional wedding songs. [Note by Ruhumbika; 2002: 93]

[16] *Enerere* or *obunerere*: Bracelets and anklets of very fine iron or brass wire worn in bundles by women on legs and arms as ornaments (ibid.: 93).

[17] *Isingiro:* Block of wood which was kept by the bedside for people to clean their feet

wife's side of the bed and pulled up the same *enkanda* covering her husband, and settled herself. (Kitereza, 1980: 57-58) [18]

This text perfectly illustrates the poetic of Kitereza's novel. The concern with detail does not simply reflect the novelist's predisposition. Rather, it builds the core of the novel. Characters' actions regularly echo the muddy and swampy substratum from which they emerge.

Kitereza's characters permanently fight against the dissolving elements surrounding them. Water is everywhere on this island: water from the lake surrounding it, water from rivers that cross the island and particularly the rain that falls throughout the year.[19] Nature is ever-present in the novel. Quite often lightning destroys houses, small boats capsize on the lake, dust and mud cause even the most beautiful dresses to lose their sparkle.

The ruinous power of nature is even shown in the intimacy between characters since their bodies are sources of all kinds of illnesses. People's stomachs crawl with worms (*michango*) which are always likely to provoke diarrhoea and other intestinal diseases. In Kitereza's novel, it is common to see characters defecating, slobbering and vomiting. These bodily expulsions are not there to give a naturalist tinge to the

---

(contd) on before going to bed, since Wakerewe normally walked barefooted so that their feet always needed such dusting before they went to bed (ibid.: 93).

[18] *Walipoingia nyumbani, wakakuta moto bado unawaka, wakaanza kukausha miguu yao itoke mchanga na matope ya mvua waliyokanyaga nje. Ilipokauka, wakajipangusa vumbi. Myombekere akavua vazi lake akampa mke wake, akapanda juu ya kitanda akalala. Bugonoka akalitundika vazi la mumewe kwenye lusika (kiambaza), halafu akaja upesi, akalikung'uta vazi lake liitwalo enkanda (yaani ngozi ya ng'ombe iliyotengenezwa na kulainishwa kwa ufundi kabisa), akamfunika mume wake. Yeye, kwa kuwa alikuwa amevaa obunelele (madodi) miguuni mwake, alirudi jikoni kujikausha miguu vizuri zaidi na kutoa mchanga uliokuwa katika udodi wake; yote hayo ni ya kutaka usafi, ati asiende kitandani na mchanga katika madodi, ukapukusikia kitandani ukawakera mwilini. Baadaye ndipo akauweka udodi wake sawasawa, halafu akatoa motoni vijinga vyenye kuni ndefu, akavichomeka mchangani kuvizima moto visije vikaendelea kuwaka na hatimaye kusababisha nyumba ishike moto. Alipomaliza kutengeneza vizuri moto mwingine uliobaki mekoni, naye pia akavua vazi lake, akalitungika kwenye olusika, akapukusa miguu yake juu ya isingiro (mti uliokuwa karibu na kitanda), akajipangusa sawasawa. Basi akapanda kitandani, akaenda upande wa wanawake wanapolala, akajifunika enkanda ile aliyomfunikia mume wake, akalala.*

[19] Months of the year in the Kerewe calendar are described according to the type of rain that falls each month (Kitereza, 1980: 250-254).

narrative. Rather, they stress the fact humanity cannot exist without a constant battle, on all sides, against these shapeless substances. The story of Ntulanalwo's childhood is all about the different diseases that he suffers. Repeated fevers, itches and abscesses put his life in danger and were treated by healers who identified the spiritual source of the evil before they suggested any treatment. The key issue in Kitereza's poetic language is the nature of the link between the world of the spirits (*mizimu*) and the world without form which humans inhabit.

Illnesses and accidents reveal the same issue: the constant presence of a threat lurking in all human societies. It is impossible to understand the narrative development of the different social customs at the heart of Kitereza's novel without a full appreciation of this permanent threat. This is the major difference between novelistic writing and the ethnographic approach which is descriptive and functionalist. This is not simply a question of understanding the part played by spirits in a system of beliefs or the role of nature in the social system, but of imagining a world where such forces threaten the very existence of life. The main point of the first volume is that a couple is endangered by sterility. The main point of the second volume is a child endangered by disease, but in the course of both volumes, healing forces are active even in minor details, as in the scene where Myombekere and his wife go to bed.

Gifts establish the social link between families. Some chapters of Kitereza's novel depict the preparation of presents and visits during which the families-in-law of different matrimonial alliances on which the story is built receive presents. Every gift is presented with the utmost care:

> On returning home from escorting Kanwaketa, the first thing Myombekere did was to take down the house screen which he made before leaving for Irugwa, bring it outside, give it a dusting to rid it of cockroaches and cowbeds and scrutinize it to make sure that mice hadn't damaged any cords. When he was satisfied that it was still all right, he beamed with happiness, gave the screen another thorough dusting and spread it on the ground and left it sunning there as he told Bugonoka: 'A courtship article should be presented when it is still in good condition like this, so that those for whom it is intended are pleased with it. That way you

too don't feel ashamed of what you have brought and can find the right words you need to converse with your hosts and speak without any anxiety as if you were in your own home.'

In response Bugonoka said, 'A courtship article is like a borrowed robe, with which the borrower cannot be too careful. For when you borrow another person's robe to wear on such and such an occasion, however careful you may be it is very difficult to return it to the owner without having damaged it in one way or another or having done something to it that might displease the owner, like wrinkling it when putting it away instead of folding it nicely the way perhaps the owner usually does, so that when you return it to him or her and he or she receives it without saying a word most probably he or she has done so only to spare your feelings, otherwise, were he or she to tell you the truth and point out how you had spoilt his or her robe in this or that way you would certainly be overwhelmed with shame, if you are sensible person, and say to yourself: 'Yes, I have indeed disgraced myself!'

A courtship article too has no room for even the slightest of blemishes, because, as people say, in courtship no blemish can be a small matter. And with you too, since courtship is your present business with Kalibata, yes, you should take to him something good, something he can receive with sincere thanks.' (Kitereza, 1980: 475-476) [20]

---

[20] *Myombekere alipotoka kusindikiza rafiki yake Kanwaketa, akafika kuangua pazia, alilosuka kabla hajaenda kuposa kisiwani Irugwa. Alipolipeleka nje, akalikung'uta mavumbi na madudu mengine kama mabuibui waliokwisha kuingia ndani yake, akaliangalia kwa makini aone kama panya pengine wamekwisha kukata kamba. Alipokuta liko sawasawa, akafurahi sana, akaongeza kusafisha zaidi, tena akaliacha pale nje akalianika kwenye mchana, na kumwambia Bugonoka hivi: 'Kitu cha kupeleka mahala unapoposa, kinafaa kukipeleka kikiwa kizuri kama hivi, na wale unaowa pelekea wapate kukifurahia; hapo ndipo na wewe huwezi kupata soni usoni mwako, hapo ndipo utasema bila hofu yeyote kama baba mji asemavyo mjini mwake.'*

Bugonoka naye akasema hivi, 'Kitu cha kupeleka katika posa, kinafanana na ngozi ya kuazima kuvaa, jinsi haikosi kupata masizi, au pengine hasa haikosi kupasuka. Kwa sababu kama ukiazima ngozi ya mtu mwingine, na kusema, acha niende nikiivaa kwa kulia sikukuu fulani na mahali fulani, ni vigumu kabisa kurudi nayo salama, bila kasoro ya kupasuka, au pasipokuwa na ubaya wowote utakaoweza kukasirisha mwenyeji wa ngozi, kwa kuchafuka kwa aina yoyote au kwa kukunja kwako labda inawezekana kuwa tofauti na mkunjo wake tena kukunja kwako kunakuwa kwa ovyoovyo tu! Na tena utakapomrudishia mwenyeji anapoipokea, kwa kuwa wewe anakuonea haya, atafurahiwa. Lakini akipenda kukufunukia wazi jinsi ngozi yake umeichafua kwa uchafu kadha wa kadha, hapo hukosi kufedheheka. Na kama ukiwa wewe ni mtu mwenye akili yako timamu utasema na majuto, 'Kumbe! Nimeaibika! Tena na wewe sasa tazama.'

Basi ndivyo ilivyo sawa kama kitu kitakiwacho kupelekwa mahala mtu aposapo, nacho hakitakiwi kuwa kama kimechakaa au kimefifia uzuri wake, hata kidogo, na jinsi watu wasemavyo kama hivi, 'Mzazi na mzazi mwenzake haifai kuingia fitina

This description of the art of giving is crucial. The gift must be perfect. Any sign of dirt or of its being second-hand may turn it into an insult. Either a gift is perfect or it is not. This high expectation stems from the fact that it is the intention that matters, and that coincidentally any kind of imperfection reveals the true nature of the giver.

Therefore, the social bond that is sealed through the mutual exchange of presents is subject to the greatest care so that it is not spoiled by corruption, wear and tear, or natural decay. No sign of contamination from the 'background of chaos' is tolerated. The utmost happiness of the recipient is at stake. Such giving clearly hightlights the importance of purity in social ties and how they are modelled on the ideal. Nonetheless, this striving for perfection does not mean that Kitereza's fiction never deals with social tension or conflict, but that such events come by way of chaotic, marginal realities: the presence of 'the evil eye' and witchcraft running throughout the text offer explanations for events that jeopardize the characters in the novel. Behind any mishap lurks an evil intent or an anti-social deed. Only the perfection of a gift is an exception to this rule. Most exchanges are tainted. Behind every contamination there is an intention of either evil spirits or an enemy. The crucial role of healers is to expose these evil intentions in order to thwart them.

In contrast, the ideal of gift exchange is that intentions do not matter. The ideal gift is one that conveys no other meaning except that of its being, perfect in itself. Accordingly, the ritual of exchanging presents between two families, at a betrothal for example, is an act of transparency, a social act of ideal purity. In such circumstances, it is easier to understand the high stakes in the so-called 'ethnographic novel'. To speak of 'society' is to describe all the forces needed to prevent this society from being corrupted and contaminated. In this kind of text, the purity of social bonds is at the heart of the task. Without doubt this explains why the issue of marriage plays a major role in the 'ethnographic novel'. A marriage that transforms the intimate relationship between a man and a woman into a public and transparent bond is a crucial public institution. Furtive encounters between men and women in the woods do

(contd) *kati yao'. Tena na wewe sasa, angalia; posa ndilo utafutalo kwa Kalibata. Ingefaa umpeleke kitu kizuri, naam, naye apate kukifurahia sana.'*

not matter once their matrimonial links are there for all to see. The structure of ethnographic novels is built on such ideals. The unusual success of Kitereza's novel is due to the fact that it displayed the impure basis of such ideals. It is not a given that Kerewe society should be shown as an image to the world. Rather, this society is the fragile outcome of an enduring fight against the forces of chaos.

To render Kerewe society as an ideal is different from making an image out of it. The image is consolidated by filtering out all the elements that damage its visibility. Even when the image looks realistic it remains abstract and calm. In contrast, idealism is always in tension and cannot cut itself off from its inherent need to distance itself from reality.

Mnyombekere is the ideal husband far away from the imperfect man who is easily unfaithful and whose belly is full of worms, prone to all kinds of illness. The novel ends with Bulihwali's lamentable death. Of a great age, she lapsed into second childhood and disgusted those around her by playing with her urine and faeces. This pitiful breakdown of the character does not create any doubt about its ideal dimension:

> They even stopped passing by or going to say hello to her in her tiny house, or going in to talk to her, even for a few minutes! Once she began putting filth in their food and dirtying the utensils, they found her repulsive and completely avoided her. Often, only sent the grandchildren over just to light a fire for her, and that's all. But on the day she died she all of a sudden became very dear to them all again and they felt the pang of her loss to the very centre of their being. (Kitereza, 1980: 590) [21]

As with all characters in Kitereza's novel, Bulihwali embodies a duality: she is at the same time pure and impure, ideal and faecal.

This proximity between the ideal and the squalid is entirely revealed in numerous binging sessions where people drink

---

[21] Na kisha wao hata kumuamkia katika kijumba chake, walikuwa wamekwisha kushindwa, wala walikuwa hawaingii ndani yake wapate kuongea naye walau kama kipindi kidogo, hapana! Alipoanza kuwachafulia chakula chao na vyombo vyao ndipo hapo wakamchukia sana. Walikuwa mara nyingi wakiwatuma wajukuu wake tu, ndiyo waliokuwa wanakwenda kijumbani mwake mle kumkokea moto tu, basi. Lakini siku alipokufa ile, ndipo alirudi kuwauma sana na kuwavunja sana mfupa wao wa uti mgongo kabisa.

a carefully prepared banana beer. A significant development in the novel's first section focuses on the preparation of the drink that Mnyombekere will later give to his family-in-law in order to get his wife back. The beer's quality lies in its purity: the two most important steps in preparing it are fermentation and filtering. A good beer must be pure and strong. The one who has beer to share holds a central position in Kerewe culture, as long as his jugs are full. Drinking sessions are thus key moments for celebrating social connectedness. When the drinking reaches its peak, polite exchanges turn into uproars, singing and dancing breaks out, until the entire party stumbles into deep sleep. In the morning guests have to clean up barf and faeces all over the courtyard. People's bodies have spoken. This grand and highly sociable event is equally a release for the basic human body. People's wild words and songs are social expressions: urine, barf and faeces are the body's emissions; each has its place when social values are celebrated. This is at the heart of Kitereza's novel.

Drunkenness at the heart of the social system is also a central idea in novels by Kezilahabi, another writer from the Ikerewe Islands. In Kezilahabi's first novel, *Rosa Mistika*, the heroine's father is a notorious boozer who never stops asserting his parental authority over his daughters. The father's tyrannical rigidity stands in contrast to the collapse of his body, as he frequently falls into his own vomit. Drunkenness is the point of disclosure between the fantasy of ideal social relations and the dark rites of body contamination. In this sense, drunkenness displays an essential truth about the ethnographical novel. In this sense, the binges in the ethnographic novel reveal an essential truth. The steady decline of social values is caused by men who drink. Kitereza's novel ends with the narrator about to take his leave from a gathering of people who drink beer: 'And now to make a long story short: Good-bye, ladies and gentlemen, keep on with your palaver. As for us, we are leaving' (Kitereza, 1980: 591).[22] [Translation by Ruhumbika; ibid.: 675].

It is worth noting that no so-called 'ethnographic' novel draws a peaceful picture of traditional society. John Buyu's

---

[22] Maneno ya mwisho ni kama haya: Miye, ninawapeni kwa heri, nyinyi endeleeni na Maongezi yenu, mimi ninawaaga, jameni, ninakwenda zangu.

novel *Mtugeni*, that portrays the life of a typical fishing village in Eastern Africa, is full of violence and conflict. Nothing is simple for the hero Mtugeni who struggles, whether in his marriage, living with his wife or bringing up their children. These problems are caused by the fact that spirits (*mizimu*) regularly intervene in daily life. Spirits are the guarantors of reverence in the traditional social order but their means of intervention is very chaotic. Spirits are great meddlers but in the service of order. In a way, spirits are always drunk.

Two united narrative schemes

I will conclude this chapter by analysing the close link between the tales of elders that express the values of the Swahili world and ethnographic novels which aim at representing it. Obviously, both types of texts do not belong to the same genealogy: texts that are purely narrative come from the collections of ancient tales published by Steere or Velten. Ethnographic texts come from collections in which the customs of the same period are described. Both the purely narrative and the ethnographic texts are rooted in a colonial literature whose objective was to provide Swahili prose texts and to acknowledge a world entrusted to them, a world that the dynamics of colonialism would ultimately destroy. A further genre that must be included is the historical chronicle, for some manuscripts of this type were published during the colonial era. It is more difficult to establish the novelistic origins of the historical chronicles perhaps due to their proximity to epic poems (*utenzi*) which among other things seek to record historical events.

Once a tale is put on paper it becomes a pure narrative utterance. The speaker is pushed aside or completely erased from the text. Thus, the reader is faced with tale in the raw, whose passing from one generation to the next will be conveyed by the book long after the notion of 'ancient' or 'elder' has vanished. As soon as a link is established between the utterance and its transmission, the real speaker of these essentially pure narrative texts is the 'book'. The elder's 'word of mouth' is the verbal utterance *par excellence*, since the aim is to pass on values from one generation to the next. Now, however, the book takes over the task. Novels that derive from tales inherit a great narrative freedom as well as a moral dimension at the heart of the story. Miraculous, magical and unexpected events are always at the core of this type of narrative, because of the need to pass on values, which as they are narrated reveal a specific world. Thus we find the unbreakable link between the tale and the proverb in the Swahili novel, a link that goes well beyond those that explicitly take on this narrative form.

The ethnographic novel seems to operate in a different way since at heart it is a descriptive form. It is possible to find tales in ethnographic texts but they are always hidden in the descriptions of people's customs. Narrative is very often embedded in this way. Tales can appear in ethnographic texts, but they are tied to an utterance which the text describes in the form of an old man addressing his grandchildren. Building on ethnographic texts, the ethnographic novel emphasizes the question of time as being central to the notion of the transmission of values from one generation to the next.

In novels from the mainland that tend more to be ethnographic, society is displayed according to the rhythm of generation change. Characters are dominated by time more powerfully than by their individual actions and the healer's task is to guarantee the transition. In Muhammad Saleh Farsy's *Kurwa na Doto* (*Kurwa and Doto*) [1960], a novel from the coast, the logic of the tale takes care of this temporality. Characters are driven by the dynamics of solving crises which comes from the tale. In one novel or the other, it might not be necessary to have recourse to a healer because the latter is already implied in a narrative plot that maps out itineraries over which characters do not have much command. The narration imposes its own law and tension. Therefore, the novel focuses much less on society itself: rather it displays its values.

There is an inversion between the narrative order and the descriptive order. In the case of the narrative order, narrative episodes are inscribed into basic description of a society whereas in the case of description as in novels from the coast, description eventually enriches a previous narrative thread.

Depending on whether the novel is from the coast or from

the mainland, modalities of culturalist presentation vary, even though the subtext remains identical. The main difference is between novels based on explicit values (proverbs) or implicit values (tales) and novels that are based on a narrative process alone. Thus, the ethnographic narrative takes on the difficult task of holding a world's values. This difference is grounded on the notion of transmission. In ethnographic novels, generation change acts as the counterpart of the enunciative transmission which characterizes the tale. In one case, transmission pertains to the utterance. In the other, transmission pertains to enunciation.

It is possible to look at this difference between novels from the coast and novels from the mainlaind from the point of view of the relationship to language. Novels from the coast can rely on the *continuum* of the Swahili language to pass on their histories. The fact that the book replaces the storyteller is a supporting frame for the story. Factors such as language modernization and the arrival of editing systems are replacing the traditional storytelling evenings. The social system is capable of absorbing the unfamiliar features of modernity. Future generations are there to receive the legacy of the past. Transmission is certainly made more difficult by changing attitudes and the role of cultural interferences. However, the book is a positive tool, open to the future, with a capacity to overcome historical conflicts and to transmit the values of survival against all odds.

Shaaban Robert's optimism, which is the subject of the following chapter, is based on his conviction that nothing can stop the dynamics of transmission which are expressed in ways as protean as life itself, and of which the book is its greatest manifestation.

Writers from the mainland have a more complex relationship to Swahili because their use of it introduces a linguistic disruption from their primary language. The narration of *hehe*, *gogo* or *nyamwezi* traditional tales in Swahili has no connection to their authentic vector of speech: in this, enunciation is central to the text. Thus, Swahili does not embody all the values of the society wanting to express itself. The language is deterritorialized. Thus, the ethnographic novel bears witness to this deterritorialization. Swahili will be used by mainland writers who do have it as the vernacular. Novelists from the mainland need to show the changes that have taken place over generations, for those who will be born after them. The fact that disorder is an underlying threat in the Swahili ethnographic novel reveals this literature's vulnerability. The enduring presence of description throughout these texts highlights the struggle to hold on to a world that the writers know to be endangered. The characters who embody these descriptions are flesh and blood. They are actually *biographical*: life flows in them like an unseeing flood heading towards to an uncertain future.

Having said this, portraying the culture of a society is not totally foreign to fiction writing from the Swahili coast as shown in Farsy's pioneer novel *Kurwa na Doto*. The novel's introduction makes this clear:

> The story in this book is fictional. It was written with the intention of explaining how people live in our villages. The aim of this story is to preserve some of our customs so that our children can know how we used to live since many of the customs that we describe in these pages no longer exist. Also this story was written to help students and pupils who are involved in classes on people's customs and their way of life (Farsy, 1982: 3).[23]

In such circumstances, the novel's task is to safeguard and to stake out a cultural territory. The novel will describe ways of life and customs. The Swahili world is recognizable through a number of encoded gestures which are called customs and which are its distinctive identity. To delineate these encoded gestures is to reveal a culture. The key notion of *custom* establishes a union between what is narrated and what is described. This union is of particular significance to the novel.

Another point to take forward from this Preface is that the novel is a means of resisting the ravages of time. The novelist wants to expose a world that is endangered. It is worth noting

---

[23] Hadithi iliyoandikwa katika kitabu hiki ni ya kubuniwa tu, nayo imeandikwa kwa madhumuni ya kujaribu kueleza namna watu wanavyoishi katika vijiji vyetu. Haya yamefanywa kwa kusudi la kuhifadhi baadhi ya mila zetu ili vizazi vyetu viweze kujua namna tulivyokuwa tukiishi, maana mengi latika yale tuliyoyaeleza hayafanywi tena. Kadhalika hadithi hii imeandikwa ili iweze kuwasaidia wana wa vyuoni na wanfunzi waliohusika na masomo ya tabia na hali za watu.

that the substrate of such texts often lies very deep. The idea is to hang on to some part of worlds that no longer exist. This is a major feature of the novel, the form that can best accomplish the description of a passing world. In such descriptive novels, there is is a deep movement that carries everything forward. Behind the often romanticized images of ethnographic novels, one can hear the hidden echoes of calamity. What is unique to Farsy's novel is the fact that the ethnographic impulse to capture a Swahili life-style threatened by colonization works hand in hand with his deep concern for the external world. The presence of the rest of the world runs through a novel such as *Kurwa na Doto*. Scenes in which marriages, burial ceremonies and religious celebrations are described are meant to emphasize a narrative in which characters evolve according to the frantic rhythm of Swahili tales. This plot brings an old tale to life, with its short-cuts and symmetries. Kurwa and Doto are twins. The first is wise and hardworking while the second is frivolous and flirtatious. Kurwa remains attached to the island while Doto leaves with Faki, the man Kurwa loves. Doto must return to the island to die, and Kurwa's surrogate husband has to disappear mysteriously in the sea in order for Kurwa and Faki to finally be united.

As for the husband who vanished mysteriously: he finds another wife during his far-off journey and returns to Zanzibar where he lives in harmony with Kurwa and Faki.

In Farsy's plot, characters disappear and reappear quite easily. The sea and its distant coastlines permeate the novel. Kurwa is the only static character: she plays the pivotal role in a narrative that is open to all horizons. The key action takes place in Zanzibar but interest is still focused on characters that are either on the move or have just arrived. It is only at the end of the novel that the island is no longer a stopping point but a place for a stable life. This will be Kurwa's victory and the novel's end. This novel's distinctive mark is the clear heterogeneity between narrative sections and descriptive breaks that focus on the customs of Zanzibar, which attach themselves to the narrative to depict a culture and a way of life.

In a paper in *Outline of Swahili Literature*, Elena Bertoncini draws a link between *Kurwa na Doto* and a short novel by Naila

Kharusi entitled *Usinisahau* (*Do not forget me*), published in 1966 in the journal *Swahili*. In fact, the plots of these two texts are very similar, since Naila's text is also about two sisters, Shadya and Nadya. In the course of the story, the more serious sister gives up her life for the happiness of the frivolous one. The major difference between these two texts is the absence of local colour in the later novel, which speaks of the fame of *Kurwa na Doto*. Naila Kharusi emphasizes the psychological relationship between Shadya and Nadya. The dominant point of view is that of the serious Shadya, who is the narrator with better things to do than worry about how she dresses, how she decorates her house or what she eats. There is no space for depicting Zanzibari society. *Kurwa na Doto* and *Usinisahau* are two approaches to novel writing in the digressive style of the old tale. Yet Swahili customs are noted in Farsy's novel. A minor difference between both narratives is Farsy's effort to insert descriptions of Swahili customs on the surface of his text. No matter how many pages are dedicated to these descriptions, they do not change the substance of the narrative. This kind of text communicates the Swahili system of values. The description of habits and customs may be added to the narrative but it merely hovers over the text.

This insertion of the descriptive into the narrative mode is one of the features of a self-conscious writing. A novel such as *Kurwa na Doto* combines features of the ethnographic novel and the tale. It integrates Swahili customs (*Desturi za Waswahili*) in a Swahili story (*Hadithi za Waswahili*). This implies that stories do not necessarily show much about cultures from which they take their material. Swahili tales such as those collected and translated by Steere or Velten do not tell us much about Swahili life itself.

The tale as a genre is resistant to its instrumentalization in the narrative. To write about customs is not sufficient to make a novel come alive. Ethnographic narrative needs a touch of the romantic to make it into the realm of literature. A narrative has to twist and turn, otherwise it will get stuck. This narrative pull applies to all novels whose foundations are ethnographic.

This disjunction between expressing a world and representing it will play a key role in the development of the Swahili novel. Two possible uses of the Swahili language will make their mark on the Swahili novel: territorializing the language by having confidence in its ability to create narrative, and deterritorializing the language by not allowing it to become fixed, thus forcing the novel to find its own territory. The space claimed back will be its new reality.

Shaaban Robert can be considered the major agent of this paradigm shift as far as prose writing is concerned.

2 Shaaban Robert
The Optimism of Writing

All specialists in the history of Swahili literature agree on the crucial role that Shaaban Robert (1909-1962) played in the move towards modernity. While efforts were being made to create a standardized Swahili that would meet the expectations of the modern world, there was an urgent need for a literature that would go in hand with such a linguistic development. Shaaban Robert's aim has been to create a literary corpus that stands as the reference point for a new language that was specifically created to be able to serve new circumstances and demands. This body of work is *par excellence* transitional. It is the meeting point for traditional forms: poems clearly inspired by the Swahili poetic tradition, tales that are retold and adapted from *A Thousand and One Nights*; and also for new literary forms such as prose fiction.

Not by chance is the father of the Swahili novel also a poet dedicated to the classical tradition. A writer such as Shaaban Robert is not part classical and part modern: he has always responded to the dynamism of Swahili poetry, with its centuries-old desire for innovation. Didactic intent applies to both his prose and poetry. His narrative style can be described as a series of scenes that reveal the process of self-development. Characters are always 'in progress' or, more exactly, they are always on the move. The function of the narrative is to describe these inner changes through the actions of the characters. They develop themselves and in so doing to improve the world, and the reader is led to understand this process. If these changes are to be expressed in narrative form, it is due to the close link between his writing and his creative values. Behind the apparently outdated phrase, 'edifying works' there lies a very original conception of prose narrative which is the subject of this chapter.

Narrative resources in changing places

Characters move a lot in Shaaban's narratives but they never set out on adventures mindlessly. They move house more than they travel, although relocating is seldom a departure. Rather, it is the cumbersome move from one environment to the other with all challenges of adaptation that such a move embodies. This is what Shaaban says about relocation in *Insha na Mashairi* (*Essays and Poems*) [1959]:

> To gather and relocate beds, tables, chairs, frames, books and the rest. When we take the last decoration off the wall and we leave the empty house, we feel just as sad as when a brother dies. Everything is in a mess in the new house. It takes several days to put some order to this sad jumble of belongings. The first night in the new house is a sleepless one. Our hearts are full of memories of former friends. (Robert, 1971: 8-9)[1]

It is worth noting that one introduction to Shaaban Robert's essays is precisely on relocation, which he compares to death. Death is understood here as the final relocation of the soul outside the body.

The theme of relocation is important to Shaaban Robert because he sees writing as deeply caught up in places. Where a character lives matters more than what he/she does. Shaaban's autobiography, *Maisha Yangu na Baada ya Miaka Hamsini* (*My life and fifty years after*) [1966] describes his relocation from Pangani to Mpwapwa, which takes place over four chapters. More significantly, his novel *Utubora mkulima* (*Utubora the farmer*) [1968] is the story of a man's move from the town to the village. Utubora suddenly realizes that he cannot stand the city any more, with its massive jumble of buildings. He needs some air and decides to change his way of life. The novel tells

---

[1] *Kufunganya na kuhamisha vitanda, meza viti, picha, vitabu na vyombo vingine. Tuanguapo pambo la mwisho ukutani tukaanza kutoka katika nyumba tupu twaona huzuni kama ile ya baada ya kifo chaa ndugu. Kila kitu huwa katika mchafuko katika nyumba ihamiwayo. Chungu ya vitu vilivyotawanyika ovyo kila upande hutaka siku kadha za kupangwa vema tena. Usiku wa kwanza katika nyumba ihamiwayo hauna usingizi.*

us how he turns this decision into action. In changing his environment, however, Utubora runs the risk of destabilizing his entire selfhood. He was an office worker with a comfortable salary: now he will become a peasant farmer with no stable income.

The novel ends with the marriage of Utubora and Radhia: the hero has found himself, and does not need to fret all the time about his decision to move: it does not matter what drives characters to move house. Utubora will never succeed in finding a proper explanation for what triggered him to turn his life around. When he tells people about it, his sudden loathing of the city always seems inexplicable to them:

> As usual he was sitting in his office. The window faced a mass of buildings through which the sun could scarcely be seen. When he noticed this he said to himself that even the sun did not shine well on Unguja. This thought awoke in him a sudden longing for pure air and freedom.
>
> This desire, inspired by a weak ray of sunshine inspired a train of thought that led to important changes in Utubora's life. Suddenly, he realized that he had never liked Unguja and did not like his life in it either. He did not like spending the whole day sitting at the office and he realized too his salary was not that important to him. (Robert, 1968e: 12)[2]

The whole novel is held by one thread: the delicate piercing of a ray of sun. In the case of Shaaban Robert's own relocation, the triggering event is a letter from his superior, notifying him of a transfer. Shaaban cannot believe what is happening to him: 'I went through every line word by word to make sure I'd got the message but every time I felt I had been struck by a bolt from the blue, out of a totally clear sky' (Robert, 1991: 45).[3] The

---

[2] *Siku moja alikuwa afisi ameketi pahali pake pa sikuzote. Dirisha lililozungukwa pande zote na majengo yaliyosongana sana lilipenyeza ndani nuru ndogo ya jua. Kuona vile alifikiri kuwa hata jua lilikuwa haling'ai vema Unguja. Fikira hii ndiyo iliyoamsha hamu ile iliyokuwa moyoni mwake ya kutaka hewa na uhuru.*

Hamu iliyoamsha na cheche ile ya nuru ya jua ilianzisha mwendo wa fikira iliyoongoza katika mabadiliko makubwa katika maisha ya Utubora. Aliona ghafula kuwa alichukia Unguja na mambo yake, kuwa hakupenda kuketi kitako katika afisi kutwa, na kuwa hakujali fedha aliyokuwa anapata kwa malipo ya mshahara.

[3] *Basi nilikariri kila mstari na neon baada ya neon tena na tena ili nielewe na kiini cha taarifa ile, lakini kila mara niliona habari yake kama shindo la radi ya mvua liliilotokea bila ya wingu juu ya mbingu.*

reason for this letter does not really matter; in the following chapters Shaaban explains what took place when he moved.

The theme of relocation clearly reveals the power in Shaaban Robert's narrative. He gives his characters the role of transposers of places. Their main function in the narrative is to bring different places together. In *Kusadikika* [1951], one of Shaaban's most perplexing narratives, six envoys are sent to six countries around the country of Kusadikika, a land in the sky: above and beneath, to the north, south, east, and west. Each trip is narrated by Karama who, on being accused of high treason in Kusadikika, publicly defends himself. However, its fossilized society progressively discovers the benefits of being open to others. As days pass by, Karama's stories captivate a wider audience.

Shaaban's novel is a reflection on the need for evolution in society. It is remarkable that this progress is conceived as combining physical places. Karama's envoys find themselves plunged into societies they know nothing about and which they describe from an external point of view.

Gaps in the society of *Kusadikika* are filled by transposing certain positive aspects of neighbouring societies onto *Kusadikika*. Progress is conceived as a relocation. When envoys return to their countries, they are systematically imprisoned by the current powers that be, who can sense the subversive potential of such trips. The envoys are dangerous just because they have been somewhere else. By merely telling their travellers' tales of various trips, the envoys will excite the masses and make themselves famous.

Mechanisms of glory

In the political vision set out in *Kusadikika*, societies do not progress according to internal constraints. Rather, social progress takes place in the course of random transpositions caused by the voyage of one character or another. The people of *Kusadikika* are present in the novel more to hear about neighbouring countries than to manifest a demand for change. People come together in ever-bigger crowds to listen to Karama's different stories and narrative arguments. Each new chapter opens by mentioning that the audience is growing in size and becoming more attentive to Karama's stories:

> The vast courtroom, the biggest in the world, was filled by a mass of people who were sitting, standing, standing on tiptoe to listen and to see the accused person. Spectators had their eyes riveted on him and their ears were wide open, carefully listening to his stories. There were no more free spaces even on the window ledges. The hall was crowded on all sides. There were people to the right, to the left, in front and behind. The very breath of the immense crowd made the air hot. (Robert, 1966: 29)[4]

Shaaban's fiction is subtly duplicated in the narrative of Karama's storytelling to the people, whose presence in the hall is a sign that he has defeated his accuser. Each one of Karama's stories falls on their ears like a little bombshell, sending shockwaves through everyone's soul. The crowd of people does not actually do anything, but their presence is necessary for the unfolding of the narrative, to which they react like an echo chamber. Only news that reaches into the heart and mind of people has any real meaning. It is the people's prerogative to say what is important and what is not.

In his collected works, Shaaban has written an entire essay on rumour. He examines different means that states have to influence people by controlling the spread of rumours. To Shaaban, radio, press and cinema seem to be the new means for controlling information rather than books: 'By these means news is spread in cities and villages at the speed of light.'[5]

Shaaban's concern in this short text is to give an account of the challenge to elites that they remain aware of people's changing opinions. To a major extent, Shaaban's political thinking is centred on this problem.

Shaaban is particularly interested in characters that people

---

[4] *Eneo lote la baraza iliyokuwa kubwa kabisa katika baraza zote za dunia liligharikishwa na umati wa watu waliokaa kitako vitini, waliosimama wima, na waliochuchumia nyuma ya watu wengine ili kumsikiliza na kumtazama mshtakiwa. Jozi za macho ya watazamaji zilimtazama bila ya kupepesa, na jozi za masikio yao zikamsikiliza kwa makini mengi. Palikuwa hapana nafasi tupu wala dirisha lililokuwa halichunguliwi. Watu walijaa pomoni pande zote. Walijaa upande wa kulia na wa kuo, mbele na nyuma, na karibu hewa yote ilikuwa moto kama tanuu kwa pumzi.*
[5] *Kwa vyombo hivi uvumi huenezwa katika miji na vijiji kwa upesi wa umeme.*

talk about – characters who became famous. When Shaaban leaves Pangani following his new assignment, he notes with pride that he is not unknown:

> On the street, the people, whether rich or poor, adult or children, waved in my direction when I passed by in my car. I responded to their greeting by raising my hat. I was neither a mayor, nor a governor nor a member of any parliament. I was a man like other men. I lived with them in good faith. The day I was leaving was a day of glory to me. If that glory was to be the last one in my life I would not complain in times to come because I had had my turn. (Robert, 1991: 48-49)[6]

Real fame does not come from the performance of one's duties, but from the reputation that one can gain among the people thanks to one's behaviour and one's manners. Shaaban discovers that he is famous where he used to live and that he is recognized and distinguished, from which he takes immense pleasure. Official and stuffy administrative or political hierarchies are supported by the principled efforts of their employees.

Shaaban Robert's elitism cannot be dissociated from his commitment to the people. One must try to understand the mechanism of this optimism that enables him to attribute this faculty of discernment to ordinary people. To Shaaban Robert, there is no usurped glory. People always recognize somebody with good reason. Negative characters are forced to compensate for their lack of glory through self-aggrandizement, or in other words, by boasting. This is the case with the one who accuses Karama in *Kusadikika*. Even his name Majivuno (boasting) carries the flaw of self-congratulation. Glory can only be given to us from an external source.

This is why there is a major difference between the biographer and the autobiographer, as Shaaban explains in the poem 'Wasifu' in *Kielezo cha Fasili* (*On posterity*) [1968].

---

[6] *Barabarani, watu na mji, tajiri na maskini, mkubwa na mdogo, mwanamume kwa mwanamke, wakati nilipokuwa nikiondoka kwa motokaa walinipungia mikono. Nilijibu heshima yao kwa kuvua kofia yangu. Nilikuwa si jumbe, liwali wala diwani wa halmashauri yo yote. Nilikuwa mtu wa kawaida tu niliyekaa nao kwa wema na adabu. Siku ya maagano hayo ilikuwa siku ya fahari kubwa kwangu. Kama fahari ile ilikuwa ya mwisho katika maisha yangu sitanung'unika kukosa nyingine wakati ujao kwa sababu fungu langu nimekwisha kuchukua.*

While the biographer is only concerned with giving a good account of the life of his subject, the autobiographer sets out on an enterprise fraught with issues:

> The one who writes about their own life faces many challenges. The author blames himself/herself by continuously recalling certain shameful actions; by bringing up happy and sad times with friends or enemies, and dredges up the many other spiteful or wrong things suffered at the hands of others. Above all, the biographer runs the risk of being labelled a hypocrite – a liar [...] The autobiographer does not have the leisure to praise his/her own actions and should not try to do so. (Robert, 1968b: 53)[7]

To speak of oneself is a tricky business because it is impossible to put oneself in the place of others and to praise oneself. The story is somehow told blindly and the actions narrated are cut short as is the telling of their impact on other people. In his autobiography, Shaaban Robert recounts actions and intentions but does not relate the impact of these actions on others. It is not for him to deal with his own reputation.

In complete contrast to Robert's autobiography, *Wasifu wa Siti Binti Saad* (*Praises to Siti Binti Saad*) [1958], his biography of the taarab singer Binti Saad was written at the height of her fame. Shaaban tells how the young girl's exceptional voice first enabled her to gather a group of musicians and later to attract a growing and passionate audience.

Binti's Saad life makes sense thanks to this audience, while Shaaban's biography justifies her acclaim. To be more precise, Shaaban's writing consists in showing that this glory does not in any sense diminish Binti Saad's humanity. The singer was born in a village to a poor family. She was not particularly beautiful and was completely illiterate. From these humble beginnings, which should have kept her in total anonymity for the rest of her life, fate stepped into the breach. The biographer's task consists of reminding us of her original situation

---

[7] *Mwandishi wa habari za maisha yake mwenyewe ana jumla kubwa sana ya mashaka. Hujiaibisha yeye mwenyewe kwa kurudia kusema tena na tena matendo yake ya aibu kwa uchungu; kuhesabu heri na shari, na rafiki na adui; na mambo mengine kadha wa kadha yaliyo maovu, au matukio ya daawa na misiba. Mwandishi huyo hushikwa na woga wa kutosha kwa kuchelea kudhaniwa kuwa mzandiki — mwongo. [...] Hana nafasi ya kusifu matendo yake mwenyewe katika dunia, wala hawezi kujaribu kufanya hivyo.*

in order to contrast it with her glorious destiny. For Binti Saad, everything begins with a relocation: she decides to leave her village and settle in town. The decision is the result of much internal conflict between her love of her people and her village, and her longing to see the world. Shaaban presents this relocation as the real starting point of her career as a singer, and it serves as the touchstone to the whole story.

Everything is evaluated from this point of departure. To Shaaban, Binti Saad is a girl from a small village whose fame will soon spread throughout East Africa and beyond. Binti Saad did not simply move from the village to the town; she passed into another dimension: '…following this sudden step into glory she had the impression that she was living a new life in a dream country, flowing with milk and honey.'[8] This land of dreams is the one Shaaban Robert chooses for his stories. It is a glorious country but a country not without its dangers.

Taking action in a foreign country

The theme of relocation is crucial to Shaaban because he always makes us catch sight of the glorious country that plays a key role in the narrative. The place that one leaves behind is transformed in the moment of saying farewell: around the one departing, neighbours and friends gather in an attentive crowd, filled with emotion, creating the event. But the story is much more about setting up in the new place. However one finds that place, it does not matter what it is like, as long as it is welcoming, it is the right place for events to break out. Binti Saad moves from the village to the town but Utubora (Utubora the farmer, discussed earlier in this chapter) moves from the town to the village. In both cases, the characters experience a relocation.

Utubora settles in a village where he does not know anyone. All the villagers take note of his arrival. A friend from his university days recognizes him, which takes him back to the

---

[8] *Kwa mkuzo wake wa ghafula sana katika sifa, alijiona kama kwamba alikuwa akiishi katika maisha mapya katika nchi ya ndoto, iliyokuwa na mito ya maziwa na asali.*

world he has just left. All the ghosts of the past will come knocking at his door but Utubora will not abandon his new status as a 'relocated' person. Against all odds he chooses to become a farmer.

Utubora puts up a notice in front of his house: UTUBORA THE IMMOVABLE FARMER.[9] Everyone can read the sign as a business venture that will help him to enter his new world. His past, one that included his varying status as student, soldier in Burma and model employee is left behind with this *curriculum vitae*. Just as Binti Saad turned into a singer, so does Utubora, as a farmer. Both will get used to a new identity that is against the tide of what previously seemed to be their destiny. The process of settling in the village will transform him to the core of his being, precisely because the newcomer is a 'relocated' person.

Utubora's behaviour is odd. He is totally indifferent and works less for money than he needs to achieve the programme he has set for himself. He takes care of his neighbour's garden, even though she is a lonely old lady embittered by misfortune, who refuses his help. To the great surprise of those around him, Utubora is now just an 'immovable farmer'. These two words justify his behaviour. The neighbourhood grows accustomed to this newcomer who is nothing more than a stubborn peasant. In fact, the lives of everyone around him will be affected by Utubora. The old lady will rediscover her *joie de vivre*. Radhia, a young neighbour, will break up with her unsuitable fiancé to marry Utubora.

Thanks to his stubbornness Utubora will succeed in creating an environment of joy of which he is the focal point. Conflicts fade away around him as he becomes the reference point of a whole world. He generates a utopia. All he had to do was to move to another place, far from a world that was too familiar, so that this perfect place would rise up. Both Utubora and Binti Saad are propelled out of their normal life to create a world in the image of their true splendour, a world that Shaaban brings to life with his words.

The new world created around these heroes is inevitably unpredictable from the start, otherwise it would not be a true relocation. Everything is possible in a foreign world. Different

[9] UTUBORA MKULIMA WA MAKATAA.

people's reactions might be explicable, but we cannot understand these reactions. The metaphor of the sea is used repeatedly in Shaaban's writing to refer to the world in which the one who left his place of origin now finds himself, facing an uncertain destiny. A much-used metaphor for being in this world is that of a ship's captain who steers his ship through heavy winds and the tides to bring it safely to port:

> For a man to keep to the course and make progress in life, he should never cease to be careful. Life is like a big ship whose captain is the pilot who must use every means to bring the ship to port, through the storm or the calm, through the darkness or the light. (Robert, 1967b: 27)[10]

The challenge lies in finding this ability that will enable anyone to keep the course in a world in which everything is on the move.[11] It is the concept of action, (*tendo*) that guides the rudder. The ability to act is the condition for any successful life; one worth the telling. To Shaaban Robert, action stands at the crossroads with ethics and literature. A. N. Shija clearly addressed this link between action and character in his article on the subject in Robert's works: 'If it is common knowledge that a man learns a lot from the actions of others, it is obvious that Shaaban Robert uses his characters as testimonies to good deeds.'[12] The idea is expressed in another work, his poem 'Matendo', where the refrain establishes the link between the action and the memory one can have of a man.[13]

The theme of good deeds is more explicit in *Insha na Mashairi*: 'Those who die in accomplishing a good deed do not die because their name and reputation will not be forgotten.'[14] Nonetheless, what might look like a commonplace in the epic

---

[10] *Kila mtu ilimpasa kukisi tena na tena kama alitaka kufaulu rasi ya mafanikio katika maisha yake. Maisha yalikuwa kama merikebu; na mtu alifanana na nahodha wa kuongoza merikebu ile katika bandari ya usitawi, haidhuru kwa hali yo yote; mbele ya tufani au shwari, mbele ya giza au mwangaza.*

[11] The 'baroque' substrate of Shaaban Robert's conception of the world is visible in a poem such as 'Mabadiliko' ('Changes') (Robert, 1967a: 55-57).

[12] *Ikisadikia kwamba mwanadamu hujifunza mengi kutokana na matendo ya wengine, ni dhahiri kwamba Shaaban Robert kawatuma wahusika wake kama vyombo vya ushuhuda wa matendo wema.*

[13] '*Matendo ni kumbukumbu ya mtu kukumbukiwa.*'

[14] '*Hawafi wafao katika tendo bora, kwa sababu majina na sifa zao hazisahauliki.*'

tradition takes on a particular meaning in Shaaban's works if one looks at them from the perspective of the 'relocated' person. The action *par excellence* is relocation or a step into the outside world, which makes it possible for all other actions to take place. To Shaaban, there is no real action unless its aim is to transform if not reorganize the world. Men who take actions are not forgotten because they give rise to a world from which they will get their glory even some distant time after their death.

In Shaaban's world, deeds are always well intended. There are no evil-intended actions. There are only bad mind sets, which is different from a bad intention. A deed is underlined by the mind set *(tabia)* that is part of the small amount of luggage that a relocated person takes to their new home. In a way, the mind-set is the intimate face of a deed but there are two types: the well-disposed one, that is fully dedicated to others' well-being and the detrimental one that is centred on the self and on what is considered to be in one's own interest. Majivuno, who denounces Karama in *Kusadikika*, is introduced as a character with an obviously negative mind-set:

> His outward appearance could attract people and he could use his verbal prowess to make a sandbank appear or a rock on which a person could hurt himself just like a shipwreck. Every human ability can turn into danger or destruction to other people if it is not well directed. This man [Majivuno] was known to all, but as this story will show, he was despicable. (Robert, 1966: 1)[15]

Two important traits of Majivuno's detrimental frame of mind are revealed here. On the one hand, Majivuno has enemies he wants to obliterate. On the other, Majivuno is famous, but will never achieve glory.

The fact that Majivuno thinks he has enemies is a stumbling block, because the good mind set is totally directed towards others; it cannot generate real enemies.[16] This philosophy would

---

[15] *Kwa haiba hii aliweza kuyavuta macho ya watu; kwa ufasaha wa maneno aliweza kufanyiza fungu au mwamba wa kuyavunja maisha ya mtu ye yote kama chombo. Kipawa cho chote cha mtu kama hakikuongozwa vema huweza kuwa hatari au maangamizi kwa wengine. Mtu huyu alikuwa maarufu na mashuhuri lakini alijaa tadi na inda kama hadithi hii inavyosimilia.*

[16] Cf. *Insha na Mashairi*, p. 37: '*mtu mwenye tabia njema hana maadui*' ('A person of good behaviour has no enemies').

sound simplistic if Shaaban did not attempt to understand the narrative mechanisms beneath this philosophy. It is perhaps in the novel *Siku ya Watenzi Wote* (*The day of all creators*) [1968] that the question of 'spiteful' people is directly addressed.

Bwana Izak is an arrogant and wealthy heir whom everyone despises due to his unpleasant behaviour. Surprisingly, he will be the main actor in a generous deed at the end of the novel. The young Sarah, who can no longer bear Bwana Izak's attempts to seduce her, is told by Binti Akili that what matters is to create the space for friendliness:

> Sympathy is like a river into which water from many little streams runs. The river will dry out if you block off these streams. If you allow these streams to run freely, the river will gain from their strength. In this world – be it the world of your choice or the world you were born in – you will find yourself among people of all kinds, good and bad people – and you will have to mix with them. Nonetheless, what young people find difficult to understand is that crooks are not on one side and saints on the other. In fact, the most wicked person is somehow endowed with goodness. Even the most hardened heart has some softness and kindness that one can reach and awaken. (Robert, 1968d: 124)[17]

The emphasis on the theme of relocation in Shaaban Robert's work comes to the fore in the distinction between a world in which one was born and a world one chooses. One must show that those who have designed a world for themselves are the ones who can best express feelings of friendliness towards others. To relocate or to leave the world one was born in means to look at the world from another perspective and to go beyond the inflexible dualism of good versus bad people. In a tale from the Arabic tradition *Adili na Nduguze* (*Adili and his brothers*) [1952], Adili's magnanimity consists in always

---

[17] *Juruma ni kama mto ambao hukusanya maji toka vijito vingi kidogo. Ukivizuia vijito hivi, mto wenyewe hukauka. Ukuruhusu nguvu ya vijito hivi kukua, khadhalika mto huo huzidi kuwa na nguvu na maji. Katika dunia hii — katika dunia iwayo yote ujichaguliayo mwenyewe kuwa au ambayo umezaliwa ndani yake kama desturi — huwa umetiwa miogoni mwa watu wa kila namna, wema na maovu — utakuwa nao wote. Lakini lililo gumu zaidi kwa kijana kutambua ni kwamba wote si dhaifu wala si watukufu; maana hata yule aliye dhaifu kabisa ana namna fulani ya ubora; na hata moyo ulio mgumu kabisa kwa choyo una sehemu yake laini ya hisani iwezayo kufikiwa na kuzinduliwa.*

forgiving his brothers despite their determination to hurt him. He finally overcomes their ill-will and reawakens their sense of brotherhood (Robert, 1968a).[18]

The power of goodness

There is no symmetry between a good and an evil deed. Kindness is the essence of life and wickedness takes the form of tensions and knots to be untied. Thanks to his good will, Utubora succeeds in in opening up the heart of the neighbour who had shut herself up in cantankerous solitude. There are no 'evil people' in Shaaban's stories. There are only problems among neighbours. Through relocation we understand that our enemies are not 'wicked people' but simply they are our neighbours:

> You can choose your friends but you cannot choose your neighbours. You can either stay with them or go wherever you wish. No matter where you settle you cannot hope to have neighbours you like. Nowhere in the world can one choose their neighbours. That is why I do not want to leave the place where I am settled now although one or two of my neighbours hate me. (Robert, 1971: 33)[19]

No one is further from blind optimism than Shaaban Robert. The point is not to ignore the troubles in the world on the premise of human nature being essentially good. On the contrary, problems are found everywhere but they are presented as differences between neighbours, from living close to each other.

Some people are poor neighbours because they think that where they live is theirs alone and that they have nothing in common with those next door. What needs to be explained to

---

[18] This tale is the Swahili version of an Arabic tale found in the first book of Galand's translation *Mille et une nuits*. The tale is entitled: 'The story of the second old man and the two black dogs'.

[19] *Waweza chagua marafiki zako upendavyo, lakini huwezi kuchagua majirani zako. Wakubali ukae kati yao au jitenge nao ukakae pahali po pote pengine. Hata katika makao yako mapya huwezi kutazamia kuwa na majirani uwapendao. Uchaguzi wa hiari wa majirani haupatikani duniani. Kwa sababu hii, sihami katika makao niliyo nayo sasa, ingawa nachukizwa na mmoja au wawili wa majirani zangu.*

these people is that all places in the world are equal and that it is only by comparing opinions with other people that one can judge their value. Troublesome people think they are the only ones in the world; they think too much of themselves. Their 'wickedness' is due to an illusion about their place in the scheme of things. Quite the opposite: a good frame of mind comes from always taking others into account when making plans. Thus a deed is only truly positive when it benefits others as well as the self. Shaaban believes that the link between this principle of good neighbourliness and consideration of others' needs automatically gets recognition.

Wealth is the outcome of hard work but only the exterior sign of any positive deed that brings about glory. For Shaaban's positive characters, glory is much more important than money. Glory has nothing to do with fame. Glory is what one gets from being friendly to the world. Our glory equals our friendliness to our neighbours.

Ayubu, the main character of *Siku ya Watenzi Wote* is a typical example of the glorious character. He starts an association for mutual aid in his neighbourhood. Ayubu's main challenge is to replace the traditional principle of charity by the principle of mutual aid. The evil-intentioned Bwana Izak despises the visionary Ayubu, who has refused his 'generous' donations many times. Ayubu's political project is to set up a network of mutual aid among neighbours, which will heal the divide between the rich and the poor given that the gap feeds into the 'them and us' of hand-outs. Alongside this political project is a religious one, aiming to break down the antagonism between Islam and Christianity created by glorifying God. The proliferation of religions prevents the free circulation of divine beneficence and thus diminishes the glory of God. Ayubu's utopia is that both God and his people will benefit when religious differences disappear, to the blessing of mankind and the glory of God.

Writing: an enlightening and open territory

Words play a key role in this conflict between the forces of separation that breed divisions between parties, churches, social classes and so on, and the unifying forces that tend to foster solidarity among human beings, ultimately serving God's glory. Shaaban Robert believes in the power of words. He often uses the image of a gun to refer to language. Words are like bullets that reach their target and cause serious damage when they are released with evil intent, but the opposite is equally true:

> Words are very powerful and can be used to help people or to harm them, to make them suffer or make them happy, to bless or curse them. Bad words can cause a lot of damage and cause sadness while good words can make people happy and bring them joy. [...] Bad words come from evil-intentioned hearts. Greedy people find it difficult to say good things, because they only think of their pleasure instead of considering the happiness of others. To be capable of saying good things, one must try to share the joy and sorrow of other people, thus forgetting ourselves. As we change for the better, we can speak good words more easily, more naturally and more sincerely.[20] (Robert, 1971: 59)

In the case of orality, one cannot separate the impact of language from the ethics of the speaker. But Shaaban is a writer, and the written word lacks this immediacy of intention since the addressee is not present. In his autobiography Shaaban tells us that he could not stop writing: 'I had to write! At all times. I wrote day and night, even in my sleep and as soon as I woke up. I certainly wrote too much – nobody is more aware of this state than me – but I could not stop writing.' (Robert, 1971: 78)[21]

The words that Shaaban wrote down in such a compulsive

---

[20] *Maneno yana nguvu nyingi, nayo huweza kutumiwa kwa kusaidia au kudhuru, kuudhi au kufurahisha, kubakiri au kulaani. Maneno maovu huweza kutenda dhara kubwa na kuleta wingi wa huzuni, wakati maneno mema yawezapo kutenda wema na kuleta wingi wa furaha. [...] Maneno maovu hutoka katika moyo mwovu. Watu wenye choyo huona vigumu kusema maneno mema, kwa sababu hufikiri habari za furaha yao bila kujali habari za watu wengine. Kama yatupasa maneno mema, lazima tujaribu kushiriki katika furaha na msiba wa watu wengine, tena tujisahau sisi wenyewe. Kadiri sisi wenyewe tuzidivyo kuwa wema, ndipo iwapo rahisi sana, wajibu zaidi, na unyofu mwingi mno wa kusema maneno mema.*

[21] *Nilijiona ilinipasa kuandika tu! Ilinilazimu kuandika katika wakati wote. Niliandika mchana na usiku, na kati ya kulala na kuamka siku zote. Hapana shaka niliandika mno — lakini hapana aliyejua hilo sana kuliko nilivyojua mimi mwenyewe— lakini sikuweza kujizuia.*

manner are self-reflexive. However, he writes poems, articles, books, and has a precise conception of being a writer. To Shaaban, writing is totally open: 'It is commonly said that there is no end to books.' (Robert, 1971: 55).[22]

This endlessness of the field of writing is the ground where young generations will form themselves. To Shaaban Robert, good mind sets are cultivated through books. Utubora has to separate himself from his important library when he decides to move to the countryside because he does not have the means to transport all his books, but one can see that he remains attached to writing, which explains why he will entrust his fate to a few words written on a board. It is a kind of 'relocation' to have access to the world of writing through reading. By getting in touch with the written word, human beings can go beyond their personal interests, lose themselves, and enter the world of words.

Shaaban Robert neither mythifies literature nor his own work. He writes to nourish this world of writing and particularly to strengthen the Swahili contribution to the field.[23] It is characteristic of Shaaban that he does not hesitate to include the poetry of other writers in his own books.

It is obvious that education lies at the heart of Shaaban's project as a writer, particularly in his narrative works where the issue of moral guidance is central. The aim is to take the reader out of him/herself, to give readers the chance to develop another mind-set through the open world of the book. This much vaunted 'well-disposed mind-set' (*tabia njema*) as the key to a better future is necessarily conveyed through this relocation, in a world of words.

---

[22] *Husemwa kuwa hapana mwisho wa vitabu.*
[23] Shaaban Robert's works were part of a great strategy to defend and to illustrate the Kiswahili language.

3 The Crisis of the Bildungsroman

The education of younger generations is a very complex issue which is a priority for Swahili novelists especially in the context of a colonial world which is bound to change and to question of rules of the game. A principal feature of the Swahili novel is the fact that the Bildungsroman has no place in its repertoire. The one who looks to the world in order to develop is doomed to failure. The world is not a teacher. It is riddled with traps that those who are not well advised will fall into. The key proverb of the Bildungsroman goes as follows: 'The one who does not listen to the elders will break his leg.'[1] A proverb such as 'What the mother does not teach will be taught by the world'[2] can hardly be interpreted positively. This proverb implies that the world (*ulimwengu*) cannot play the role of a teacher, which means that the result can only be a disaster (Ndalu and King'ei, 1989; Wamitila, 2001).

This brings to mind the title of a Kenyan novel: *The World is a Saw* (Simani, 2002). Formation is impossible: either one is educated or undeveloped. A person is either raised well or is lost. As far as education is concerned, prose literature takes over from poetry in offering advice on good behaviour. In prose literature, rules of good behaviour in society are explained (Dumila, 1972, 1979); and readers are warned about bad behaviour (Baka, 1969). It is noteworthy that this kind of didacticism did not find its way into romantic fiction. Just like the Bildungsroman, the educative novel did not find its mark. We have seen that Shaaban Robert's works could not be limited to a didactic approach despite the fact that ethical issues are ever-present in his works. Utopianism precedes didacticism in Shaaban Robert's work in which social evolution depends on

---

[1] *Asiyesikia la mkuu mwisho huvunjika guu.*
[2] *Asiyefunzwa na mamaye hufunzwa na ulimwengu.*

the quality of interpersonal ties. Significantly, one of the only didactic Swahili works of fiction is a prison novel, as if isolation from the world outside was needed for a correct transmission of moral values (Haj, 1990). It is from being isolated from it that someone can be trained to face the world well prepared. Rules of good behaviour are learnt outside the world but they should be used in the world. Whatever comes from the world can only ruin the person who does not start out learning the rules of good conduct. This is the message of *Mbio za sakafuni* (*A race on the floor finishes at the wall*) (Ndumbu, 1976) and from *Kanayago la Maisha* (*Life's stagnation*) (Nyandini, 1991). These two novels tell of the disappointment of children who were left to their own devices too early.

Families in crisis

In such conditions, the main challenge will be to find the good teacher in a modern world in which parents are not always a safe bet. There is no guarantee that parents will be concerned with their children's education. Many novels feature parents who are confused by the eager embrace of autonomy that education instils in their child (Kondo, 1985). Deforming forces of the world can be at work within the family. Such is the case with a mercenary father who tries to corrupt his daughter's teachers so that she fails her exams. His motive is that he wants to marry her off so that he can get hold of the dowry (Wambura, 1990).

The most notorious example of a disgraceful father in Swahili literature is Zakaria, Rosa's father in *Rosa Mistika*, Kezilahabi's first novel. This drunkard abuses his traditional paternal authority and rules his daughters with a rod of iron. As a consequence, Rosa becomes incapable of having a balanced view of the world and her progress to adulthood soon turns into disaster.

Fathers who deny their children or who neglect them completely are also the starting point for several Swahili novels. The characters' names are Fuad (Suleiman, 1976), Bwana Maksuudi (Mohamed, 1980b), Bwana Juba (Mohamed, 1988a) although the topic of corrupted parents is absent from all the earliest Swahili novels. It is not found in Shaaban Robert's works nor in works of Mohamed Abdulla (the master of the Swahili detective novel). Furthermore, in Mohamed Abdulla's works, a father's mistreatment of his natural son is the best evidence of the absence of a true parental bond. The detective Bwana Msa bases his case on what he sees in the relationship between parents and children. The development of the modern Swahili novel comes about through further debate on such issues.

In an article that deals with mistaken identity in Swahili literature, Carol Eastman remarks that this theme is not used for a moral or educative purpose but for the sake of the narration, which signals an evolution in African literature. The theme of mistaken identity has been inherited from oral traditions especially from the folk tale. A child's bad behaviour is not the sign that he received a poor education from his parents but an indication of an error in his line of descent. Likewise, when parents do not treat children well, it is the sign that they are not their real parents. This explains the significant status of orphans. Generally, an orphan is not left to his or her own devices. The child is given to foster parents who are responsible for their education. In George Mhina's *Mtu ni utu* (*To be human is to act humanely*), an uncle is given the task of educating the little Sozi whose father has died and whose mother has been sent back to her village. It does not take long for people to understand the uncle's real intentions:

> People finally found out that the uncle Samesozi had started to use up the orphan's goods that he had been entrusted with. Sozi, the poor child, did not know anything about it. The money that came to the household benefited everyone except Sozi. (Mhina, 1971: 7)[3]

Little Sozi is dispossessed by those who had a duty to educate him. The same goes for little Mwiti in *Damu ya ulimi* (*Blood from the tongue*). He is mistreated by his uncle who wants to steal his fortune:

[3] *Watu walikwisha ng'amua kuwa mjomba Samesozi alikwishaanza kutafuna mali ya mtoto wa marehemu ambayo alikibidhiwa kumtunzia. Maskini mtoto Sozi alikuwa hana habari. Pesa zinazobaki zikipelekwa nyumbani zinawatumikia wote isipokuwa Sozi.*

Mwiti saw that the world had cheated him. The world and its people turned their backs on him. He was besieged with tragedies. Who else could they turn to, to claim back their due? He did not have a father or a mother. People had no other choice but to be satisfied with what God gave them even if it were to be the body and the blood of Mwiti. (Muridhania, n.d.: 15-16)[4]

These poorly treated orphans, on the brink of life, are at the centre of a whirlwind. They suffer from being in the wrong place but they can still build better relationships. In both novels the orphans manage to leave the home where they are poorly treated and to rebuild a family and ordered life. Sozi will support the development of many villages based on the principles of justice and equality. He becomes a defender of *Ujamaa*.

Mwiti's fate is similar to Sozi's. He will succeed in creating an ideal home after his uncle's family is struck by lightning during a storm (Muridhania, n.d.), or again, a new life comes to Ochieng in a novel set in Luo society (Wambura, 1980). In both these novels the hero is not formed by contact with the world, but participates in its formation. The impossibility of parents passing on the right values to their children leads to the possibility of the world's renewal. Marthe Robert's analysis, developed in *Roman des origines et origines du roman* on the myths about 'the child who is found' and the 'realist illegitimate' as a source of the romantic genre seems very relevant to those novels in which orphans are in the grip of unworthy proxy parents.

The 'neurotic family novel' therefore seems to fit perfectly here: a child develops himself in the world despite his parents (in the case of the illegitimate child) or in a new world (in the case of the foundling). The style of the ethnographic novel that builds on the idea of the transmission of values from one generation to the next seems to be of limited value as a model for the novel which is much closer to the narrative styles

---

[4] *Mwiti aliona kuwa ulimwengu ulikuwa umemghilibu. Ulimwengu na walimwengu walikuwa wamempa kisogo. Viroboto walianza kumshambulia; tena kwa wingi sana. Walikuwa kama vile walikuwa wanamdai haki yao. Ama kwa kweli hao viroboto wangalimlilia nani mwingine? Hawakuwa na baba wala mama. Ilikuwa hawana budi wajikimu kwa kile Mungu alichowapa hata kama kilikuwa mwili na damu ya Mwiti.*

of the modern Western world. Yet Mhina and Muridhania's novels which are apparently archetypal of the break with the ethnographic tradition surprisingly take another turn.

The narrative seems to pay more attention to what becomes of disgraceful parents than what happens to their ill-treated children. Sozi's exemplary actions for the development of the region and in support of a new social harmony has the primary effect of putting his uncle on the right track (Mhina, 1971: 71-72). Heaven's punishment of Mwiti's uncle at the conclusion of the novel exemplifies this concern with determining the fate of the generation that failed. The destiny of a child cannot be fully realized in the novel without a deviation into what befalls their parents.

Children can bring about a new world which takes into account the previous generations. In a story by Mwaduma published in 1974, *Simbayavene*, which has some mythological features, the eponymous hero disobeys his mother's order not to go hunting, since his father died doing the same thing. The boy flees to an unreachable village where he kills a monstrous snake, before he marries a young girl who obediently accompanies him to his village and is introduced to his mother. Simbayavene overcomes many obstacles and develops a new personality. He finds the means to shape a world more suited to his needs but his main concern is to include his mother in it, and to let her reap the benefits of his creation. Exactly the same progress appears in *'Mkumba vana' mwamba wa Mauti* (*'Mkumba vana' The rock of death*) in which an infant who must be sacrificed at birth is stolen away by his parents, raised in the bush, and returns to his village to re-establish the social order (Mcharo, 1988). The theme reappears in *Baadha ya dhiki faraja* (*Joy follows pain*) (Mushi, 1969). The problem with the interpretation offered by Marthe Robert lies in her attribution of a neurotic tendency to the family novel that developed from the rejection of the classic myth of origin. In the novels discussed here, parents are fully part of the narrative; indeed they are even its main theme.

As soon as one thinks in terms of generation, it is all the same: foster parents belong to the same one as true parents. If they behave poorly and refuse to pass on values to their offspring, they create a stumbling-block for the entire next generation. Children absconding, their education in another context, and their return to their initial society leads to the regeneration of values. From the moment that parents are not in a position to pass on values, children become responsible for creating their own. Otherwise they will sink into chaos.

Sentimental education

A major flaw of parents is their obsession with seeing their children, especially their daughters, married off. Marriage as an event often conceals a love relationship that precedes marriage. And yet, love or at least the relationship between girls and boys is one of the main issues in education. It is known that a father's disapproval on this issue causes the ruin of heroines, such as those of *Rosa Mistika* (Kezilahabi, 1971) and *Kitanda cha Mauti* (*The death bed*) (Mukajanga, 1971). Asumini, the heroine of Said Ahmed Mohamed's novel is distressed by a love relationship. Her escape is no better than Rosa's (Mohamed, 1990). The hardening of the paternal attitude to relationships between their daughters and boys is the only thing left to pass on to the next generation when values are uncertain. This is the case with Susan's father in *Nguvu ya sala* (*The power of prayers*) (Wamitila, 2003): he tries his best to prevent young people from drifting into romantic entanglements rather than planning their future.

People often fall in love in the Swahili novel. Romance between a young girl and boy figures prominently or marginally in all the novels discussed so far. A major feature of the love interest in Swahili novels is its strong social roots. One cannot imagine falling in love outside the real world. Love is not absolute and lovers do not create a world for themselves. Falling in love challenges for good or for ill, all social ties. It is exactly the fact that romance slips out of control that makes it socially decisive. Every romance is portrayed as going to the edge, not because love is absolute, but because it unsettles the web of social ties around the lovers. Katama Mkangi's first novel *Ukiwa* (1975) is about the love affair between a student and a young girl from his village: it relates the strength and sincerity of their love and the agreement of both families to a marriage in the future. But all this good fortune comes to nothing when the couple is confronted by a mysterious power that will in the end destroy their relationship:

> The disagreement that caused us to part seeped into us like a contagious disease. It caught Lila like a delirium, made worse by alcohol. Drink temporarily deranges one's thoughts and then the effects wear off. In the case of young girls it makes them lose their heads for a while and quite often leaves them depressed for good. (Mkangi, 1994: 87)[5]

Once again, the young people's splitting up is caused by love. The expression used by Mkangi is literally 'the world's confusion' (*mzozo wa ulimwengu*) as if the whole world was affecting this romance. Mkangi's narration unfolds at two social levels. From the point of view of the family, the love between the two young people is accepted and will lead to marriage but there is another perspective which is more difficult to define, and which makes such a marriage impossible.

The story is told by the student: his relationship to Lila disturbs his studies. After their split he goes back to his studies with renewed zeal:

> I returned to the university with a new kind of determination – I only relied on myself and I wanted to do better in my examinations than I had before. Lila's cruelty did not torment me any more, although I sometimes thought of her. For three months I concentrated on nothing but my studies. There was no girl to drive me crazy by not writing to me. I felt completely free – free to choose and to be chosen, free to choose anyone I wanted. This freedom came to me at dawn, and left me at sunset. This freedom went from where the wind rises to where it blows and this freedom spread itself from the bottom of the earth to the sky's limit. The world was mine! (Mkangi, 1994)[6]

---

[5] *Mzozo wa ulimwengu uliosababisha kutengana kwetu ulitunyemelea kama maradhi ya tambazi. Nyemeleo lake lilimshika Lila akiwa kwenye maruerue ya werevu wa kisichana; na maruerue ya usichana hupumbazisha mtu kwa muda mrefu, na mara nyingi huzinduka na hali hii ajikutapo katika mkosi usiotokeka.*

[6] *Nilirudi Chuoni na ghera aina mpya — ya kujitegemea na kutaka kushinda mitihani yangu kwa kima cha juu kuliko siku nyingine zote. Hiana ya Lila haikuwa ikinikera sana ingawaje mara kwa mara nilikuwa nikimwaza. Kwa miezi mitatu niliendelea na masomo na kujitosa maishani bila simile. Sikuwa na msichana ambaye kutopata*

Obviously one has to take into account the autosuggestion in this speech but the essence of the problem is made clear: romance entails a loss of liberty in one's choice of actions. Love is a passion in the proper sense of the word. Everything goes well if it ends with marriage but otherwise it leads us all to disaster.

The lovers' split is due to the fact that Lila had gone to the city when her schooldays were over. She wanted get a training in a professional school. Despite her love for Matano, her confidence in the future and her respect for her parents, she falls into the wicked ways of the city. Her relationship with Matano starts to fall apart when she embarks on a series of affairs that leads to their separation. This worldly confusion is concentrated in the city, where girls and boys come into contact outside the rules that marriage will bring. Love is liberated from the future; in cities, young people can take pleasure in the moment.

This explains why marriage becomes a private affair in novels seeking to present the social complexity of urban life as a space where different worlds overlap. The function of the marriage is modified in cities because these places are obviously where different worlds collide. The city widens the scope for potential marriage partners. Whole novels deal with the difficulties in making a choice, which is a personal matter. In the urban setting, to get married means to make a future for oneself. Love, as the intimate criterion, plays the first role, of course, along with money. The question of whether a marriage is self-serving or not is also raised. In the novels of Burhani and Habwe, couples come together, split up and try again in a continuous movement until the right formula and the ideal balance are found. (Burhani, 1981; 1987; Habwe, 1995). In this constellation, self-interested or greedy characters find themselves left out in the game of musical chairs.

The immediacy of love is matched by the dedication to study that will guarantee the young people's future. The school

(contd) *barua kutoka kwake kungenitia kichaa. Nilijiona nina uhuru usio na kikomo — uhuru wa kuchagua na kuchaguliwa na mwisho, uhuru wa kuchuja. Uhuru huu ulianza Mashariki pachomozapo jua na kukomea Magharibi pa machweo ya jua, Kusini chanzo cha upepo na Kaskazini uvumako; na urefu wake ulianza ardhini kama msingi na kukomea mbinguni kama dari. Dunia ilikuwa yangu!*

or the university is responsible for designing a professional future for the young. Education plays a different part in these issues since it takes no account of personal relationships. Love is experienced in the shadow of studies. Young people are students but are also at the age of falling in love. The two experiences are not supposed to come together. City dwellers are certainly not more libertine than village people but their romantic relationships are no longer tied to a future project, and can become chaotic. George Mhina's *Kovu* (*Scar*) tells how Mwingi, a brilliant medical student is completely knocked sideways by his simultaneous relationships with three young girls: Juliana, Maria and Katerina. Things end very badly for Mwingi who has no other choice but to hang himself in order to escape from the dead-end he has created (Mhina, 1986).

The narrator of Simbamwene's *Kivumbi uwanjani* (*Dust on the ground*) finds himself in exactly the same position and manages to extricate himself by putting aside all thoughts of marriage and by banking on his future as a professional football player:

> I decided to wait and to see what would come out of all this. Jasinta told me that she would tell her parents to go ahead right away with the wedding plans. Meanwhile Suzy had already told her parents that we were going to get married. I was getting confused, my head full of worries. I realized that I was getting into a state for no good reason with all these marriage plans. The most important thing was to wait for my leg to heal so that I could go back to playing football as before, and make my name in the world of soccer. Finally, I fell into a sweet dream about my leg healing up and getting back my reputation as a football player. (Simbamwene, 1978: 160)[7]

Good management of a romance means putting aside all

---

[7] *Uamuzi wangu wa mwisho ulikuwa kungoja na kuona nini kitatokea mwisho wa yote haya. Jasinta ameniambia kwamba atawambia mazazi wake ili mipango ya harusi ifanyike mara moja. Suzy naye alikwisha waeleza wazazi wake kuhusu harusi yetu. Usingizi ulininyemelea na mawazo yalikuwa bado yamejaa kichwani mwangu. Niliona ninajihangaisha bure na mawazo mengi juu ya kuoa, jambo kubwa na la maana ni kungoja na kuona kama kweli mguu wangu utapona na nitaweza tena kuchez mpira kama zamani na kulifufua jina langu katika ulimwengu wa kandanda. Mwisho usingizi ulinitawala na nililala usingizi mtamu wenye ndoto nzuri na nikiwa na tegemeo la kupona mguu wangu na kuufufua umaarufu wangu wa zamani katika mchezo wa mpira.*

thoughts of marriage. Thinking about the future does not go with all-consuming passion. Problems arise from the difficulty of managing one's studies and love-life. This applies particularly to girls who risk becoming pregnant and then being expelled from school in novels such as *Jeraha ya Moyo* (*Heartwound*) (Kiango, 1974: 22-27), *Doa la mauti* (*Death wedding*) (Geranija and Muwanga, 1976), *Upotevu* (*Perdition*) Mbatiah, 1999b: 36), *Mkondo wa maisha* (*The course of life*) (Njama, 2000), or *Nguvu ya sala* (*The power of prayers*) (Wamitila, 2003: 192).

An illness can also put a stop to characters' future plans (Kezilahabi, 1974; Merinyo, 1998). There is no tragedy in love itself in the Swahili novel but the ties of love can have dramatic consequences for the young people involved. Suicides that occur at the end of many stories on philandering are linked to the social consequences of love relationships: young people find themselves without a future (Kezilahabi, 1971; Komba, 1978).

The tension between the intimate and the social face of marriage is a powerful source of inspiration at the heart of the complex plot of *Nataka iwe siri* (*I wish it could remain a secret*) (Kirumbi, 1971). It seems as if there is nothing against the happy marriage of two lovers except the secret kept by their parents about an adultery that means the lovers are siblings. The impossibility of the marriage cannot be exposed. The situation will only be resolved by a secret inside a secret: the unfaithful husband had also been betrayed by his wife and the daughter he thought to be legally his own is not in fact his. Thus, the marriage is made possible thanks to this secret at one remove: the lovers are officially allowed to marry. In a final twist, the young girl refuses to get married and commits suicide, leaving behind a secret that will never be revealed.

The novel's internal architecture relies on the hidden twists and turns of secrets which eventually disentangle, so that a public and transparent event can take place in which the whole social body is involved. Kirumbi's novel emphasizes the irreducible role of privacy at the heart of every story. Marriage as a public event *par excellence* is the cornerstone of many stories which derive their tension from unveiling secrets that this bright event casts into the shadows.

A curious little novel by the detective writer Muhammed Said Abdulla with the title *Mke mmoja waume watatu* (*A woman for three men*) (Abdulla, 1975) focuses on a jealous husband who manages to trap his wife and get proof of her infidelity. This discovery confirms an insecurity that started when he was four, when by accident he was present at a female initiation ritual during which young girls were taught that a pot needs three stones to keep it upright. It is through this secret that the true nature of marriage is revealed. Women's infidelity is not simply a narrative device that allows good stories to be told. Their deception is at the heart of the social system regulated by the institution of marriage.

Making a connection with time is the main aim of education. What matters is to learn to adjust one's behaviour to time. Short-lived pleasures are dangerous because they do not open into any future. This recognition of the temporal dimension of behaviour transcends any other moral criterion. It is very difficult to find moral judgements in terms of being good or bad in the Swahili novel. Bad deeds cannot be condemned as such, but only to the extent that they lead nowhere and are doomed to perish (Mbega, 1982). Girls sink into prostitution. Boys turn to crime and gangsterism as in the most famous Tanzanian popular novel, *Mwisho ya mapenzi* (*The end of love*) (Simbamwene, 1971).

The failure to pass on values to the next generation leads to crime: there is no alternative. The question is therefore to know which values shall be transmitted in a world facing complete revolution. The great question of the Swahili novel is how to choose a mentor, or teacher, once parents and partners have been disqualified. The world of adults is not to be trusted. It is contaminated by the realm of instant gratification and has lost all sense of its educational responsibilities. Adults who are well-established professionally and within the family may venture into pleasures without personal risk. However, what they fail to see is that they run the risk of dragging future generations into the abyss. This is the case with Mzee Tamaa in the novel by Yusuf King'ala entitled *Anasa* (*Pleasure*). An apparently respectable adult carries on like a hunter in the bush and but his prey is the schoolgirl:

> Such a hunter never missed his target. When he was stalking his prey, he waited for exactly the right moment and lunged like a

leopard. He never missed his target. He did not waste his arrows: he was as patient as a cat waiting for a mouse to pop out of the hole where it was hiding. (King'ala 1984: 42)[8]

Such a perversion turns into a crime as is the case in a novel by Ali Njama about a professor who rapes one of his students and kills her, throwing her corpse into the sea (Njama 1995). Being around grown-ups is even more dangerous since one expects them to be wise and to give sound advice to younger people. However, they are just as likely to lead younger people to perdition. Several novels feature the theme of an adult getting a young girl drunk in order to abuse her (Habwe, 2000: 13-24; Mukajanga, 1985: 69-77; Mumg'ong'o, 1980: 59-60). Kezilahabi's novels are obsessed with the figure of the unworthy elder such as the school headmaster and the elder brother who corrupts his younger brother in *Kichwa Maji* (*Empty head*).

It is in *Mzingile* (*The labyrinth*) that this theme is developed with the utmost power. The hero takes a trip to the house of an old man who proves to be the creator of the world. The latter openly admits to the narrator that he has entirely lost interest in the fate of mankind (Kezilahabi, 1991: 10-16).

On the difficulty of finding a teacher

Schools deliver certificates, and universities degrees, but neither have any educational value when, as we have seen, nothing stops even brilliant students from falling into the abyss. Schools in many of these novels are places of learning, not places for the development of character, which explains why they do not figure prominently. Characters may often be pupils or students but this is only mentioned in the background. More important is what takes place during the school holidays or at least outside a place of study. What young people learn at school cannot serve as material for the novel.

---

[8] *Mwindaji wa namna hii hakosei katika shabaha yake. Hii ni kwa sababu hatupi mishale ovyo ovyo; huwa mvumilivu mpaka wakati uive ndipo mradi wake utekelezwe. Huwa mvumilivu kama paka anayemgojea panya aliyetokomea tunduni mpaka anapojitokeza na kutiwa kuchani.*

The only thing that matters is the ability to pass examinations less because of the students' competence to do so, than for the social status they gain from getting a degree. The school plays its role as social differentiator to the full. Thus a new and unique situation arises: the educational establishment is only responsible for professional apprenticeships. The world outside is abandoned to the quest for pleasure and the dictates of greed. All previous drivers of the transmission of values have been left behind. The novel will thus be the place for testing future values since there are no other values that will lead people into the future. This stake in the future explains why authors are obsessed with social values in their fiction. What novelists and their critics call 'society', the vision of every novel, should guarantee a future to the individual.

Modern Swahili literature is profoundly conscious of the threat that this future may vanish. To fight for the future is to fight for life. The mere transmission of the values of the past no longer suffices when these precepts do not serve the future. Education guarantees a personal future to its successful students but it does not protect them from the threat of the breakdown of society. Better yet, current schooling and the principle of selection that goes with it is the symptom of this decay. Education is the best assurance against the dangers of the world but it is a guarantee that only works at an individual not a collective level.

In other words, education cannot fully develop the younger generation. It is a structure that makes it possible to learn skills for working life and which gives social status but it does not serve as a social foundation. The school requires the existence of a coherent society in order to play its role as differentiator. The whole issue is to find what can hold a society together once the failure of adults regarding the transmission of values has been registered. One can read the history of the Swahili novel, at least since *Utubora mkulima*, as a remarkable effort towards restructuring the society. Young people have to take action, given that the chain of transmitting values has been broken.

The younger generation has no choice but to design a mythical plan. They are directly involved in a fight against chaos. Kezilahabi's first four novels tell of this tragic impossibility to truly take action. It was only with the publication of *Nagona* and *Mzingile* that an understanding of the conditions for this restructuring of society was made plain. Kezilahabi, who was quite often read as a pessimistic writer suddenly reveals himself as mystical one.

After a long journey of initiation, *Mzingile*'s young narrator takes care of his sick grandfather. He chooses a wife, whose chief merit is to be the only woman available, and he becomes aware of a new land, through the realm of the animals. His aim is to create a new world from the ruins of the old. The notion of a *tabula rasa* is entirely foreign to the Swahili novel. Fiction in the Bildungsroman genre has characters who withdraw from the world. The purpose of such novels is to reveal what the hero will discover at the end of his perilous wanderings. Some heroes are totally desperate, as is the central figure in *Fimbo ya Ulimwengu* (*The rod of the world*) (Ndibalema, 1974). Others reject the world for religious reasons, as does the hero of *Kuishi kwingi ni kuona mengi* (*To live long is to see a lot*) (Somba, 1968). The world is not for self-realization but for perdition. However, to cross over a world in decay is the prerequisite for a re-opening of a future provided that one does not find oneself caught up in this world. Thus characters develop the art of travel. In this regard, Ndyanao Balisidya's *Shida* (*Troubles*) is a somewhat unique Bildungsroman because the hero goes to a city where he meets a young girl he has always loved. He rescues her from a disastrous situation in which she is entangled. He returns to the village as a transformed person, ready for anything. He is quite satisfied to merely watch what is going on. Characters do not develop through action, but by observing. The desire to get involved can soon lead to being caught up by the world, to be led astray; real action can only be taken by someone who has taken time to weigh up the situation. This explains why a journey is the best master.

It is more appropriate to call these books 'novels of distanciation' rather than Bildungsroman. To find the right distance from a world that is caught up in the 'now' is the only possible future-oriented approach. Dadi, the narrator of Mbelwa's *Donda Ndugu* (1973) is a teacher whose emotional life is non-existent due to his constant work transfers and the ups and downs of his life. He loses touch with reality. The novel's third chapter is devoted to Dadi's stay in Nairobi and to his attempt to forget an unhappy love affair by going to a library as often as he can. The hero needs to place books between himself and reality before he can face reality again. The main character of *Njozi iliyopotea* (*The disoriented dream*) by Mung'ong'o is a young disabled consultant engineer in agriculture, who is appointed by his administrators to put reforms into practice. However, he fails to find his place in his new environment or to be accepted by the villagers. He becomes a keen observer of all the abuse of power and the shady dealings of his neighbours. One could provide many more examples of such characters who are in some disharmony with society and who function as a sounding board for reality. Such characters perform the role of witness to what really happens in the social body, which the political watchwords tend to conceal.

4 Euphrase Kezilahabi
An Initiatory Realism

The main subject of Kezihalabi's first four novels is Tanzanian society. Each character is fully integrated in this world where there is little place for fools or marginalized people. This is not to say that everybody is in the right place. Kezilahabi writes fiction precisely because society is an arena of tensions. Conflicts are intrinsic to society. They arise from within, not from the external world. The title of his third novel, *The world is an arena of chaos*, displays the author's sharp awareness of the presence of disorder at the heart of every aspect of reality. A society can be the subject of a novel because it embodies disorder in its fundamental nature. The reader must go beyond their usual ways of thinking to read Kezilahabi's fiction, because the narrative has nothing to do with a breakdown in societal values and does not conclude with their restoration.

Beyond the apparent realism of Kezilahabi's four early novels,[1] there is a theme of initiation that I would like to examine in the third and fourth works of this early phase, both published in the early 1990s. It is evident that they break away from the realistic mode.[2] *Nagona* (also the eponymous heroine) and *Mzingile* are two texts that are explicitly ritualistic. *Nagona* is about the spiritual quest of a mysterious half-woman half-deer. The first person narrative of *Mzingile* concerns a man's difficulty in returning home to deliver a message to the old man, who is in fact God, the creator of the world who has become a human wreck. Two initiatory models are displayed in these two texts: the never-ending pursuit, and the challenge of the return.

Each model shapes the space according to its needs. In

---

[1] These are, in a chronological order: *Rosa Mistika* [1971], *Kichwa maji* (*Empty head*) [1974], *Dunia uwanja wa fujo* (*The world is an arena of chaos*) [1975] and *Gamba la nyoka* (*The snake's skin*) [1979].

[2] *Nagona* [1990] and *Mzingile* (*The labyrinth*) [1991].

Nagona, the narrative space is crossed by an infinite line of flight compelling the narrator to follow. Through this neverending quest all places in the world lose meaning: the quest for what the future holds reduces the present to unreality. In contrast, the heroine's space in *Mzingile* is marked by stagnation. The narrator fails even to leave the old man's house, constantly returning to it, although he thinks that he is getting away. The vanishing point has turned back on itself; it has become a journey without end.

I do not think that Kezilahabi finally turned away from sociopolitical questions that were at the heart of his first four novels to immerse himself in a kind of mystical meditation. To me, it is more interesting that *Nagona* and *Mzingile* reveal the narrative structure of his first novels. It is evident in these two novels that Kezilahabi is concerned with the status of human society, its place in the order or disorder of the world. *Nagona* raises the question of a rejection of the social system. This text reconsiders the problem raised in *Rosa Mistika* and *Kichwa maji*: how can a character find him/herself while caught up in the radical process of desocialization? How can a narrative reveal the 'Beyond' within the order of society? Mzingile also raises the opposite question: what are the conditions for a society to be able to establish a new social order? How does the shift from a former order to a new order take place? How does a character experience this shift?

Entering the circle to get out of the social

Rosa Mistika describes the student years of the protagonist and her eventual suicide shortly after she has become a primary school teacher. The routine of her life, in the period between her studies on the mainland and then holidays at home on Ikerewe Island, which is followed by the period of her examinations, provides the external framework of this novel. Underlying it, however, Rosa is deeply disturbed by her wild sex life. Her relationships and her promiscuity lie at the heart of her confusion, close to destroying her very sense of self. She cannot come to terms with her life. The originality of the novel is that the narrative is not driven by Rosa's wild sexual encounters; rather it focuses on the studies that sustain her, despite all her distress. As she has one abortion after the another, her life seems increasingly aimless, with less and less chance of turning it round. The steady stream of awards and degrees fill her with the illusion that she is moving up in the world, and will be able to improve her lot, but this is in stark contrast to the increasing list of disastrous affairs that destroy the core of her being.

The person who is actually responsible for this situation is Rosa's father. Zakaria is a notorious drunkard who consistently forbids his daughter from having anything to do with boys. Zakaria keeps her away from them not because he wants his daughter to remain single but because youthful love affairs are a sign of disorder:

> Zakaria was very severe in the education of his girls, but he wanted to see them married as soon as possible. For this reason, he was very happy when he heard that Rosa had a fiancé. He wanted to get rid of his burden. He used to say, 'What a nuisance it is, having daughters! One's home is invaded by all sorts of people: some come to the house for directions when they are lost, others drop in to ask for water and so on and on.' Five daughters, it was really too much, and the young people treated his house like a zoo. (Kezilahabi, 1971: 47)[3]

The problem with Zakaria is that he cannot accept his daughters' adolescence, in other words, their becoming women. The only thing he believes in is moving up in the world. In this sense he only thinks of his family's social status. Yet the strict order he imposes on his family is matched by the disorder that his heavy drinking brings to his private life. The drunkard who cannot cope with his disordered life clings to his authority as a father and husband and brings down a reign of terror on his household. This type of power comes directly out of the social order. There is a close link between Zakaria's abuse of

---

[3] *Zakaria alikuwa mkali sana katika mambo ya malezi ya binti zake, lakini alipenda sana binti zake waolewe upesi iwezekanavyo. Kwa hiyo aliposikia kwamba Rosa alikuwa amekwisha pata mchumba alifurahi. Alitaka kupunguziwa mzigo begani. Wakati huu alizoea kusema, 'kuzaa wasichana tabu sana! Unapata wageni wa kila aina: wageni wanaopita tu nyumbani na kuuliza – njia ya kwenda kwa fulani iko wapi? Wageni wanaopita nyumbani kunyiwa maji tu na kwenda.' Kweli wasichana watano walikuwa wengi na vijana sasa walizoea kuita mji wake 'Zoo'.*

his paternal authority and his misuse of alcohol. Order and disorder are separated yet face to face. In Kezilahabi's novels, a man never drinks alone, only in company. Zakaria gets drunk on the local beer at a spot outside the village. The men form a circle, most often around a fire. Men always feel free to say what they like at these gatherings. Similarly at parties where people gather round musicians and dancers. The third chapter of *Nagona* features a group of people searching for truth, sitting in a circle around a column of light that they cannot touch. The circle reveals a very precise centre, but one that is always out of reach.

The obsession with the circle in Kezilahabi's novels is a sign that this shape is closely linked to chaos. Characters sit in a circle as soon as they step out of the social order. In the fifth chapter of *Gamba la nyoka* (*The snake's skin*) villagers who refuse to be relocated to *Ujamaa* villages hide in the bush after they have attacked a government convoy:

> At this point, the fire started to go out in each group. At first, people had built large circles because they were afraid that the flames would burn their eyebrows or the hairs on their legs. But as the fires in each group weakened, people moved closer, gradually forming a smaller circle. In the end, in every one, they cuddled up.
>
> 'Who's this kid, pushing me?' One could hear old Chilongo's voice, grumbling at a young boy. The boy was edging up to him, trying to get closer to the fire. (Kezilahabi, 1979 : 38-39)[4]

While the people are crouched in circles trying to get warm, the state troopers come up behind them and take all their weapons. Society, whose 'centre' is remote, has come to destroy such circles.

In Kezilahabi's novels, there is a constant dialectic between the square and the circle, between the structure and the

---

[4] *Wakati huu moto ulikuwa umeanza kufufia katika vikundi vyote. Ulipoanza kuwaka pale mwanzo, watu katika vikundi vyao walikuwa wameuzunguka moto kwa mbali wakiogopa ndimi zake zisibabue nyuso zao au manyoya yao ya miguuni. Lakini sasa kadiri moto ulivyofifia ndivyo watu walivyousogelea na kufanya duara iwe ndogo. Mwishowe watu katika vikundi vyao walianza kubanana.*

'Mtoto gani huyo anayenisukuma?' Sauti ya Mzee Chilongo ilisikika akimwambia kijana mmoja kwa ukali. Kijana huyu alikuwa akimbanabana ili awe karibu zaidi na moto.

cell. The village meetings imposed by *Ujamaa* are about the structure, while resistance is organized from the circle:

> Now, someone speaking very low chose twenty people and told them to move further away from the meeting spot. These people were arranged in a wide circle so that they could keep watch on all sides for any sign of a police raid while the meeting was going on. (Kezilahabi, 1979: 14)[5]

The circle is also used as defence against intrusions to the social structure. The circle is thus a centrifuge, so that no one should look directly into it. But in both cases the circle is built against the structure. Another feature of the circle is that people squeeze into it, so there is a good chance of misbehaviour:

> Anastasia could not see well because she was rather short. They were all standing up and huddled together when a man – a young man – moved in behind Anastasia. He pretended to be watching the dancers but Anastasia knew very well why he stood behind her. She felt his hand on her bottom. (Kezilahabi, 1975a: 72)[6]

One has to regard the circle as an asocial principle. Contrary to appearances, communities do not cut themselves off from the outside world, in a huddle, but open themselves to the grand Outside. A distinctive feature of circles in Kezilahabi's works is that they close in on a vertiginous centre.

The narrator of *Nagona* is caught up in a line of flight that gradually tears away all his social conditioning. His tries to get into a circle that keeps moving away from him. The theme of *Nagona* is this continuous movement of deterritorialization. The space around the protagonist shifts away at the same pace of his own forward movement so that everything around him becomes unreal. The narrator loses his social bearings for the sake of this point of intensity, which is Nagona, the young girl/antelope. The circle acts as a magnet. One can consider the

---

[5] *Sasa, kwa sauti za chini chini, watu ishirini walichaguliwa na waliambiwa kwenda mbali kidogo na mahali pa mkutano. Watu hawa walipangwa katika hali ya duara ili kutazama pande zote kama kulikuwa na dalili ya kuingiliwa na polisi wakati wote wa mkutano.*

[6] *Anastasia alikuwa hawezi kuona vizuri kwa sababu kimo chake kifupi. Walikuwa wamesimama kwa kubanana mwanamume mmoja – kijana – alipokuja na kusimama nyuma ya Anastasia. Alijifanya kama mtu atazamaye mchezo, lakini Anastasia alielewa nia yake. Alisikia mkono wake ukimgusa matakoni.*

dynamism of the novel to be centripetal if one bears in mind that the centre is always pushed to the edge of the circle.

The apparatus invoked by Kezilahabi is very particular: the centre of the circle that is always evasive pulls the circle to the opposite of social organization. Everything is escaping imperceptibly as if this situation reflects what is taking place on the wrong side of reality. Citizens no longer gather in circles to turn their backs on the social structure. This circle exists on its own and sucks people up into an infinite and vanishing vortex. Thus, the narrator's problem is to enter the circle and get to its centre. This will only happen at the end of the novel when he joins in the chaotic dance of people driven mad by their fate.

> I was dragged into the circle by a wave of intense desire. I stared at the centre of the circle. I danced and I lost consciousness. Then I saw the old man coming closer to me. He looked into my eyes, he raised his cane and touched my necklaces. He seized me by the hair and dragged me to the centre of the circle. He touched my body with his cane and said: 'Dance!' Suddenly I was taken over by an immense force. I knew what I had to do. I began to spin like a top without feeling dizzy at all. 'Dance!' The old man filled me with energy. I danced till I lost all my senses. Finally I blacked out.
>
> Just as I was falling down, the old man touched me again with his cane, reviving me. I heard him say, 'Look up!' Still spinning, I looked up, then my eyes closed. I felt an immense light beating into my eyes from above. I had the feeling that a new life coursed into my blood and veins. The light was powerful. 'Kneel down!' the old man commanded, I stopped dancing and did as he said. 'Look down!' Suddenly, I felt something heavy pressing down on my shoulders. 'Stand up! Dance!' I danced. The old man touched me once again with his cane. 'Dance! Dance! Celebrate your life!' I began to spin fast like a top. I felt that tremendous weight lift from my shoulders. Suddenly I saw a great flash of lightning and I heard the roar of thunder. (Kezilahabi, 1990: 59-60)[7]

[7] *Nilijikuta nakokotwa na mkondo wa utashi kufuata duara. Macho nikayakazia katikati ya duara. Nilicheza ngoma, nikajisahau. Niliona kizee kinijia pale nilipokuwa. Kilinitazama machoni, halafu kikainua fimbo yake na kugusa ushanga wangu wa shingoni. Kilishika nywele zangu za kichwani kikaniburuza hadi kwenye kitovu cha duara. Kiliugusa mwili wangu kwa fimbo kikasema: 'Cheza!' Ghafla nilipata nguvu za ajabu. Nilijua sasa la kufanya. Nilizunguka pale katikati kama pia na bila kuona kizunguzungu. 'Cheza ngoma!' Kizee kilinitia hamasa. Nilicheza nikajisahau. Nilianza sasa kuona kuzunguzungu.*

The centre of the circle is a source of energy. No one can stand at this centre without losing his entire self. The trance state that overcomes the narrator is epiphanic, revealing the nature of all his previous wanderings. The novel concludes in a climax of meaningless words. Everything that happens in the novel is a narrative device to define meaninglessness. The remarkable outpouring of energy that concludes the novel defines the interaction between energy to chaos, revealing a ferocious strength that can take hold of anyone who is in the right frame of mind, and finds the right place.

In *Mzingile* it is revealed that that this final trance has brought on unimaginable disaster. One could call it a nuclear explosion. The entire narrative is driven towards this denouement. Similarly, *Rosa Mistika* is driven towards a disaster that will force Rosa's family into total destruction. Zakaria is stabbed with a spear on his friend Ndalo's grave because of his appalling behaviour at the funeral. Beer-drinking has made Zakaria lose all sense of decency. During the funeral, he cracks jokes as he used to do with Ndalo:

> Nobody said a word. Zakaria did something incredible. Everyone was stunned. It just wasn't the time to say such things. He was drunk but the way he spoke was not simply because he had been drinking; it was because he loved to crack a joke. Zakaria was an irredeemable comedian. Nothing he said could be taken seriously. When he noticed that people did not appreciate his humour, he just took it further. He stepped up on Ndalo's grave. Everyone looked at him with total amazement. Even the women came out of their houses to watch him. (Kezilahabi, 1971: 108)[8]

(contd) *Nilipokaribia kuanguka kizee kilinigusa tena kwa fimbo. Nilipata tena nguvu za ajabu. Nilicheza na kuzunguka kama pia. Nilisikia kizee kikiniambia, 'Tazama juu!' Nilitazama juu hali nikizunguka kasi kama pia. 'Cheza!' kilipiga kelele. Nilicheza nikitazama juu, halafu macho yangu yakafunguka. Niliona mwanga mkali ukishuka machoni mwangu kutoka juu. Nikajihisi kama kwamba mwilimzima ulikuwa umewekewa damu mpya. Mwanga ulikuwa mkali. 'Piga magoti!' Kizee kiliniambia. Niliacha kucheza nikapiga magoti. 'Tazama chini.' Ghafla nilihisi kitu kizito kimekaa juu ya mabega yangu. 'Simama! Cheza!' Nilicheza. Kizee kilinigusa tena kwa fimbo. 'Cheza! Cheza! Cheza maisha yako!' Nilizunguka kama pia. Sikusikia tena uzito wa kile kilichokuwa mabegani pangu na mlio mkubwa wa radi ukasikika.*

[8] *Watu wote walikuwa kimya. Zakaria alifanya jambo la ajabu. Kila mtu alishangaa: huu haukuwa wakati wa kusema maneno kama hayo. Zakaria alikuwa amelewa; lakini siyo tu ulevi uliomfanya aseme hivi lakini hasa kwa kuwa alikuwa amezoea mizaha. Zakaria alikuwa mtu mwenye mizaha mingi. Alifikiri kwamba alikuwa*

In truth, Zakaria's misbehaviour was not caused by alcohol but by his over-familiarity. He is incapable of distinguishing between his drinking mates and a group of villagers in mourning. He has lost all sense of proportion due to too much idle socializing. Zakaria makes the fatal mistake of losing all recognition of the social order and how he should behave. He goes beyond all social bounds not simple through his actions, but by transgressing the internal code of intimacy.

Zakaria's loss of control can be compared to Kalia's – the younger brother of *Kichwa maji*'s narrator. Kalia is still a child when Kazimoto takes him along to his assignations with his lovers. Kalia loses his way because of these women. He discovers that behind the normal behaviour regarding women and sex, as sanctioned by marriage, there is in fact a secret world of illicit behaviour, disorder and deceit. Later, he embraces this disorder and turns into a sexual predator. He starts raping young girls on the outskirts of the village and goes as far as to get into their rooms. Eventually his body is found on the banks of a river, stabbed with two spears. Kalia embodies the swift decline of Kezilahabi's characters. In an idle conversation with Kazimoto, Kalia reveals that he was taken up to heaven in a dream. When Kazimoto asks him whether he saw God, his answer is 'No! But we knew there was a power beyond us, which I think was God.'[9] Kalia is at the centre of that circle which is constantly renewed in energy by the old man's cane, at the conclusion of *Nagona*. The weapons that pinion Zakaria and Kalia are like scalpels cutting out a tumour. They prevent the disorder that leads to disaster. Thus, in *Nagona*, everyone decides not to call the police because the language of law is irrelevant to the situation. Zakaria and Kalia are not criminals; they have not broken the law, but slipped away from it. They have moved into an intimate micro-space that knows no limits, which is indeed the chaotic foundation of all human societies. There seems to be an invitation to chaos that is fundamental to Swahili social structures and the

(contd) *akifanya mizaha. Alipoona kwamba watu hawakufurahia mizaha yake alijaribu tena. Alikwenda akapanda juu ya kaburi la Ndalo. Kila mtu sasa alikuwa akimwangalia kwa mshangao mkubwa. Hata wanawake walitoka ndani ya nyumba kuja kumwona.*

[9] *'Hata! Isiokuwa kila wakati tulikuwa tukifahamu kwamba kulikuwa na nguvu fulani juu yetu, ambaye nafikiri niye Mungu Mpenzi.'*

self-realization of the people. Kezilahabi draws his narrative dynamism from this tendency to chaos. In reply to a question by Lars Bernander (1977) on the number of dead people in his novels, Kezilahabi replied, 'It's how I conceive tragedy. Death puts an end to a tragic trajectory; yet it is an end from which it is possible to revive.' Death and chaos are integrated in Kezilahabi's characters. Their life trajectories can be regarded as death in motion.

Dunia uwanja wa fujo opens in this chaotic space:

> A bird whose foot was hit by the stone from a sling was flying very fast to save its life. It flew very high, which made the squealing children give up hope that it would fall to the ground. But it did not go very far and its wings got tired. The bird needed to rest. It saw a tall tree not very far off. It landed on this tree but it could not stand on one foot and began to lose its grip. Slowly the bird slipped. Feebly, it tried to fly again and ended up in the thick foliage of a mango tree. There, the bird recovered its breath.
>
> This mango tree had been planted right at the centre of Kasala's compound [...]. (Kezilahabi, 1975a: 3)[10]

The wounded bird in the opening scenes of the novel disappears from the narrative. The bird has led readers to the compound of Kasala, one of the novel's main protagonists. A drama that is at once domestic but with savage implications has been played out between the group of children and the bird. Children's cruelty incurs no consequences; it occurs with a sort of innocence towards animals and remains with the domestic sphere. However, what Kezilahabi reveals is this delimiting of the private sphere from the public space, which brings such conflicts to the surface.

In a strange way, *Nagona* begins with a very similar scene in which the victim is no longer a bird but the narrator himself:

---

[10] *Ndege mmoja aliyekuwa amevunjwa mguu kwa jiwe la manati alikuwa akirika juu angani kwa kasi sana kuokoa maisha yake. Aliruka juu sana na kuwakatisha tamaa watoto waliokuwa wakipiga kelele wakimtegemea kuanguka chini. Lakini hakufika mbali sana mbawa zake zilipochoka. Alihitaji kupumzika. Karibu naye aliona mit mrefu wa aina ya mvule. Alitua. Lakini hakuweza kusimama juu ya mguu mmoja. Polepole alitelemka chini. Alijikaza. Alijaribu kuruka tena. Alitu juu ya majani mengi ya mwembe. Hapa alipumzika kwa maumivu katika kifua chake juu ya majani.*

Mti huu wa mwembe ulikuwa umepandwa katikati kabisa ya mji wa Kasala (...)

My hip started to hurt. I fell to my knees. The pain made me crawl about. I heard people laughing. I tried to go faster. I heard laughter all around me from every tree. The whole forest started laughing at me. I saw its branches dancing in the breeze. Then suddenly, all trees stopped laughing and there was no more mockery. Everything went quiet.

Here and there one could hear a bird singing. I went on crawling about about to no purpose. Suddenly I felt someone caning me on my buttocks and my back. I tried to speed up because of the pain but then I could not take it anymore. I was beaten with no let-up and I could not get away from it. I grew weaker and weaker, in body and in spirit, and I went numb. (Kezilahabi, 1990: 1)[11]

From the start, the narrator is at the centre of the circle, in this space of initiation where no laws apply and no holds are barred.

The eponymous protagonists in *Rosa Mistika* and *Kichwa maji* (Rosa and Kazimoto) are pivotal in their respective spaces. As young adults they are part of the social sphere, each one hoping to find a job and get married. Still, these concerns are not intimate concerns, it is precisely the private sphere that will dash all their hopes.

The opening scene in *Kichwa maji* perfectly expresses the close affiliation between the social and the private sphere:

Many people were lining up in front of the District Head's office: old and young men and women. They all sat on a long bench close to the entrance, like patients in a doctor's waiting room. As soon as one of them went in, others shifted along bottom to bottom, to fill up the space. I liked this exercise because I was sitting between two young girls but the young girl who was sitting on my left did not seem to like it: she was next to an old man and she held a handkerchief to her nose all the time. (Kezilahabi, 1974: 1)[12]

---

[11] *Kichomi kilianza ubavuni. Nilipiga magoti chini. Kwa maumivu nilianza kutembelea mogoti. Nilisikia vicheko vya watu. Nilijaribu kuongeza mwendo. Nilisikia vicheko kutoka karibu katika kila mti. Msitu mzima ulianza kunicheka. Niliona matawi ya miti yakianza kuchezacheza kwa upepo. Ghafla miti yote iliacha kuchez na vicheko vikaisha. Kukawa shwari.*

Milio ya ndege ilisikika hapa na pale. Niliendelea kujikokota kwa magoti kuelekea nisikokujua. Nilistukia napigwa kiboko matakoni na mgongoni. Mwanzoni nilisikia maumivu, nikajaribu kuongeza mwendo, lakini baada ya muda kichomi kilinizidi. Nilipigwa viboko mfululizo, lakini sikuweza kujitingisha. Polepole nilijiona naishiwa guvu na fahamu, na mwili ukafa ganzi.

[12] *Watu kuliokuwa kuingia ndani ya ofisi ya Mkuu wa Wilaya tulikuwa wengi.*

There are no principles of order in this haphazard queue in which body contact can evoke pleasure or disgust. The people lined up at the door are bodies outside any social protocol. The rule according to which the person who arrives last waits the longest is a principle of self-regulation in a crowd, and not a principle of social organization.

In the same way, these bodies are lined up on a bench in an expression of the social power of the district head: people wait there because they hope to get something from him. Bodies are not assembled in a circle, but lined up as a function of the social order. The man they wait for embodies a rule of alignment not a principle of social organization. Zakaria's authority over his daughter is of the same nature; he operates on the principle of abstract paternity, having abandoned his role as guardian of the home.

In concrete terms, Rosa and Kazimoto both live in a world without order while keeping up some abstract sense of its social rules. It is possible to view Kezilahabi's novels as intimist works provided that one understands that to Kezilahabi, privacy is a frightening space that works against the social order. Characters believe they can marry and start a family without taking into account their previous sexual activities. Their bodies betray them: Rosa is no virgin, while Kazimoto has infected his wife with a disease he picked up from prostitutes. Each of them will commit suicide at the end of their story. This action comes from outside the private sphere. The dream of becoming real social people leads them to kill off their 'wild child' traits, even though this behaviour is totally at one with the clandestine intimacy of their world.

Kezilahabi shows that privacy is not an individual matter but deeply social. Societies have an intimate aspect. Characters are never who they think they are because they live in a society that does not know its own intimate life. This private yet solid space, pulsing with details, lies in the foundation of

(contd) *Wazee kwa vijana, wanawake kwa wanaume. Wote, kama wagonjwa wangojeao kumwona daktari, tulikuwa tumekaa juu ya bao refu karibu na mlango uingiao kwa mkubwa. Mmoja alipobuwa akiinigia ndani tulisukumana kwa matako ili kuziba nafasi. Kwa kuwa nilikuwa nimekaa kati ya wasichana wawili, mchezo huu niliuona mzuri sana. Lakini msichana aliyekuwa amekaa karibu nami mkono wa kuo hakuonekana kuwa na raha: alikuwa amekaa karibu na mzee, na wakati wote msichana huyu alikuwa ameweka kitambaa juu ya pua yake.*

Kezilahabi's novels. Personal stories will always be told against this background of all-encompassing impersonality, yet such a background is not merely a passive setting but a dynamic one. It is never forgotten, even for a moment. Kezilahabi's novels are filled with parallel scenes that disrupt the main narrative. In a way, they are novels without plots, relying on characters for their coherence. Such chaotic underlying material is the real substance of these novels. It discloses the inverse of all societies in history – it is the mystical foundation that is so close to us and at the same time so far away. It bears the name of the lady-antelope: Nagona.

Leaving the circle to rebuild the social order

The narrative in *Mzingile* follows a logic quite different from that of *Nagona*. In *Mzingile*, the only problem is to how to get out of the circle. The narrator, who is sent to deliver a message to the old man, cannot find his way home and is unwillingly drawn back to the old man's dwelling place. The circle's centre exercises some magnetic force that destroys the narrator's pathway.

The narrator's wanderings in the old man's circle are explained by the fact that no world is ready to welcome him. The old world was destroyed by a nuclear explosion, while the new world has not yet been born. The time-space in *Mzingile* is set between two worlds. Kezilahabi's narrative takes place in this transitional zone between one world and the other. The opening of the novel reveals the particular attention that Kezilahabi pays to epochal changes, and to the traces that former eras leave to those following:

> On Lake Victoria – as it is still being called today – there is an island known by the name of Ukerewe, thirty miles from Mwanza. If there is no fog, it can be seen from Sukumaland. At the centre of the island there is a huge building constructed by the Germans. Next to this building there is a tree that was used as a gallows – for the Blacks. This building stands at the centre of Namagondo village. It was not far from there that Regina had her home. (Kezilahabi, 1971: 7)[13]

[13] *Katika ziwa Victoria – kama liitwayo mpaka sasa – kuna kisiwa kijulikanacho kwa*

Regina is the mother of Rosa, whose chaotic life is the centre of the story. She lives in an unstable space where the place-names, architecture and even the vegetation are subject to the vagaries of history.

There are two kinds of stories of a quite different nature. One displays a world: revealing and manifesting a vision of a society, they give testimony to that world. Other stories record the movements from one world to the next. Such stories of necessity speak of an Outside to both worlds in which the movement from one world to the other takes place. Kezilahabi's stories fall within this second type. This explains why former worlds leave marks on new worlds as ghosts do, and just as a snake sloughs off its old skin.

Gamba la nyoka is about the real change to the world of *Ujamaa* and the political turbulences that went with this campaign. Mamboleo and Mambosasa are the two young men who dedicate themselves to putting their competence and energy into the *Ujamaa* policy. To both of them the success of *Ujamaa* is a personal matter, for their social status depends upon it. The two men endlessly discuss the shape of the new world, the socialist society they want to introduce, and the strategies to adopt in order to convince people that they should accept this new model of society. Their main foe is not Kidevu's father, who as a CIA agent works for another development model; rather it is Mzee Chilongo who is hostile to any new debate as if he has an intuition about the destructive power of words. Chilongo always speaks from the interior of a world, for his resistance to *Ujamaa* is not ideological. He embodies the will to survival of a society that is menaced by death. *Gamba la nyoka* relates the battle between an existing world and a world that only exists in words, debate or slogans. Mamboleo and Mambosasa are characters who live by the word while waiting for the world they want:

(contd) *jina la Ukerekwe, maili thelathini hivi kutoka Mwanza, na kama hakuna ukungu unaweza kukiona kutoka Usukumani. Katikati ya kisiwa hiki kuna jengo kubwa la Wajerumani lisilosalia mpaka sasa. Karibu na jengo hili kuna mti mpaka leo uliokuwa ukitumika kunyongea watu – watu weusi nafikiri. Jengo hili liko katikati ya kijiji cha Namagondo. Si mbali na jengo hili alikuwa akiishi Regina.*

Mambosasa and Mamboleo were very famous young men to the village of Bucho. They were the first from there to have reached university level while others who came after them were still in primary class. They were held in high esteem by the people of Bucho who took care of them like the seeds from a new harvest. The villagers thought that these seeds would bring them a new crop; maybe not in the following year but for the harvests in years to come. (Kezilahabi, 1979: 29)[14]

While waiting for these future harvests, Mambosasa and Mamboleo are lost in the labyrinth of words. Like the narrator of *Mzingile*, they are trying to escape the circle of life to create a new world. *Gamba la nyoka* and *Dunia uwanja wa fujo* are about the movement from one world to the next. The stories are set in this zone of turbulence, this labyrinth, this circle from which they must escape. The main protagonist of *Dunia uwanja wa fujo* (Tumaini) is a young heir who squanders his fortune before taking control of his life and starting to grow cotton. But the *Ujamaa* revolution destroys all his efforts. He is stigmatized as a profiteer and his land is expropriated. Tumaini's mistake is that he thought it was possible to build something in a world in flux. His friend Dennis reminds him several times that 'the world is a chaotic place' and that happiness is not something we can take hold of: 'Tumaini, happiness is just a thought that can drive a man either to destruction or to progress but a man will never seize happiness in his hands' (Kezilahabi, 1975a: 163).[15]

Happiness is a utopia. Here, the important idea is that happiness is a thought. Its realization is only possible in the world of words. In Kezilahabi's novels, characters only speak when they have some idea of what makes for happiness. For these characters, the word is much less expressive than the cause.

---

[14] *Mambosasa na Mamboleo walikuwa vijana waliojulikana sana katika kilili cha Bucho. Ni wao pekee yao katika kijiji hicho waliokuwa wamesoma mpaka Chuo Kikuu na vijana wengine waliowafuata walikuwa bado katika kidato cha sita. Wana-Bucho waliwathamini sana vijana hawa, wakatunza kama mbegu za mazao mapya. Wana-Bucho waliamini kuwa mbegu hizo zitafaa, kama si katika kilimo cha mwaka ujao, basi katika kilimo cha miaka yo yote itakayofuata mbeleni.*

[15] *'Tumaini, furaha ni wazo tu ambalo linaweza kumsukuma mwanadamu mbele ili kumwangamiza ama kumwendeleza. Lakini mwanadamu hatalishika mkononi.'*

This explains why Mzee Chilongo mistrusts speeches from young people. He has realized that these young men are talking to themselves. He has a good formula for letting only the old folk speak: 'I don't want to hear words from a tongue unless it's been in a mouth for more than fifty years!'[16] Words must be controlled by the way they are used in speech. When words are not freighted by the age of the bodies that articulate them, there is a danger that they will turn into a maze of deceit, in the false hope of a happiness to come.

These self-created words are, in the first place, found in books: the Bible, the Koran and *Das Kapital* are the three texts that plunged the world into the greatest deterritorialization. These books haunt the pages of *Nagona* and *Mzingile* – the two most initiatory works of Kezilahabi – hounding them from beginning to end.

The first chapter of *Nagona* opens in an ominous city in which all books are banned and thrown into the woods to rot away. In a house nearby the narrator finds a dead body, splayed out in a disturbing pose:

> It was dark in the house, but once my eyes got used to it, there was just light enough to see to see what was in it. The room was full of books covered in dust, and those that has fallen to the floor were riddled with termites. My attention was caught by the sound of a cat mewling as it crept out of a corner somewhere. I headed towards it. I heard a coughing outside so I knew someone was following me. The cat was sitting on a corpse that appeared to be a human being. I leaned over to get a closer look: it was indeed a human being. One could say that it had been embalmed to stop it rotting because there was no bad smell in the house. The corpse held a Bible in one hand and a Koran in the other. The mouth of the corpse was stuffed with a white handkerchief on which it was written: 'Silence is wisdom'. (Kezilahabi, 1990: 2-3)[17]

---

[16] *'Sitaki kusikia maneno ya ulimi ambao haujakaa kinywani miaka hamsini!'*

[17] *Ndani kulikuwa na giza, lakini baada ya macho kuzoea, kulikuwa na mwanga wa kutosha luweza kuona vilivyomo. Nyumba nzima ilikuwa imejaa vitabu vilivyokuwa vimeenea vumbi. Vile vya chini vilikuwa vimeanza kuliwa na mchwa. Mawazo yangu yalivutiwa na mlio wa paka kutoka pembe moja ya nyumba. Nilitembea kuelekea huko. Kutoka nje mtu fulani alikohoa, aina ya ukohoaji iliyoonyesha kuwa nyendo zangu zilikuwa zikitazamwa. Paka alikuwa amekaa juu ya kiwiliwili kilichoonekana kuwa cha binadamu. Nilipoinama kukitzama vizuri niliona kwamba lilikuwa kweli kiwiliwili cha binadamu. Yaelekea alikuwa*

At the end of *Mzingile*, when the narrator returns home to find his village totally destroyed after a nuclear bomb has wiped out the world, he finds a copy of *Das Kapital* amongst the ruins. It looks as if this copy of *Das Kapital* will rot with the remains of the old world and that the narrator who has finally succeeded in getting out of the old man's circle will inaugurate a new space, a new world.

The last paragraph of *Mzingile* however, annihilates this fine hope, reminding us of the obstinacy of words:

> We stood for a while exchanging glances with the children. They were obviously twins: a girl and a boy. When I first looked at them, they resembled two ancient gods. The second time I looked at them, I saw my features in their faces. The third time I looked at them they looked like my companion. We looked at each other, falling into each other's arms, smiling. Then we just stood together. One looked north, the other looked south. One looked east, the other looked west. Together, we raised our hands to the sky in a sign of peace.
> On the top of the hill four lights illumined the four corners of the world, and down in the valley animals grazed the meadows.
> Then, just as I glanced down the hill, I thought that I saw the old man crawling on his knees towards the summit. He had a book on his back. The animals were laughing! (Kezilahabi, 1991: 70)[18]

It would be wrong to try to interpret this final appearance of the old man finally with his book. It is impossible to know

---

(contd) *amepakwa mafuta asioze maana hakukuwa na harufu mwbaya ndani ya nyumba. Katika mkono mmoja alikuwa amepakatishwa Biblia Takatifu na mwingine Korani Tukufu. Modo wake ulikuwa umefungwa kwa kitambaa cheupe na juu ya kitambaa hiki kwenye mdomo palionekana maandishi yaliyosema 'Kimya ni Hekima'.*

[18] *Tulisimama kwa muda tukitazamana na watoto. Ilionekana dhahiri kuwa walikuwa mapacha, wa kike na wa kiume. Mwanzoni nilipowatazama, wote wawili walifanana na mzee. Nilipowaangalia tena mara ya pili sura yangu ilikuwamo. Mara ya tatu, wote wawili walifanana na mwenzangu.Tulitazamana, wote wanne tukaanza kukumbatiana kwa zamu hali tukitabasamu. Tulipomaliza tulisimama. Mmoja akitzama kaskazini, mwingine kusini. Mmoja akitazama mashariki na mwingine magharibi. Kwa pamoja, tuliinua mikono yetu juu kama ishara ya amani. Juu ya kilima pakawa na mianga minne katika mmoja ikimulika pande zotz za dunia, na chini bondeni, wanyama wakila majani.*

   Halafu, kwa bahati, nilipotazama kwa angalifu chini ya kilima ni kama niliona mzee akitambaa kwa magoti kuelekea kileleni. Juu ya mgongo wake, palikuwa na kitabu. Wanyama walikuwa wakicheka!

why the animals laugh. Is it for better or worse? The only thing that matters is the distinction between verbal and non-verbal communication. In all his novels Kezilahabi reveals that all societies find their deepest soul in the latter. Social structures are implicit. The social fabric is satisfied with silence. People only talk at the edges of life, and most of the time they do it all wrong and at cross-purposes, in drinking bouts, in dark dirty corners, and in moments of crisis. Once words are let loose, they do not go up in smoke but form a savage core out of which society must be reshaped.

5 The Political Novel

Historical circumstances easily explain why political questions have been at the heart of the Swahili novel in Tanzania in the years since independence. Patricia Mbughuni has argued that Swahili literature followed the path of a politicization that steadily became more explicit (Mbughuni, 1978a). The years under Nyerere's regime fall within this scheme. Tanzanian society was shaped by political sloganeering for at least three decades. This society was subjected to a pronounced political thrust. The Arusha Declaration of 1967 that launched the *Ujamaa* politics of grouping villages is an example of a discourse that is closely connected with basic social transformations.

The direct impact of words fired the imagination of writers of that time. In an article on the effect of the state's ideology on Swahili language and literature, Jan Blommaert shows

> ...how and to what extent *Ujamaa* provided an overall orientation for literary practice in Tanzania, how it structured this field by determining the relevant topics of literary discussion and debate, how it influenced criteria of quality in assessing literary products, and how it came to be used as a default mode for discussing social themes in literature... (Blommaert, 1997: 254)

The setting of a new society would turn out to be an obsessional topic in the novels and would address two questions: how to do away with the past and its traditional society, and how to found a society ideologically promoted by political slogans which were spread throughout the country at this time.

The political world in search of an anchor

To critics, there seems to be an equivalence between the literary word and the political word; each category is meant to have the same social impact. Since writers are professionals of the written word they are necessarily politicians. Making political statements is part of writing novels. Without doubt Shafi Adam Shafi is the Swahili novelist who has best succeeded in linking political discourses to fictional ones. His novels depict militants involved in a clear battle.

His 1978 novel, *Kasri ya Mwinyi Fuad* (*Landlord Fuad's Palace*) has as its theme the 1964 Zanzibar revolution. Published the following year, *Kuli* (*Dockworker*) tells of the 1948 dockworkers' strike at Zanzibar port, while a third, *Vuta N'kuvute* (1999), tells of a young girl who is in love with a member of an independence movement during the colonial era. Nonetheless, real characters in Shafi's novels are not militants. The militants are not the protagonists: they play rather the role of guides.

In *Kasri ya Mwinyi Fuad*, Fuad's old slave called Kijakazi is totally committed to her master despite his constant rebuffs. The novel tells how she slowly becomes aware of her alienation. The militant line will progressively take hold of Fuad's employees but will not influence Kijakazi who is stubbornly loyal to her master. Before they become men of action, revolutionaries operate through words. Marijani, a militant, travels all over the countryside to spread his ideas among the farmers:

> ...they were listening to him with passion, their eyes wide open so that they could make out his features through the darkness that prevailed that night. There was only silence that night. Once in a while one could hear the sound of an owl or a bush baby singing, drunk on palm wine. Marijani was the only one speaking. (Shafi, 1978: 50)[1]

It takes more than the individual to become aware of the condition of being alienated. Adam Shafi's novels show that discourses precede any struggle for liberation. One of the major activities of militants is the distribution of propaganda leaflets that are political statements in their purest form.

---

[1] *Wote walikuwa wakisikiliza kwa hamu, wamefumbulia macho ili wamwone katika giza lililokuwa limetawala usiku huo. Kimya; mara moja tu ilisikika sauti ya bundi au ya komba, wakiimba baada ya kunywa tembo. Marijani pekee ndiye aliyekuwa akisema.* (Shafi, 1978: 50).

Rashidi, the dockworker in *Kuli* is forced to ask his co-workers to read such material to him. He can only join in militant action if he learns to read. His political awareness is inseparable from discovering writing. Denge, who is member of an independence movement in *Vuta N'kuvute* is mainly in charge of circulating propaganda on the two islands of Zanzibar:

> Denge stood up and went to look for something under the bed. He pulled out a box that was hidden under it. He opened it, rummaged around for a while and took out a bundle of papers. Then, he closed the box and put it back under the bed. He sat down again and put the papers on his knees. 'What is it about, in your opinion?' he asked.
> 'Was is it?' he insisted.
> 'Propaganda.'
> 'No doubt... it is propaganda...' He took one flyer out of the bundle and gave it to Mambo: 'Read it.'
> Mambo read these words, written in big characters:
> WE WILL FIGHT TO THE DEATH FOR FREEDOM
> 'Oh yes! we'll fight to the death for freedom!' Denge repeated, word for word. 'Now listen to me. These propaganda brochures will get to every corner of Unguja and Pemba – that's the job I've been given.' (Shafi, 1999: 186)[2]

These papers are the only treasures Denge has hidden under his bed. He fully expects sudden political awareness to transform the people and that a revolutionary impetus will arise from this propaganda.

This trust in political statements shapes the writing of the

---

[2] *Denge aliinuka pale alipokuwa amekaa akainamia mvunguni. Alilivuta sanduku lililokuwepo mvunguni kule. Alilifungua na kuanza kupekuapekua na kutoa chungu ya makaratasi. Baada ya kuyatoa alilifunga na kulisukumia tena mvungunikwa mguu. Denge alirudi na kukaa juu ya kiti akayapakata yale makaratasi pajani.*
'*Unaona, nini hiki?' aliuliza.*
  '*Nini hiki' aliuliza tena.*
  '*Makaratasi*'
  '*Barabara, ni makaratasi.*'
  Alichukua moja akampa Mambo. 'Soma,' alimwambia.
  Mambo aliichukua karatasi moja katika chungu ile ya makaratasi iliyokuwa imechapwa kwa maandishi makubwa. Aliisoma, 'Kufa au kupona tunataka uhuru.'
  '*Ndiyo, kufa na kupona tunataka uhuru.' Denge aliyarudia yale maneno. 'Sasa sikiliza' alisema, 'makaratasi haya yanatakiwa yafike katika kila pembe ya Unguja na Pemba, kazi hiyo nimekabidhiwa mimi.*'

novel. Characters do not have the last word in the plot. Their role is to respond to such political statements with a totally different frame of mind. Characters' stories, their bodies, their feelings and emotions will enable these statements to become reality; this is the metamorphosis that Shafi Adam Shafi depicts. Thus there are two quite different characters in Shafi's works: militants who are the agents of propaganda, and others who are the object of their political desires. This explains why Denge, the militant in *Vuta N'kuvute* does not have any chance of a future with the beautiful Jasmin, although she is head over heels in love with him. In the course of the novel Jasmin leaves one husband after another but only meets Denge from time to time. The illegitimate child she conceives with Denge will be brought up by another father. For Denge to start family life he has to give up his political commitment. Denge is a kind of Holy Spirit of the political message. He embodies 'The Word', but it will not come to life unless he continues to spread it. (Incidentally, these words do bear fruit: Jasmin's child is the result, but she has to go on with her life in exactly the same way or be crushed by the reality of it.)

Shafi Adam Shafi's novels occupy a central place among Swahili novels because they raise the difficult question of the link between the political statement and the social body. In one way or another all Swahili novels, at least since Shaaban Robert's *Siku ya watenzi wote*, have raised this question: how to set a link between political statements and daily life in a way that the latter will not distort the former, and vice versa?

Adam Shafi's fourth novel *Haini* (*Forbidden*) describes the months a journalist spends in jail in a contemporary African country, after being accused of a political conspiracy – all this long after the struggles for independence that have been the subject of so many novels up to this point (Shafi, 2003). This prison novel is full of people who have been torn from their families, held by a political power, and are in dire straits. The novel alternates between Hamza's prison life and the troubles that his wife Khadija faces in carrying on with normal life. Khadija faces social problems. She should, for example, reject the advances of other men. Hamza, however, is absorbed in very abstract problems of legal strategies for a plea of innocence against a charge so intricate that he cannot grasp it. He has become a political prisoner in spite of himself, and has to put up some sort of a defence. Several chapters of *Haini* deal with conversations among prisoners in their cells, where close relationships develop among the men. Conversations, friendships, gestures of solidarity, courage or even of cowardice all take place in this prison but are never to be part of their world outside.

The prison as narrated by Adam Shafi is a realm of discourse. Those found guilty are removed from the social body and put behind bars. This results in their total dependency and excludes any possibility of their reconstituting the social body except by building on the power of discourse. The prisoners in Adam Shafi's novels are cut off from any society, but they discuss ideas about society. Hamza discovers that much humanity arises from this fraternity in prison. He understands that political solidarity is tied to the social body. Those in power are unaware that prison produces militants, that is, people who have bound themselves to the life of the word. It is interesting to compare this to Ben Mtobwa's account of his own imprisonment. Mtobwa's story is that of a social person. From this perspective, it gives an account of the traumatizing impact of the prison experience with all its pains and humiliations. Mtobwa's text is obstinately concrete because it sticks closely to direct testimony. Adam Shafi's text puts the prison experience into a fictional perspective and is concerned for the future of these prisoners, deprived of social reality but at the same time kept alive, thanks to the abstract form of discourse.

The political fable

The political issue of a duality between a discourse and the social body makes it possible to take a fresh look at the prologue of a novel by the Kenyan Katama Mkangi, entitled *Mafuta (Oil)*. Two children retrieve a poor man's coat after a crowd has attacked him for stealing a piece of fruit. They find a bundle of papers in one of its pockets that turns into the narrative of the novel (Mkangi, 1984: 1-7). It is a political fable on power. The prologue sets out two themes. On the one hand, the point is to generate a statement without a speaker. On the other hand, this prologue aims at subordinating characters to this statement by converting them into readers.

The author of the manuscript which becomes the core of the novel has completely vanished: the two children cannot say anything about him, not even about his life or death:

> They did their best to find out whether [the old man] was still alive but they were only left in doubt. On the one hand, they were told that he had been set upon, then stoned to death by the crowd. When the crowd was done, it vanished! It was impossible to find out where they had buried the corpse.
> ...On the other hand, it was said that he managed to escape. The crowd could not catch him because he was fast and cunning. It was said that he escaped but then later mingled with the mass of people. It appears he changed his clothes, melted into the melée and imitated them, shouting: 'Stop thief... stop thief..!' No doubt he was still alive but no one knew where he was. (Mangi, 1984: 91)[3]

Thus it is thus unclear whether the actual author of the story exists. The one who stole a fruit is also the author and death-defier. He becomes a legend: he may be dead but may also be alive, unbeknown to us. The political narrative finds its deepest foundation in this uncertainty. It is crucial to the story we are being told that it has no reference to the spectrum of political opinions. Political stands are not necessarily the guarantee of a narrative that is political. What Mkangi tries to invent through this novel is the possibility of slipping a text into the political machinations that generate power. This novel is not an attempt to substitute a new political ideology for a previous one, but is dealing with the mechanisms of power.

The impossibility of stabilizing an enunciation is the driving force behind the whole novel. Through the technique

---

[3] *Walitia juhudi zote walizoweza ilikugundua ikiwa alikuwa yu hai ama la, lakini pasi na uhakikisho wowote. Kwingine, walihakikishwa ya kwamba ule umati wa malofu ulimsulubisha kwa kumng'ung'uta na mawe. Walipoona kuwa wamemmaliza, walitoweka namna ya mvuke! Alikozikwa haijulikani.*
Kwingine, waliambiwa kuwa aliepuka. Hawakuweza kumpata kwa mbio na kwa ulaghai wake. Yasemekana kwamba aliweza kuwahepa na kuwazunguka. Eti aliwahi kujivalisha nguo zingine na kujifanya mmoja wao na akawaiga kwa kupiga mayowe ya 'mwizi huyoo... mwizi huyoo...!' Bila shaka alikuwa yuko hai lakini haikujulikana wapi!

of successively interlocking narrators in the novel, readers can cross all classes of a pyramid-shaped society that is in the hands of a minority of elected people (Bertoncini, 1995). At the top of the pyramid, there is a 'Bed' that is always empty; everyone heads towards it.

This Bed is the epitome of power. It is the empty but haunting structure of a society that holds to its hierarchies. The problem is that these hierarchies are founded on lies. The 'Oil' to apply to the body in order to get to the 'Bed', or to reach a higher level in the hierarchy is nothing else but cat's pee. This reference to Andersen's tale 'The Emperor's New Clothes' is introduced in the narrative to display two obvious facts in politics: truth is always subversive; and truth does not come from the better informed social circles.

This scrutiny of the political order is provoked by a person from the lowest orders: Matope, 'the mud-man'. Since he is outside the hierarchical system he senses in a vague way that only falsehoods and lies can be the base for a hierarchical order. The truth that Matope claims to be his is an inappropriate tool for creating a new social order. Rather, it is an obvious and unassailable fact that reveals itself to everyone in moments of incarnation. By spraying water on a female candidate for 'ascension', that is, to reach the Bed, Matope ruins the oil that is meant to effect the transformation and exposes the social lie. Matope's impulsive action is as irrational as the child's exclamation in Andersen's tale. This deed will bring about the collapse of the power pyramid.

The narrative of Mkangi's novel springs from Matope's action and the inevitable change of heart that results from his action. The novel's characters belong to different levels of the social hierarchy. The higher one is situated up the hierarchy, the longer is the work of decontamination. The abstract framework of power that allows the elite to prosper is based on deceit. To dig out the lie jeopardizes their way of life. Ti, a young woman from the elitist milieu must submit herself to an initiation in order to get rid of the lie that forms her whole personality. This initiation is a step towards a concrete life. Step by step Ti discovers the warmth of being anonymous. She will drag herself out of the abstraction of the political lie in order to rediscover the concrete sense of the political. In the political perspective outlined in Mkangi's novel, the duality of truth/lie is aligned with that of the concrete/abstract.

In *Walenisi* (1995), Mkangi extends the political themes set out in *Mafuta*. The hero, Dzombo, is a political activist who is sentenced to death by the regime. He is strapped to a rocket and shot into space. Miraculously, he survives and takes a journey through all sorts of planets and reaches a society of dreams whose operating mode is revealed to him through the subsequent chapters. In the society that Dzombo discovers, there is no form of hierarchy. *Walenisi* is an utopian novel that draws an idealistic picture of a society in which everyone is happy. This idealistic vision is revealed bit by bit through an account of the processes of liberation that led to the collapse of the Wachura's domination under the former regime. The society Dzombo discovers exists as a counterpoint to this lie. To Wamitila, the opposing metaphors of hell and heaven embody the deep stylistic structure of the text. The seventh chapter provides three versions of the myth of foundation of the non-egalitarian regime that was established by the Wachura. Each version portrays a founder/hero who was either a liar or a trickster (Mkangi, 1995: 154-166).

The Wachura's downfall represents a rejection of lies and all abstract structures that uphold them. Money is the novel's main target. Money is the agent of the fraud that perpetuates the split between the rich and the poor. As a counterpoint to money as an abstraction, people who live in *Walenisi*'s utopian society argue for concrete wealth that is a common good. Just like any model, wealth is not measurable. A particular feature of wealth is that it is of its nature, a social substance. This wealth can only flow, to be shared without limits in the social body. Money may be the divisive agent between rich and poor people, but wealth is made collective by the mere fact that it is incalculable.

The political act *par excellence* consists in refusing to measure wealth. The great lie consists in presenting money as 'wealth'. This false definition facilitates and consolidates the domination of a class of 'rich' people (Mkangi, 1995 : 82-85).

Mkangi's Kenyan utopian novel resonates with several Tanzanian novels that have dealt with the *Ujamaa* experience under Nyerere's African socialism. Tanzania was the ideal of a society of wealth-sharing for almost two decades. Literary creation had to play a leading role in this political project. Key characters of novels about *Ujamaa* are, like Nyerere, people who succeed in influencing people's behaviour thanks to the power of words. The sixth chapter of *Ndoto ya Ndaria* [*Ndaria's dream*] by John Ngomoi is devoted to the discourse of a politician who comes from Dar es Salaam to enlighten some villagers on the real value of money:

> What is money? My brothers and sisters, I think we're all agreed, now, on the answer to that question. First and foremost, we'll agree that money doesn't have value in itself. The story I told you about what happened to us in the bush makes it clear that money doesn't have any value of its own... we had money, but we couldn't use it. Money only has value when you have something to buy with it. (Ngomoi, 1977: 35)[4]

Bwana Manoti's discourse is supported by anecdotes. The function of an anecdote is to show how clear a thesis is. In a way, Bwana Manoti's discourse covers the same ground as Ngomoi's novel. The idea they are defending is that of the supremacy of a society of wealth over a society of money. The story, whether it is an anecdote or a fable, operates less as an illustration of a thesis: rather, it aims to provoke a way of thinking that reveals the thesis. In other words, it embodies the political function of literature. The social ideal of the benefits of shared wealth are made real with the fable as the privileged tool for this enunciation.

The criticism of money echoes a tradition of the utopian novel that goes back to the 1960s, as in Paul Ugula's *Ufunguo wenye hazina* (*The key to the treasure*). It is a morality tale about the search for a key to a great treasure. 'MAS'ALA, that is to say ELIMU or 'Education' was written on this huge key.' (Ugula, 1969: 43)[5] The treasure will bring prosperity to the whole society. It is the mythical element that will transform their world into a land of plenty at one stroke. This fabulous

---

[4] *Ndugu zanguni, sasa nadhani tunaweza kushirikiana kujibu swali lililotushinda – fedha ni nini? Kwanza kabisa nafikiri tutakubaliana kuwa fedha ni kitu kisichokuwa na thamani chenyewe. Hii ni wazi kutokana na hadithi niliyowasimulia kuhusu yaliyotupata kule porini, tulipokuwa na fedha basi tusiweze kuzifaidi. Faida yake ingeonekana tu kama tungepata kitu cha kununua.*

[5] *Na ufunguo ule mkubwa uliandikwa MAS'ALA, yaani ELIMU.*

narrative shows that reality as experienced is not a matter of fate or the result of destiny, but that the world can be transformed. For this to be realized, those who are fond of the status quo have to be killed. Kiimbila's novels also deal with this conflict, whether they are fairy tales such as *Lila na Fila* or realist novels such as *Ubeberu utashindwa (Capitalism will fail)* (Kiimbila, 1971).

The apparent realism of the fable works well with the constraints of socialist literature. The ideal of *Ujamaa* can be conceived of as a study of nature, as in *Fimbo ya Mnyonge (The poor man's cane)*:

> There was a big tree next to me. I looked up the tree and saw a hive of bees. I observed these bees carefully, thinking about their life: they lived in harmony. I saw them helping one another to attack dangerous insects that threatened them. They came and went to the place where the food they would all share was stored. Without a doubt, I was enormously attracted by the life of these bees. (Nshiko, 1978: 53)[6]

The spectacle of the bees is lifted out of reality and transposed onto the idealistic plane. The image of the hive of bees derives its political effectiveness from this ideality. The world of the bees turns into an concept and later a model.

Utopian society is a projection. It is a way of transforming a reality embodied in characters who identify with the project. The clarity of this ideal society is matched by the conviction of the characters who fight for its realization. An ideal society means ideal people. Tanzanian critics have debated at length on the issue of 'flat characters' (*wahusika bapa*) who are static (Madumulla, 1987; Mlacha, 1985). This type of character comes directly out of the tradition of the fable. Historians of Swahili novels trace this type of character back to Shaaban Robert as well as to this ancient source. The fact that such characters have persisted over the development of the Swahili novel is linked to the political project of narrative writing. All

---

[6] *Karibu yangu kulikuwa na mti mkubwa. Nilipotazama juu ya mti huo niliona kundi kubwa la nyuki. Niliwaangalia kwa makini sana nyuki hao nikichunguza maisha yao: walikuwa wakiishi pamoja kwa upendo mkubwa. Niliwaona wakisaidiana kuwashambulia wadudu waharibifu waliofika karibu yao wakitaka kuwadhuru. Walitoka na kurudi mahali hapo wakiwa na chakula cha kuwafaidia wote. Hakika, maisha ya nyuki hao yalinivutia sana.*

critics agree that 'flat characters' cannot fit into a genre that claims to be holding a mirror up to society.

Novels in which characters become gradually more politically aware, and those in which the militant actions of purposeful characters are depicted, belong to the same writing project. These two types function perfectly in Shafi Adam Shafi's novels. The evolutionary path of characters whose awareness grows over time readers are told is a trick in the development of the narrative. Contact with the world leads these characters to the discovery of their innate radicalism. *Gongo la umma* (*The people's bludgeon*) tells of the metamorphosis of a character into a legendary revolutionary hero. Juma becomes aware of the oppression suffered by the whole country while he is in jail after being wrongly accusation of theft. Juma sets up his headquarters in a cave and launches a guerrilla war throughout the country (Chiume, 1980). The novel ends with the victory of the liberation movement, Juma's appearance before the public, and his address to the crowd.

Activists are 'flat characters'. They do not need to develop; it is society that must change. Their static position is the lever that sets in motion the social revolution. The formation of an an activist goes hand in hand with the political discourse that becomes the character's centre of gravity. In Kenyan novels on the Mau Mau guerrillas, the oath is the instrument of privilege that transforms a character into an activist. Mau Mau warriors are at first looked upon as savage beings who have transgressed all the bounds of human behaviour. Hidden deep in the forest, they look like wild beasts to the villagers. This is how a young female villager called Mumbi in *Kaburi bila msalaba* (*Grave without a cross*) regards one of these glorious militants:

> As she stooped to cut the grass she heard a slight rustling. She looked up quickly and there in front of her stood a man, staring at her with ferocity of an animal. His long hair reached his shoulders. His hair had plaits like a young girl. His clothes were dirty and war-torn. He squatted on his right knee, pointing his gun at Mumbi. (Kareithi, 1969: 19)[7]

---

[7] *Mara tu alipoinama kukata jani, alisikia huko ndani sauti ndogo ya majani yaliyokauka. Upesi alitupa macho hapo mbele yake, na mara tu akaona mtu amemkodolea macho makali kama ya mnyama. Nyele zake ndefu ambazo zilifika mpaka mabegani, zilikuwa zimekuwa zenye uchafu na zimerukaruka. Aliketi*

Fighters threaten the established order from the wild, however, their exclusion from the social order does not mean they cannot engage in the rules of discourse – quite the reverse. These wild and hairy apparitions take an oath that they repeat with utter conviction, for it is the driving force of their commitment: 'Freedom and our land' (Ngare, 1975: 134).[8] This is the essence of the guerrillas' cause. It gives them purpose and is embedded deep within their souls. A rebel can survive many years in the forest, utterly cut off from the world. His oath is his shield, guarding him from the animalization to which he is exposed. Indeed, it will project him into the starry sky of mythology.

The oath is a discourse couched in a formula. It draws its strength from its irreducible fixity. In the public sphere, it becomes the slogan of uprising. Thus, militants do not make up slogans. Rather, slogans shape militants. In order to study the political novel one has to analyse the discursive status of this word. The study of the political novel begins with exploring the notion of the formula. Political actions rely more on 'slogans' than on state apparatuses or political parties. A formula is a given level of a statement around which the crowd can gather. The slogan is a political formula. The power of the formula is that it can free people from the thrall of prevailing social discourses. The slogan can unite people and push them into taking actions. In this regard, coming up with a slogan has nothing to do with a communication advantage. The slogan will turn out to be a tool for propaganda and will lose any credibility as soon as it emanates from an apparatus of the establishment and serves its aims instead.

The slogan 'Freedom and our land' is by itself powerful. It is mediated by these 'creatures of the wild', these mud-caked monsters who will be transformed into heroes, heralding the future. During the *Ujamaa* period a 'slogan-genre' became the ambition of many Tanzanian writers. Their aim was to insert delimited statements that would shape a political world vision. Nyerere's discourses of that period were published under the eloquent and suggestive title: '*Ujamaa ni imani*' ('*Ujamaa is*

(contd) *akapiga goti kwa mguu wake wa kulia, na mguu wake wa kuo umesimama. Mkononi alishika bunduki tayari kumpiga Mumbi.*
[8] '*Uhuru na ardhi yetu.*'

an act of faith'). *Ujamaa* is a political agenda but is also the soul of a social revolution. The whole of society is called to reform itself around such political statements.

A literature that believes in its heroes

This harmony between political writing and the fable makes it possible to establish a link between the genre of novels we have just explored and the rising popularity of spy fiction, which is becoming very successful in Tanzania. Ben Mtobwa and Aristablus Musiba are popular writers. The blurbs on all their covers promise that their plots deal with violence and love, betrayal and revenge, which means that sensationalism is always guaranteed. Joram Kiango is the hero of a crime series by Mtobwa; in Musiba's the hero is Willy Gamba. In both cases, these cool-eyed characters are always ready to foil international plots hatched at the highest level against Tanzania or another African country such as Rwanda. Joram and Willy belong to that genre of heroes who work behind the scenes and fight with stubborn persistence against the evil forces of the world.

In other words, they are pure but not perfect – the precise description of a popular hero. They are activists, of a sort. The ideal of purity is the underlying theme of many popular novels; it is the basis of an unshakeable conviction that the most sordid plotlines can be played out, thus guaranteeing their popularity with readers. On first reading Mtobwa's detective Joram will never put his reputation at risk; this guarantees the credibility of the hero. Thus the hero may reveal all kinds of faults in himself, but in fact they may come in useful when he is in a jam. Joram yearns for a peaceful life, preferably by the sea, where he will pass the days caressing the perfect body of Nuru, his *alter ego*. The couple's physical perfection is echoed in the world around them:

> If water from the Indian Ocean was blessed with feelings, it would be proud to wash cool waves over the bodies of these two creatures, as they played and laughed at the edge of the sea. They looked particularly beautiful as their fine shapes emerged from

the waves, their faces bright with laughter as they frolicked in the waves. After playing in the sea for a while, they went back to dry land, stretching out on the sand and letting the warmth of the sun dry their bodies. The beach, like the sea, would have every reason to be pleased, to have such creatures lying in its warm embrace. (Mtobwa, 1987b: 5)[9]

Joram and Nuru have a mythological dimension: they are as beautiful as the gods. They yearn for endless holidays beside the sea, or on desert islands. They are as lazy and lustful as the elite in their world. It is their absolute right to be happy.

They are above any glory that they might receive, because they must live in hiding, and conceal their real identities. They are national heroes because they have saved their country from danger many times, but they have always firmly refused any honours. Their names are on everyone's lips but they are elusive. They wish to remain anonymous heroes. They do not expect anything from society: their only pleasure is in each other's bodies. Joram and Nuru live in a hotel. They travel by plane or by car. They are definitely modern but this taste for modernity is directly linked to their relationship to the world. They have a self-confident approach to the modern world, using it only as a means to make their life easier, or to increase their pleasure.

Joram has no one. His parents were killed by thugs and their house was burnt down (Mtobwa, 1988: 27-35). From that moment onward, Joram became the 'righter of wrongs' fighting against crime. Nuru does not pin him down; she is just his partner in his nomadic existence. Simply, Joram and Nuru are happy to make love but they are not a couple – they are just accomplices. Nuru does not stop Joram from taking risks; with her he is more effective. In contrast, Musiba's Willy Gamba plays the field, and finds a new partner (for

---

[9] *Kama maji ya bahari ya Hindi yangekuwa na hisia, basi yangejisikia fahari sana kwa kupata fursa nyingine ya kuiburudisha miili ya viumbe hawa wawili ambao walikuwa wakiogelea kando kando ya ufuko huku wakicheza na kucheka. Walifanya picha ya kuvutia sana hasa sura zao nzuri zilipoibuka toka majini na kumezwa na tabasamu ambalo lilisababishwa na mzaha waliokuwa wakifanyana chini ya maji. Baada ya kuogelea kwa muda walirejea nchi kavu ambako walijibwaga juu ya mchanga kuliruhusu joto likaushe maji miilini mwao. Ufuko pia ungekuwa na kila sababu ya kusherekea fahari ya kulaliwa na viumbe kama hao.*

example Mwadi or Bibiane) for each operation. His sexual partner may also be his enemy. This is true also with Joram in *Mikononi mwa nunda* (*In the beast's hands*). In another very telling scene from *Tutarudi na roho zetu?* (*Zero hour*), Joram and Nuru reach South Africa, incognito. After being interrogated by the police they are put in a hotel room (with surveillance cameras). The first thing the officers on duty have to watch is the couple making love with great abandon. These private images, splashed across the screen, are sent on to South Africa's highest authorities.

What is peculiar to Joram and Nuru is that they are always watched by the state authorities. This is testimony to their exceptional place in the social body. Joram is not just a common citizen: he is a hero. His most private moments are known to everyone. More precisely, his loss of privacy is the price he pays for his constant involvement in affairs of state.

Joram longs to lose himself in the ordinary world but the state will not let him go. All sorts of issues come landing at his door. People come to look for him at the hotel. Sometimes people even die right in his hotel room after they have given him some mysterious message.[10]

Joram and Nuru find themselves involved in all kinds of complex and dangerous affairs involving the highest branches of government. Ordinary African life is particularly absent from these novels, which are always about African states. The preferred settings for these novels are hotels, administrative buildings and basements where state officials do despicable things.

This absence of civil society is an effective device to assure a modern feel to these political thrillers. The business world has no place in them. Joram and Nuru turn from their idle lifestyles to confront groups of political manipulators specialized in state crimes. The issue at stake is the survival of civil societies, but the action takes place without anyone's knowledge. It is only after the fact that people will learn that they were saved by someone called Joram Kiango, who will become a hero. Joram and Nuru fight alone. At the beginning of *Tutarudi na roho zetu?* Joram needs money for his current operation

---

[10] This is how *Malaika wa shetani* begins.

in South Africa. He robs a bank in Tanzania and escapes by plane. An international arrest warrant is issued for him, and he gets into South Africa as a social outcast. Similarly, Joram can do nothing in *Salamu kutoka kuzimu* (*Greetings from beyond the grave*) once news of his death is reported in the press. He is a more lonely figure in *Malaika wa shetani* (*The devil's angel*). Joram and Nuru reach an imaginary African country where they receive tacit support from the president, Abdul Shangwe. Through their investigation, they reveal that this president is a criminal. In fact, Shangwe's support was a trap, especially because Joram was working alone. Joram and Nuru are singularly disoriented in this novel. Throughout the plot they are victims of accidents and kidnap attempts and they fail to understand fully what is going on. All they can do is to react in the heat of the moment to the series of events that befall them. Both detectives are deprived of any initiative. They are carried along by events that finally bring them to solving the case. Their contribution to the enquiry is limited to gathering secrets and getting out of immediate danger. But their presence in Pololo lets certain cracks in the president's official and well-protected image appear on the surface.

Joram's reputation goes before for him. He understands this when a man from a remote place dies in his arms: 'I think that I have become very famous in the world. If a man can come from such a remote place to die in my hands! My mother can be proud of having a child like me' (Mtobwa, 1988: 10).[11] Two famous people of a different nature face each other in this novel: Joram and the President Shangwe. Shangwe is the 'Father of the Nation'. He participated in the independence struggle. His authority depends on the image constructed of him during that period. Contrary to Shangwe's fame, Joram's does not depend on any image. His reputation is disconnected from any idea of reinforcing a given power.

The man without an image, Joram Kiango, is the only one who can foil Shangwe – the man who is all image – in his manipulations. Thus we see that Shangwe is at a disadvantage in their feud, despite the technical tools at his disposal. Dark

---

[11] 'Nadhani sasa nimekuwa mtu maarufu duniani. Kama mtu anaweza kusafiri toka umbali wa kilometa nyingi kuja kufia katika mikono yangu! Mama yangu ana haki ya kujipongeza kupata mtoto wa aina yangu.'

forces that Shangwe pushed into the background in order to build his image serve as objective advantages to Joram. These forces will guide Joram whenever he hesitates. The first official contact with the president is soon followed by a second clandestine meeting, at which the president shows his true demonic nature. All the characters in the novel that Joram comes across after this share the president's corrupt state.

Behind Shangwe's public image as an angel, there is an inhibited devil who tries to confront Joram. The latter perceives at once, that these threats are a sign of the opponent's fragility and a symptom of his fear. Just at this point, Joram discovers the body of a young girl – who intended to pass some secrets to him – drowned in her bathtub. At that very moment the phone rings in her flat:

> He picked up the phone and gave the number written on the handset.
> Someone asked, 'Who's that?'
> 'Who do you want to speak to?'
> There was a brief silence. Finally the voice answered: 'Are you Joram Kiango?'
> 'Maybe.'
> 'Listen,' someone growled. 'Are you listening? D'you know who you're after? You're looking for your own death.'
> With these words, the line went dead.
> Joram put the phone down and smiled a little to himself. It was a smile of satisfaction. He had made a step forward, a step towards victory.
> If the person who called wanted to impress him, he had made a huge mistake. When your enemy starts threatening you, it means that he is begging to be afraid. (Mtobwa, 1988: 51)[12]

---

[12] *Akainua Mkono wa simu na kuitikia akiitaja namba iliyoandikwa kwenye simu hiyo.*
'Nani mwenzangu, sauti iliuliza.'
—*'Wewe unamtaka nani?'*
Kimya fupi ilifuata. Kisha sauti hiyo ilizumgumza tena: 'Wewe ni Joram Kiango?'
—*'Kama ndiye?'*
—*'Sikiliza... iliunguruma. Unasikia Joram? Unajua unachokitafuta? Unatafuta kifo chako.' Baada ya maneno hayo simu ilikatwa.*
Joram akatua yake na kutabasamu kidogo. Hili lilikuwa tabasamu la furaha. Ilikuwa hatua moja mbele. Hatua ya ushindi. Kama aliyeipiga simu hiyo alikusudia kumtisha, basi alikosea sana. Alichofanya ilikuwa kumtia ari na matumaini zaidi. Adui anapoanza kukutisha ameanza kukuogopa.

The fact that the enemy is afraid of him is a sign that there is something to be discovered. Joram is now sure that there is something going on and that he will pursue his enquiry. There is a secret affair of state. Behind the image of a kind Father of the nation, there is a murky area and some shadowy business going on. The title of a novel by Ben Mtobwa that deals with criminal dealings underlying the setting up of multipartism in Tanzania is explicit: *Nyuma ya mapazia* (*Behind the curtain*) (Mtobwa, 1995). Joram looks behind images; a man of action only recognizes actions.

After finishing their job, and once the president has been exposed and dealt with, Joram and Nuru watch the news on television to find out what official version of the president's death is being reported. All the action in the novel is covered up by this new 'official' version.

> Joram and Nuru looked at each other and burst out laughing. Joram mutters, 'Africa!' But other people watching with them shudder in amazement and shock, looking at Joram and Nuru, wondering what was so funny about this news. (Mtobwa, 1988: 154)[13]

Through their joviality, Joram and Nuru show the gulf between them and civil society. They are heroes who are totally foreign to the world of deceit, which explains why Joram is not afraid of anything. Fear is linked to an awareness of the narrow gap between a current state and a threatening event, because this only arises in a character who is party to the plot. Joram can be in danger but he is not afraid of it. He lacks that deep human attachment to what happens to him. He is unable to visualize the consequences, which makes him a particularly dangerous enemy because he plunges into battle with every fibre of his being.

The fact that Joram is fearless does not mean that he cannot anticipate what will happen. On the contrary, the fact that he is free from any undermining thought processes makes him ruthless in action. He is entirely free of anxiety that might

---

[13] *Joram na Nuru walitazamana; mara wakaangua kicheko. 'Afrika!' Joram alinong'ona katikati ya kicheko hicho.*

Watu waliokuwa pembeni, wakiisikiliza habari hiyo kwa hofu na mshangao walitazama kwa chuki huku wakijiuliza; lipi la kuchekesha katika habari mbaya kama hiyo.

arise. He is a dauntless and irreproachable upholder of the law, at liberty to act as he wishes, ignoring all threats or evil rumours. This explains why Joram can be violent and even cruel, because he does not fight against human beings but against officials of a criminal state.

His typical target is the minion in thrall to the state. Everything takes place in a murky world beyond civil society and the ordered life. Joram functions in a mythic world of the utmost violence.

Violence is at the heart of Ben Mtobwa's *Zawadi ya ushindi* (*The reward of victory*) that deals with the war between Tanzania and Idi Amin Dada's Uganda. The issue at stake is the survival of Tanzanian society, brought to its knees in the period of Amin Dada's criminal rapacity. The battle takes place on a large scale. It cannot be left to specialists like Joram and Nuru but has to be led by all Tanzanian citizens, one of whom is Sikamona. *Zawadi ya ushindi* provides the space for interrogating the nature of a hero: Sikamona becomes one in spite of himself. He decides to join the army after hearing a speech given by Nyerere, but also to try to impress his fiancée Rusia. But he is not remotely heroic. He is terrified, all the time. Only the model of the hero helps him to overcome his fear:

> What if he were to die! The very thought filled him with fear. But he overcame it by thinking of all the people who had died for their country. What about Mkwawa, Mirambo, Kinjekitile and their soldiers? What about all heroes whose names would never be remembered for their bravery? [...] They were not dead. Their names and their reputation would last forever, because they had sacrificed themselves for the cause. If he were to die, his name would be among these martyrs. It would be thousand times better than dying in one's bed, or propping up a bar (Mtobwa, 1992: 28).[14]

Sikamona comes out of the war disfigured, the result of his

---

[14] *Vipi kama angekufa! Swali hili likamtia hofu kidogo. Hata hivyo aliishinda hofu hiyo kwa kuiuliza wangapi wamekwishakufa kwa ajili ya taifa. Wako wapi wakina Mkwawa, Mirambo, Kinjekitile na askari wao? Wako wapi mashujaa wengi ambao majina yao hata hayakubahatika kuingia katika kurasa za historia. [...] Hawakufa kamwe. Majina na hadhi yao, inadumu na itaendelea kudumu milele, kwa ajili ya kujitoa kwao mhanga. Naye akifa, jina lake litabaki katika orodha ya mashujaa. Ni bora mara elfu kuliko kukutwa na kifo kitandani, au kilabuni.*

bravery in action. He will not die but his face will never be the same. Thus, the problem is how to return to society. Sikamona is afraid of failing to rise to this challenge. He goes back to Rusia hoping to integrate the two sides of his personality – the hero and the citizen. The young girl welcomes him back as a hero. She offers him her body as 'the prize of victory'. Sikamona and Rusia, portrayed as intimate lovers at the beginning of the story are transformed: Rusia is imbued with Sikamona's heroism and marries this glorious but disfigured man.

The figure of the resolute hero is common to both the political and the popular novel, and is reflected in the close relationship between fiction and fable. Political ideals are better expressed through myth and fable than by flesh-and-blood heroes. The tension between reality and the dream will be explored in the next chapter which focuses on the work of Mohamed Suleiman Mohamed.

6 Mohamed Suleiman Mohamed
Narrating a Dual Reality

I have chosen to analyse Mohamed Suleiman Mohamed's works through the critical lens of the French philosopher Clément Rosset, whose book *The Real and its Double,* one of his most noteworthy works, begins with the following sentence: '*Rien de plus fragile que la faculté humaine d'admettre la réalité, d'accepter sans réserves l'impérieuse prérogative du réel.*' (Rosset, 1976: 7) (*Nothing is more fragile than the human faculty of recognizing reality, of accepting unreservedly the imperative of the real*). Most characters in Mohamed Suleiman's novels face this challenge because they are full of hopes and dreams. The title of his first novel *Kiu* (*Thirst*) exemplifies his creative works. The hunger for the realization of their dreams is the driving force of all the characters in the narrative. It transforms reality, obliterating it in order to create an unstable space that is explored in all his works.

Absent characters

Mohamed Suleiman Mohamed's stories are open-ended. Quite often there is a *fuite en avant*, or headlong rush, an escape, or a disappearance. In *Kiu*, the heroine, Bahati, disappears at the end of the novel. She leaves her mother's home for a meeting with her ex-husband and never returns home. The last scene of the novel focuses on the mother, waiting for her daughter to come back.

What happened to Bahati after she had crossed the threshold of her ex-husband's home is never divulged. She disappears in the night and is probably caught in a snare or trap, but no one knows for sure. The title story of later collection, *Kicheko cha ushindi* (*Victorious laughter*) published in 1978, narrates the disappearance of a woman whose husband searches for her throughout the night. He swears that he will send her packing if she does not return home before dawn. He has to wait until his wife reappears at first light, in 'victorious laughter', which ends the story of this woman in flight.

Characters can disappear at any time in Mohamed Suleiman's stories, to reappear several years later. *Nyota ya Rehema* (*Rehema's star*) is one such. Rehema runs away from the family home where she is treated as a servant. She is taken in by the lonely farmer, Sulubu, who gives her food and takes cares of her. She spends some time at the farm but later decides to move to the town. Sulubu walks some distance with her down the road. Then comes the time to say goodbye:

> While she could still see Sulubu's back as he walked away, she opened her eyes wide to see a new chapter in her fate. Now, right now, she had to take the steps to what had to be.
> The future started with a young girl who was fetching water near a crossroads. Rehema called back to Sulubu and bid him farewell. Once again she thanked him for everything he had done for her and she headed to the well to meet the young girl. (Suleiman, 1976: 39)[1]

Sulubu simply disappears from Rehema's life without further ado. This new chapter in her destiny is set in a different landscape, with other partners and characters. It seems as if Sulubu has vanished from the plot. He has continued on his own path and disappeared. Several years later, while Rehema is at a new turning point of her life and is looking for a partner to mark this new phase of her life, she remembers Sulubu and sets about finding him. She will go back to the very spot where they had last met and she had set off on her quest:

> Very early one morning she got into her car to go looking for Sulubu, but everything she knew about him was wiped from her memory at Mwembeshomari, where she had met Kidawa getting water from the well with a leaky bucket. Returning to that spot,

---

[1] *Na Rehema, huku bado yungali mbele ya mgongo wa Sulubu, alikodoa macho tu kuyatazama majaaliwa yake yakifungua ukurasa mwingine. Sasa, karibu tena, itampasa aifwate herufi moja moja iliyoandikwa humo.*
Ilianzia kijana moja wa kike aliyekuwa akiteka maji kisimani, masafa mafupi tu karibu na panda ya njia. Rehema alimwita Sulubu, akamwaga, na kumshukuru tena kwa yote aliyomfanyia, na tena akaelekea kisimani kwa yule kijana.

she saw tiny tracks covered by grass and leading to places she did not know. She asked two or three people about Sulubu but it was as if nobody had ever heard of him. (Suleiman, 1976: 92)[2]

Finally, she finds Sulubu who agrees to go with her right away. One could give many examples of such characters since they are the hallmark of Mohamed Suleiman's stories.

A world replaced by emptiness

At the beginning of the short story with the title '*Mji*', the young Adam, just arrived from the countryside, is completely lost when he gets out of the car which took him to town, because he cannot find the hospital that was to be his reference point for locating the house of his cousin Hamadi: 'Everything looked identical; there were people everywhere, cars and blocks of flats. He did not even know which way the taxi that had dropped him off had taken, The hospital was nowhere to be seen'. (Suleiman, 1978: 35)[3] Adam finally understands that he has been left in the wrong place, which explains the mysterious 'disappearance' of the hospital. This incident reveals Mohamed Suleiman's aesthetics of a world always on the run.

In the novel *Kiu,* characters move in a shifting world because they are in the grip of an unspecified desire. The old Mwinyi is ready to sacrifice his huge wealth for some furtive encounters with the beautiful Bahati. This young girl betrays her mother and agrees to sleep with the old man, Mwinyi, in order to obey her greedy husband, Idi, who clearly despises her, and uses her for his own pleasure. Idi is a manipulator who succumbs to drink once he has achieved his aims and sabotages his intentions by repudiating Bahati. All these characters are driven by a state of absence. Even Bahati's mother Cheusi is

---

[2] *Asubuhi mapema, Rehema aliinigia garini kwenda kumtafuta Sulubu, lakini fahamu yake yote juu ya njia ilimfikisha Mwembeshomari, ambapo siku moja miaka kadha iliyopita alimkuta Kidawa akiteka maji kisimani kwa ndoo yenye kuvuja. Baada ya hapo aliviona vijia vyembamba vimekatakata majanini na kuelekea asikokutambua. Aliwauliza watu wawili-watatu, lakini ilionesha kama kwamba hapana aliyewahi kusikia jina la Sulubu.*

[3] *Pande zote zilikuwa sawa sawa; kote kulikuwa kumejaa watu, magari, na majumba. Hakujua hata basi alilojia upande gani. Na spitali imekaa kujitokeza.*

emotionally destabilized by the disappearance of her husband – whose return after six years is the denouement of the novel. It is impossible to find a haven of peace or stability in a world distorted by an absence or flight.

It is exactly because marriage ought to be a refuge of security that Mohamed Suleiman subverts it to convey the essential instability of the world. Before Bahati marries Idi, she pays a visit to two female friends who tell her about the failure of their marriages (Suleiman, 1972: 57-61). The women go through hell with their husbands, whatever their social station. Marriage generates frustration. One of them is faced with a jealous husband who does not give her any freedom. The other woman is married to an alcoholic who abandons her. Both women think of leaving their men. We know that Bahati and Idi's marriage will also fail.

The second novel, *Nyota ya Rehema (Rehema's star)* features a couple in the same situation. The wedding of Karim and Salma is described in detail. The couple inherits considerable wealth which they squander in order to allow Karim to fulfil his dream of going around the world. Karim is the prototype of the person on the run:

> One day when he was at home, he told Salma needed the money: 'I'm planning a big trip', he said. Salma's heart began to race. Where did he want to go off to again? He said nothing. He kept quiet until she started bombarding him with questions, until she went down on her knees, because he liked to see her suffer.
> 'Where are you going?' Salma asked.
> 'To see the whole world. *Around the world*', he explained, twisting his fingers in the garlands that hung from the ceiling. 'Europe, America, Asia and the whole of Africa.' (Suleiman, 1976: 129)[4]

---

[4] *Karim alipokuwa nyumbani siku moja, alimwambia Salma kwa nini alizitaka pesa zile. 'Napanga kisafari kizuri' alisema.*
   Moyo wa Salma ulishtuka na kuanza kwenda mbio. Alitaka kuyoyomea wapi tena mtu huyu? Lakini hatosema. Hatosema mpaka aulizwe, aombwe, kwani akiona raha kumwona Salma anateseka juu yake.
   'Kisafari cha wapi?' alisema Salma.
   'Dunia nzima. Around the world, alisema, akielekeza na kukizungusha kidole chake chini ya therea lililokuwa likining'inia darini. Europe, Amerika, Asia, na baadhi ya nchi za Afrika.'

Karim abandons Salma who raises their child on her own until he runs out of money and has to come back, only because he wants to steal his wife's money – in fact, to rob his wife, Salma, the heroine of the story.

The presence of the real

As opposed to Karim and Salma who inherit quite a fortune, Rehema and Sulubu initially are not rich, but they manage to prosper by dint of hard work. It seems that Rehema and Sulubu form a totally atypical model of the couple in Mohamed Suleiman's works. Contrary to Karim, Sulubu is a man who is present:

> …it was the same with Sulubu. He spent his days working, singing and laughing. Rehema finally understood that she had found the friend she had been looking for. She was surprised by how much this man meant to her. She remembered all the troubles and disorders she had to face several years ago, the four days she had spent in his hut, how they lost touch for eleven years, then found each other with joy, and got on so well. In all those years Rehema had not experienced love and did not even believe that love existed. She tried to know love with the various people she had met. Then she met Sulubu again. When Sulubu stood there, in front of her, she saw his face, reminding her of the innocence of a child, his clear gaze hiding neither dishonesty or cunning. She knew that she loved him and would never want to be separated from him again. (Suleiman, 1976: 108-109)[5]

Rehema, who has so far been running away, finds a place at Sulubu's side. From this moment the couple can be happy. The innocence and the fullness of Sulubu's face are needed to keep

---

[5] *Sulubu hali kadhalika, siku yake nzima ilikuwa ikipita katika kazi, nyimbo, na vicheko. Hatimaye Rehema alihisi kapata rafiki aliyemtaka. Alipokaa akafikiri jinsi mtu huyu alivyogeuka kuwa muhimu sana katika maisha yake akistaajabu yeye mwenyewe. Alikumbuka jinsi ajali na msukomsuko ulivyompambanisha naye miaka mingi iliyopita, na jinsi alivyopitisha naye siku nne katika kibanda chake, wakapoteana kwa miaka kumi na moja, na wakakutana tena katika hali ya furaha na kufahamiana. Rehema katika umri wake wote alioishi hakuwa akiyajua mapenzi, wala hakuamini kuwa yapo. Alijaribu kuyatafuta kwa watu wa kila aina aliokutana nao, na kuyakuta kwa Sulubu. Sulubu alipokuwa mbele yake, akauona uso wake wenye umayale wa kitoto, na macho yake meupe yasiyoficha ulaghai na ujanja, alijua kuwa akimpenda na asingeweza kutokana naye tena.*

Rehema's attachment and to stop her from her headlong flight. Well before being attracted by his face, Rehema is prevented from wandering by Sulubu's black, broad and muscular back: 'Rehema passed huts the length of the field when she suddenly saw the black and broad back of a man with strong shoulders: she recognized Sulubu' (Suleiman, 1976: 94).[6]

Sulubu is one of the few characters with a thick-set body in Mohamed Suleiman's stories. The density of his body is directly linked to his innocence, to his refusal of any kind of plotting. He only believes in one principle: work. He is not distracted by Karim's manoeuvres to get hold of the fruits of his labour. The world around him collapses several times but this never affects his passion for hard work. Sulubu does not work to be happy but because his muscular body forces him to do so. Rehema, who started being corrupted by money that can be made far too quickly in town, finds in Sulubu the compass that will redirect her life. Sulubu is truly 'Rehema's star'. He will give life to her true destiny.[7]

Bahati, the heroine of *Kiu* is disheartened by Idi's contempt and takes comfort in her conversations with a fisherman whom she meets while he is draining water from his capsized boat. 'That fisherman was busy, he neither saw nor heard anything as if his boat was the world and as if life was all about escaping its hardships' (Suleiman, 1972: 86).[8]

Yet, contrary to Sulubu's very present physicality, the body of the fisherman will disappear in the story so that only his words are given precedence. The fisherman desperately wants to escape poverty just as Bahati and Idi did before their cunning plan succeeded. Bahati meets an acquaintance who is still poor and she tries to convince him of the fact that wealth will not make him as happy as he wishes to be. *Kiu* is more hopeless than *Nyota ya Rehema* because all the characters are in the grip of this 'thirst' or craving for something else, which

---

[6] *Rehema alipita lando kando ya uwanja hadi kwenye mabanda, na mara tu alipouona mgongo mweusi, uwazi, wa mtu mrefu mwenye mabega yaliyojikweza, alimtambua Sulubu.*

[7] Rettová (2011: 439) draws attention to the ambiguity of the character. Suleiman's text gives the reader to understand that he raped Rehema when he found her in the forest. Therefore, there is a dark side to this character that needs be taken into account in a deeper analysis of this very rich text.

[8] *Yule mvuvi alikuwa kashughulika, haoni hasikii, kama dunia ilikuwa ngawala yake, na uhai wote ni kuchota na kumwaga maji.*

cuts them off from reality and reduces them to types in an unfolding plot.

In the last short story of the collection *Kicheko cha ushindi* entitled 'Uhuru wa siku moja' (One day freedom), Mohamed Suleiman returns to a protagonist similar to Sulubu. His name is Mambo. He is a farmer who is completely cut off from social manipulations. Mambo has decided to live off the land against the will of his father who wanted him to be become a citizen and 'an office man'. Mambo's resistance to the social order is not couched in words but held in the tension of his body:

> Once more he remembered his life at the office – how he did his best to fulfil his father's wishes and how one day he found himself stuck rigid in a chair, his joints refusing to follow his orders. Outside there were people waiting for him to serve them; in front of him the phone rang; from one side a colleague called him but he could not raise a finger! His colleagues took him home, his seniors declared that he could no longer work, everyone said, 'Mambo has lost his mind.' Not at all! Mambo was in full possession of his mind. He would have loved to continue working. But it was a call from his deep interior. (Suleiman, 1978: 47)[9]

This story of the resistance of Mambo's body takes to the limit a principle that underlines all stories by Mohamed Suleiman: the opposition between the spirit and the body from the perspective of their link to the duality of society and territory. Through dreams and desires the spirit is a factor of socialization as well as a factor of deterritorialization. The more a character is integrated in the social network, the more he misses something. This is threaded through Bahati's words to the fisherman when she tries to convince him that wealth will not fulfil him (Suleiman, 1972: 88). It is also symbolized by Rehema's journey in leaving behind her city pleasures to set up a new life in the countryside with Sulubu.

[9] *Tena alikumbuka maisha yake ya ofisini — namna alivyojitahidi kutekeleza dhamiri ya baba yake, na jinsi siku moja alipojiona kang'ang'anaa juu ya kiti, maungo yake hayataki tena kufuata amri yake... Kule nje watu wakimngojea awahudumu; mbele yake simu ikipiga kelele; ubavuni mfanyakazi mwenzake akimwita, lakini hakuweza kunyanyua kidole! Ile ilikuwa amri iliyotoka katika roho ya maumbile yake. Wafanyakazi wenzake wakamrudisha kwake; wakuu wa kazi wakamwona hafai tena; walimwengu wakasema 'Mambo kapotewa na akili.' Sivyo kabisa! Mambo alikuwa timamu. Kwa akili yake alitaka kuendelea na kazi. Lakini ilikuwa na amri ya roho ya maumbile yake!*

The earth has a powerful fixity that transmits its unchanging nature to those who work its lands. On the other hand, the town that is woven by social games hollows out the bodies of characters depicted, transforming them into people who can only dream and are good at playing with words. Mohamed Suleiman's stories are underlined by a dialectics of presence and escape. In the short story, 'Uhuru wa Siku Moja', Mambo is accused of cultivating marijuana and ends up in jail after a trial from which he was completely excluded.

Mambo serves his sentence and seizes the moment to escape on the eve of his release. He is immediately caught and put back in jail: '…he had to appear before the judge two days later in the morning for having tried to escape. When guards came to look for him they found his body nestled in a corner. His spirit had escaped' (Suleiman, 1978: 53).[10]

One has to remember the context of the story to understand this escape is not a flight but a return to the real, far from the prison which is an abstract and a highly social environment. Mambo's body, so huddled up, is a cumbersome leftover that holds up the machinery of justice. Before he was caught Mambo tried to run away without any real plan. He was just driven by the fact that he breathed some air and saw some greenery through a door that was left open by accident. What justice regards as an escape is to Mambo just a return to purity, something as irrepressible as a spring that is artificially blocked up.

The real against its double

The earth embodies the presence of self that foregrounds any involvement in a society, while the sea is the completion of social itineraries. In Mohamed Suleiman's stories, cities always surround a port from which ships sail away. In the short story 'Mji', Adam's itinerary takes him from the countryside to the town, where he will pass through several of its social layers before ending at the quayside:

[10] *Asubuhi siku ya pili alitakiwa na Msimamizi Mkuu kwa mashtaka ya utoro. Walinzi walipokwenda kumchukua, walikikuta kiwiliwili chake kimejikunja kipembeni. Roho yake imekimbia.*

He did not see his friend Kitwana nor did he try to again. He meandered alone, hunger gnawing at him throughout the day. This city was not as he thought it to be. But he was not mature enough to differentiate between good and evil. There was only one thing he did not wish to do: go back to the village. He found himself at the port and looked for some work. Luckily he got a job on a ship that was leaving for a far distant place. He was very happy to go to a much bigger city. Maybe that would be where he would find his good fortune. (Suleiman, 1978: 42-43)[11]

The sea is a direct extension of the urban fabric. To embark on the sea means to connect one port to another, one city to another. One gets to know many former sailors in Zanzibar. These sailors can describe all the big port towns of the world. Cities are connected by the sea, which is obviously a way to escape but one that immediately follows on from an urban escape. Therefore, it seems that Mohamed Suleiman's stories emphasize a clear ideology that plays upon the duality of city versus countryside. Nonetheless, this apparent clarity is clouded by the fact that this opposition is radical. The point is not to compare two types of society or two models of socialization but to bring face to face society and its underside.

Both Adam and Sulubu are solitary characters. Sulubu creates a loneliness even when he is with Rehema. Thanks to their hard work they prosper but this happens away from society. While working the land they do not even need a language. What would be the use of this valuable asset of communication in a universe devoted to harmony? One only hears songs and laughter from their voices. Both solitary characters live in a sub-language. Better still, they ignore any kind of law. This is the case when Sulubu has the feeling of being intensively harassed by the covetous Karim who wants to embezzle their fortune on the basis of suspect papers drawn up by a suspect notary. Sulubu does not hesitate for one moment and slices

---

[11] *Hakumwona tena rafiki yake, Kitwana, wala hakumtafuta. Alizurura majiani peke yake, hana kazi, na kuteseka na njaa siku chungu nzima. Mji huu haukuwa kama alivyoutarajia. Lakini bado alikuwa mtu nzima mwenye kuweza kujichagulia jema lake na baya lake. Jambo moja tu Adam hakulitamani: kurejea kwao maporini. Sasa alipita katika bandari ya majahazi na kuuliza kazi. Kwa bahati njema, alipata kazi katika jahazi moja iliyokuwa ikisafiri miji ya mbali. Alifurahi sana kuwa atapata kwenda katika miji mingine mikubwa zaidi. Labda huko ndiko iliko bahati yake.*

Karim with his machete: Karim did not expect Sulubu to react so violently and he pays for this attempt to seize Sulubu's and Rehema's fortune with his life.

He thought he was dealing with an honest farmer concerned only with his well-being, but he has to face an archaic character who only knows the language of working the land. Karim dies, sliced in two, still holding the land register in his hand. He was killed while he was locating the plot he wanted to seize. Rehema looks at his remains after the act: 'She saw Karim's body lying flat on his stomach, cut in two parts, wide-eyed and staring at the border of their land, mouth wide open...'(Suleiman, 1976: 168)[12] The only solution to Karim's endless greed is Sulubu's archaic violence. Karim's body lacked substance because he was possessed by a desire that could not withstand Sulubu's sharp machete.

Karim dies holding a legal document, lying at the border of the land he coveted. He is not interested in the earth but in the financial value of the plot. He is very concerned with measures and limits. Similarly, in *Kiu*, Idi is also a man who dreams of plans and tries to make Bahati dream of a sketch:

> 'And there outside, do you see?' Idi reminded Bahati of his sketch. 'The garage will be there and on this side there will be flowers and a fruiting hedge. We will plant jasmine and rose bushes aside... do you see? We will live a wonderful life.'
>
> Bahati acquiesced but did not understand anything. She was looking sadly at the map Idi had sketched just as an exhausted traveller contemplates desolate places that he/she still has to pass through before reaching the destination. She hated that house, sketched on a map. (Suleiman, 1972: 57)[13]

Bahati will not be lucky enough to get to know a man like

---

[12] *Sura aliyoiona ilikuwa ya kiwiliwili cha Karim kimeanguka fudifudi, vipande viwili, macho yamekodoka kuutazama mpaka wa shamba lao, kinywa chake kiwazi.*

[13] *'Na huku nje, huku, unaona?' Idi alimkumbusha. 'Hapa patakuwa na banda la gari, na kwa upande huu nitafanya kitalu cha miti ya maua na matunda. Na kwa huku kidogo, itakuwa sehemu yao ya kuatikia miasumini na miwaridi. Basi... umeona. Tutaishi kwa starehe ajabu.'*

  Ingawaje wakati wote akiitikia, Bahati hakufahamu cho chote. Aliitazama ile ramani ya nyumba aliyoazimia Idi kwa uzuni, kama msafiri ya jangwani aliyechoka anavyokitazama kipande cha safari iliyobaki. Alichukia nyumba ile aliyochorewa ramani.

Sulubu. She will be obliged to live in permanent divergence from the real, to live in a world of dreams never fulfilled and with vacillating aspirations. The novel's title is explained in the symbol of crossing the desert which is exploited in the scene above: characters are burned up inside by an unquenchable thirst which causes them to see the world as a desert. Maps or plans are equally reminders of the desert.

It is understandable why Karim, who dreams of the map of the world, cannot measure up to Sulubu whose attention focuses on working the land. The problem is that Karim reflects the whole social organization and the fact that Sulubu's murder cannot go unpunished. According to the law, Sulubu has no defence. Only a popular upheaval and its ensuing turmoil can save Sulubu from this misdeed. Sulubu will then be able to resume his tireless work and to forget the incident when he sliced a human body instead of ploughing a furrow. But to Sulubu, defending his land in this harsh way also meant to tend it well. Mohamed Suleiman's story is written from Sulubu's perspective, in other words, detached from symbolic projections.

In another strange short story with the title 'Kijana Yule' a young woman is head over heels in love with a young man she knows only from what his friends say about him:

> Subira had never had the opportunity to meet this young man. She only knew him from what others said about him. It does not matter! The body does not really matter as far as love is concerned. This explains why people wonder when somebody falls in love with another person. Love is stronger when it is not concerned with appearances because it does not fade when bodies wither away. Love experts have proven to us that love is a matter of the heart to which eyes are only witnesses. Subira's heart did not need these witnesses. (Suleiman, 1978: 16)[14]

---

[14] *Lakini Subira hakupata kukutana na kijana huyo uso kwa uso. Akimsikia tu vinywani mwa watu.*

  Haidhuru! Katika mapenzi umbo si kitu muhimu sana. Ndiyo maana fulani hustaajabiwa kumpenda fulani. Mapenzi yasiyoshughulika na sura au umbo ni mapenzi makubwa sana, kwa sababu hayachakai pamoja na vitu hivi. Wataalamu wa mambo ya mapenzi wametuhakikishia kuwa kupenda ni kazi ya moyo, macho ni shahidi tu. Bali moyo wa Subira mara hii haukutaka hata shahidi. Kama alivyojiona yu mkubwa wa wakati umefika wa kupata uhuru, basi pia moyo wake uliweza kujitegemea wenyewe katika mapenzi ya kumpenda kijana yule.

Subira's love for this young man will be deepened by the fact that she is not in a position to learn anything about him. She does not know his name, where he comes from, nor where he lives. Subira is in love with an abstraction. She is totally consumed by this love which turns her life into a long wait for him. They meet at the end of the novel, when Subira finds out that the young man is illiterate. Thus her 'house of cards' collapses in a moment. Her love cannot persist in the *presence* of the young man. Her love relied on vague aspirations. The young man's illiteracy is the stumbling block to Subira's love. Being illiterate makes him a person who is detached from a world that is built on maps and plans.

Mohamed Suleiman is not condemning these characters who are at the mercy of their desires. Rather, the point is to show how fantastical their life is. Mohamed Suleiman's world of fiction is, as Clément Rosset has said, a kind of dual reality. This world is full of phantom figures who keep on appearing and disappearing, according to the twists and turns of the plot.

7 Criminals & the Corrupted

Mohamed Suleiman's works show how people are always caught by a reality that they want to escape. One of the tasks of the popular novel is to explore the depths of a social reality, which is the polar opposite of the task of the fable with its ideal character-types. Thus, the criminal takes the role of the hero in novels which allow no room for fables and whose plots unfold in the bowels of the social system.

The police v. the criminals

The Swahili popular novel develops the fantasy theme of a society ravaged by crime. Under the guise of an ordered social organization lies a network of violence, as described in the novel. The popular novel tends to position the world of crime as under police control. The enormous success of a novelist such as Godfrey Levi is due to the reassuring plots in which crimes will be duly punished thanks to the effectiveness of the police. In his novels, police methods are very violent and justice equally rough. In *Mpelelezi hodari na genge la wahalifu* (*The courageous detective and the band of thugs*) murderers confess their crimes after being tortured and they all swing for it. The three thieves in *Fedheha ya fedha* (*Money of shame*) are shot dead and thrown to the crocodiles. Indeed, Godfrey Levi's novels invite readers to a world of legalized lynching as if society had no other means of fighting crime but violence. The police take the last stand in a society dominated by crime; however, they are always threatened by contamination because they are in direct contact with criminals, and attempts to corrupt officers feature in the plots (Moyo, 1990: 41). Then too there are the inevitable failures of inadequate policemen. Take, for example, the conclusion of one of Levi's novel which deals with illegal trading in bootleg brew:

> Reader, you can learn three things from reading this story. First: 'If you don't listen to the old men you'll break a leg.' Had Saguti obeyed the law and paid attention to his what his wife was telling him, and had he given up selling *chang'aa* he would not have ended in court.
> Second: 'Sooner or later, a thief will be caught' and 'the long arm of the law [*lit.* government] reaches everywhere'. Masanja [the policeman] did not do his job. He was corrupt and broke the law. So now comes his day of reckoning, and the long arm of the law nabs him. He's sentenced to several years in prison and to penal servitude. On top of that, he'll never go back to the force.' (Levi, 1981: 62)[1]

However violent crimes are, they will be described in great detail. Popular novels by Sam Kitogo and Jackson Kalindimya are published in serial form in the press and never hesitate to give every gory detail of any outburst of violence usually between rival gangs. Violence is piled on violence in criminal circles. In one of Edi Ganzel's most successful novels, members of an organized gang kill one another after a successful hold-up. The police intervene only at the end of the novel, when the killing is over, to recover the money (Ganzel, 1971).

The police and the law hold the line in the popular novel. A society can be rotten to the core at the highest level but order is guaranteed as long as these criminal activities take place under the watchful eyes of the police. In a little story book for children by Ben Mtobwa, a policeman is disguised as a blind beggar and keeps an eye on the criminals from behind his dark glasses. The figure of the blind person illustrates the status of the police in a society that is overrun by drug dealers.

---

[1] *Msomaji, baada ya kusoma hadithi hii umegundua kuwa inafundisha mambo matatu, ambayo ni: Asiyesikia la mkuu huvunjika guu. Kama Saguti angetii sheria za serikali na pia kuzingatia kikamilifu onyo alilokuwa akipewa mara kwa mara na mkewe, kuacha kujishughulisha na chang'aa, hangeweza kuhukumiwa mahakamani.*

   Pili inafundisha kuwa: siku za mwizi ni arobaini na serikali ina mkono mrefu. Masanja alikuwa hatekelezi wajibu wake hata kidogo. Alizoea kupokea hongo kutoka kwa wakaidi wa sheria. Mwishowe siku ya arobaini ilimfikia, kwani serikali yenye mkono mrefu ilimnasa, akahukumiwa kifungo kirefu gerezani na kazi ngumu. Pia aliamriwa asitumikie jeshi la nchi maishani.

The police are always there, in hiding, but ready to take action in the name of the law (Mtobwa, 1998). The main character of *Kikulacho* joins the police after barely escaping from a shipwreck; he pursues his case right to the end even though his seniors put him under great pressure. In a society where corruption runs right to the top, even through the police, justice hangs by a thread: it is up to one central character in the novel, threatened on all sides and miraculously surviving all dangers, to win out in the end (Abdul-Wahab, 1985).

This reassuring presence of some principles of justice and order is a romantic device that prevents the criminalization of society from turning into a political issue. The policeman or the upholder of the law are in one way or another externalized social ideals. Many crime writers have created underground networks in their novels, with dealers in precious stones (Ole Kulet, 1990), drugs (Abdul-Wahab, 1975), ivory (Nkussa, 2001: Nyaruba, 1987) and so on. Such activities may have penetrated the highest spheres of the state, but that does not make any of these networks less criminal – they are still to be eradicated. Honest citizens may be involved in exploits beyond their control and may find themselves being used in the war waged between the police and the criminal underworld (Mfaume, 1993).

Understandably, the nerve centre of this criminalization of society is money, flowing through endless illegal channels. In itself, money does no harm, but becomes dangerous when it overtakes social relationships, especially romantic ones. Thus, the romantic genre is taken over by crime fiction. Many novels take up the theme of love destroyed by the lure of money (Kalindimya, 1988; Simbamwene, 1972). It can be dangerous to fall in a love in a world where everyone is chasing money. A character in love is the ideal victim for all kinds of swindles, (Mvungi, 1975; Nyasulu, 1974; Omari, 1976; Simbamwene, 1988) while on the other hand, a romance is the best plot device to get an honest citizen into the criminal world, at great cost to that character. Mganga, the narrator of *Mfu aliyefufuka* (*The resurrected*) finds himself drawn into the parallel world of witchcraft because he falls in love with a young girl who is under the spell of a sorcerer (Mbelwa, 1974). Through the frailty of love and the human attraction to the illicit or the unnatural, society is laid open to crime.

In his other novels, without his hero Joram Kiango, Ben Mtobwa raises the question of the criminal underbelly of society. Kandili Maula, the protagonist of *Pesa zako zinanuka* (*Your money stinks*) is torn between the two sides of his nature, the decent and the criminal. His conflict is played out in the novel through his dealings with two women. On the one hand, there is Dora, who raises their love child on her own and loves him without return. On the other, there is the prostitute Maua who lives with him and profits from his illegal earnings. Kandili grows rich trafficking drugs, an activity that reaches into the highest ranks of state officialdom. The rich and arrogant man that he has become is merely the personification of his anti-social, deviant self. The other side of his nature harks back to his younger days when he was a student and untouched by crime. That was when Dora conceived their little boy, Chema, who died because there were no medical supplies to treat him. Kandili is directly answerable for his son's death. He can only regain Dora's love if he gives himself up to the cops and turns himself into a decent citizen.

Ben Mtobwa's novel derives its originality from the nature of the love relationship between Maua and Kandili. She is not simply a profiteer; she can also be devoted and in the end sacrifices herself to prevent Kandili being arrested. Maua uses her charms to get rid of difficult people. She uses her body as if it is a tool in Kandili's service. This couple (Kandili/Maua) are similar to the couple (Joram/Nuru), discussed previously. Both are action-oriented. In this novel, the two women, Dora and Maua love Kandili but Dora's love drives him towards social reintegration whereas Maua's love drives him into the world of crime and the dark side of heroism.

Women always play a key role in Mtobwa's novels. They act as the regulatory connection between their men and their society. Rukia is the central support of the trio in the plot of *Dar es Salaam usiku* (*Dar es Salaam by night*). Rukia is the pivotal force, as two men fight over her: Peterson, the settled family father who is ready to give up everything for her beautiful eyes, and Hasara, the former street child, the marginalized man who sees in his love for her a way of bringing new meaning to his life. Rukia will lead one lover astray; but with the other, she will help him find his way.

A special feature of this novel is that the narrative is set within the social body. The actions of the three protagonists are related side by side in every chapter, accompanied by reminiscences from their earlier lives. Rukia, Peterson and Hasara hold on to memories of childhood. They make contact with each other, borne down by the weight of the past. The reader is witness to each character's feeble attempts to find a way out of their predicament. Significantly, no real action takes place in *Dar es Salaam usiku*. The only truly dynamic character is Hasira, Hasara's childhood friend who has turned to a life of crime. Hasira has been ordered to kill Peterson but lacks the nerve. His failure to act is directly linked to the pull of the past, the call of the family. *Dar es Salaam usiku* turns out to be a family novel: in the final chapter, all the protagonists discover that they are related to each other.

From a different perspective, this novel gives readers a better understanding of the background to Mtobwa's action novels featuring Joram Kiango. Within Mtobwa's narrative schema, actions are free from any social conditioning – they should be raw. Rukia, Peterson and Hasara obscurely aspire for something beyond the world of action. They want to heal the breaches within themselves, the legacies of their childhood. These characters have no desire to be sacrificed for the sake of some violent code of behaviour.

On the difficulty of action: the logic of corruption

C.S.L. Chachage's novels ask whether it is possible to take any action in a society which is in permanent disruption and mostly in the grip of individual conflicts of interest. These novels take as their theme the collapse of the idea of collective interest and more widely of the need to pass on values from one generation to the next. Crime is no longer the business of a few marginalized people, who act outside the social sphere and are pursued by upholders of the law who in turn hover above and beyond the whole of society. Chachage shows us that crimes are diffused throughout the social system. *Sudi ya Yohana* (*Yohana's fate*) relates a desperate attempt to stop a collective social drift by taking decisive action, the failure of which ends in an utterly loathsome deed. An honest young man by the name of Yohanna finds himself in jail for the attempted murder of his corrupt and perverted brother. The latter is well set up in the social system, giving him the power to harm everyone around him.

Yohana's act of revenge is ridiculous. It is a 'just crime' in a world that has lost all belief in myths or their power to effect change. Mythical heroes are always criminals but not all criminals are mythical heroes, however pure their intentions. Yohana is a victim who tries to take action but his action traps him: he becomes the victim of his own deed.

There is a similar case at the end of *Kivuli* (*The shadow*) when the head of a family sets his house on fire on the orders of a sorcerer. He intended to get his daughter back, after she had run off with her lover. Lighting a match turns out to be one of very few real actions that this self-interested and corrupted character ever takes:

> He went quickly to his room to get the powder and matches. He got water from a jar in a corner of the living room, then he put some of the powder in a cup. He lifted the can of petrol and poured the whole lot over the hot charcoal, grabbed a match, struck it, and threw it on the fire. It blazed up surprisingly fast and before Hiliyo knew what was what, the flames had licked right up to the can of petrol and it exploded on the spot. The blaze spread wildly over the whole place. Hiliyo's clothes caught fire. (Chachage, 1981a: 113)[2]

Hiliyo dies of his burns. The minimal act of lighting a match proves fatal for him. Chachage's extremely detailed description of this incident reflects a world in which no one believes that actions have consequences. No matter how insignificant Hiliyo's action is, it goes far beyond the scope of his plan. To

---

[2] *Alikimbia hadi chumbani na kuichukua dawa na kiberiti. Kisha akaenda penye mtungi wa maji ya kunywa uliokuwa kwenye pembe moja ya chumba cha maongezi na kuchota maji kikombeni. Alirudi tena dukani. Akachukua unga kidogo wa dawa na kuutia katika kikombe. Alilinyanyua tena debe la mafuta na kumwagia katika ule mkaa ambao ulikuwa umekaribia kuzimika. Kisha hapohapo, alichukua kiberiti na kukiwasha. Moto ulilipuka kwa nguvu ya ajabu, na kabla Hiliyo hajajua kunatokea nini, ulikuwa umerukia katika debe la mafuta ambalo lilipasuka hapohapo kwa kishindo cha bomu. Moto ulikuwa umeenea chumba kizima, na ulikuwa umeenea chumba kizima, na ulikuwa umesharukia katika koti la Hiliyo.*

his surprise, the fire spreads out of control and turns against him. In a world where material reality has gained so much solidity and value, characters are reduced to small gestures, with very little sense of how they will turn out.

This disqualification of action is the cause of widespread corruption. What was regarded as a 'criminal act' in the popular novel becomes wholesale corruption in these novels, where no trust or faith is placed in the efficacy of corrective action. In other words, corruption takes over when the notion of 'crime' is paralysed. Corruption falls within an all-too-different narrative scheme.

When crime lies at the very heart of the social system, it is transformed into depravity and loses all contact with (re) action. A corrupted character does not need to act. Quite often such a character just has to close their eyes and let things happen. What counts as an action in such a system is the refusal to be corrupted. If a person does nothing, then he or she will become depraved or debased. This explains why Chachage's novels, in exploring the machinery of corruption also reflect on the difficulty of doing anything about it.

The main character in Chachage's third novel *Almasi ya bandia* (*Fake diamonds*) is Morton Mitie, a fine example of a depraved character who blossoms in a system that suits him to perfection. It is said that he is a *'mtu wa bandia'* or 'fake man'. A diamond trafficker, he is the son of a strong-fisted man who had refused to join in the 1947 dockers' strike in Dar es Salaam. However that era of serious political action is long gone and Morton has no other means of living except smuggling fake diamonds, and in his free time raping young girls whenever he feels like it. Morton is a sordid and shallow individual trapped at the centre of the new social system. 'Perhaps Morton was the true reflection of disorder in that society' (Chachage, 1991: 113).[3]

Chachage describes a world where everyone is trapped, in which even guilty people are victims, and where everyone is overwhelmed by the prospect that nothing real is ever going to happen.

The narrator of *Makuadi wa soko huria* (*The pimps of the free market*) is an old journalist who has decided to become

---

[3] *Labda Morton alikuwa ni kioo halisi cha mikanganyiko ya jamii hii.*

a serious writer in order to give an account of what is really happening in a country where only fake news circulates:

> As far as I am concerned I have been a journalist since 1975. I have not given up this job. But what I want to write about now is not news but facts, realities. When certain people heard that I was planning to write about these realities, they asked my friends to persuade me not to do so. They said that it was pointless since these realities dishonour our country which has a good reputation as a place of peace, unity and solidarity. They said that such stories could frighten investors and donors who supported the nation in the framework of the new world economy, led by the system of globalization which has spread throughout the world and whose foundation is the free market. They told me to forget these things because they did not help in developing the country but played a part in destroying it. (Chachage, 2002)[4]

Even the words used here are trapped in the general regime of corruption. The novel relates what happens when the population of the Rufiji Delta is threatened by wheeler-dealers who succeed in pressurizing the political powers-that-be to implement a project for the exploitation of local mangrove swamps, by privatizing the Delta. The globalization of corruption makes it sensitive to condemn local practices that everyone regards as shameful but which are thought to be indispensable. It is better in the common interest not to take any action, which in this context means here not to write about these issues.

As opposed to the rationale of criminality that develops on the margins of the system, corruption penetrates all spheres of the society. It proliferates incessantly and in the long run overturns all principles until it threatens even the principle of humanity:

[4] *Mimi mwenyewe nimekuwa nafanya kazi kama mwandishi wa habari tangu mwaka 1975. Sijaacha kazi hiyo. Lakini ninayokusudia kuandika hapa si habari, baili ni mambo, ni matukio. Baadhi ya watu waliosikia kuwa naandika kuhusu matukio haya, waliwaambia marafiki zangu waje wanishauri kuwa nisifanye hivyo. Walidai kwamba hayastahili, kwani yanaipaka matope nchi yetu ambayo inasifika kwa mema mengi kubwa likiwa ni amani, umoja na mshikamano. Walidai kuwa mambo kama haya yangeweza kuwafadhaisha wawekezaji vitega-uchumi wa wafadhili wa kimataifa wale ambao ndio tegemeo letu kitaifa na sehemu muhimu ya uchumi mpya wa dunia unaotawaliwa na utandawazi, ambao msingi wake ni masoko huria. Waliniambia haya ni mambo ambayo inabidi tuyasahau kabisa, kwani hayajengi nchi, bali yanabomoa.*

What he wanted to say was that the real sense of human relationships, the real sense of love, dignity, and respect of human life was being forgotten. This is the greatest danger we are facing. The greatest proof is this: the measure of a man today is not how humane he is, but how cruel and corrupt he can be. (Chachage, 2002: 143)[5]

While crime novels may pay lip service to the vitality of a society that can limit crime, novels about corruption depict a world on the road to ruin. Real criminals do not exist in a corrupted society: only profiteers.

Paradoxically, there is nothing more human that trying to profit from a system but the result is catastrophic when the system cannot contain this urge. Many novels of the *Ujamaa* period take as their theme the little schemes that men devise which slip into the great idealist machine. The self-serving fiddles of some regional or district chiefs are contrasted with Nyerere's moral integrity and his resolute idealism. Bosi, the spineless character nominated as a regional chief in *Nyota ya huzuni* (*The star of sadness*) is found out at the end of the novel. This enemy of progress is then relieved of his duties, which is very good news for society (Liwenga, 1981). As in Mung'ong'o's novel, corrupt people *are* criminals because their self-interest goes against the ideals of a socialist society.

In one of his first short stories, Gabriel Ruhumbika narrates the progressive decay of a young medic who sinks into alcohol after his career is blocked by a tyrannical senior who misuses his position to exploit women and get rid of his rivals (Ruhumbika, 1978: 30-56). Ruhumbika's novels show the consequences of such actions on the fate of a whole group of people, and the close links between depravity and power. *Miradi bubu ya wazalendo* (*The patriots' hidden agenda*) juxtaposes two Tanzanian families who are political militants through the colonial era, the period of liberal economy, and then through the *Ujamaa*. Whatever the regime, the novel shows the chasm between the people who know how to

---

[5] *Alilenga kusema kwamba maana halisi ya mahusiano, maana halisi ya mapenzi, hata ya heshima na hadhi ya maisha ya binadamu inaelekea kusahaulika. Na hii ndiyo hatari kubwa inayotukabili leo. Ni mitihani mkubwa: kwani kipimo cha utu si utu tena, bali mienendo na tabia za kikatili na ufisadi.*

exploit power and those who defend it in the interests of the whole country.

Ruhumbika's disenchantment with life is expressed through his theme that profiteers always have the upper hand over idealists. In the last scene of the novel above, Mwalimu Julius Nyeyere pays a final visit to the country before his resignation. He is accompanied by the opportunist, Mzoka. He is covered with medals and titles and finds himself in front of a mass of people in which Saidi is just another face, still militant to the core, but aged and impoverished. Saidi finds it difficult to get closer to Mwalimu, but he can hear the words of the speech being distorted by Mzoka, the adviser who has the ear of the president (Ruhumbika, 1992: 159-166).

The choice to present corruption from the point of view of its victims leads Ruhumbika to establish a parallel between corruption and witchcraft. The two themes of profit and personal enrichment is deadly. In *Janga Sugu la wazawa*, Ruhumbika paints an apocalyptic picture of a society that is devoured by death and the exploitation of it:

> There were shops where human organs were sold. The organs were dried in the sun or grilled while they were still 'fresh'. Human skin was cut away like a slice of gazelle or any other edible flesh! There were shops that specialized in private parts, female and male, of girl virgins and even of breast-fed babies, both girls and boys. There was even a place where one could order this or that fresh limb of the human body, and get an extract, a magic powder from it the same day. The trade of corpses and human organs from hospital mortuaries increased to an extent that these places had to be closed because they were no longer of any use to the country. In fact, nobody would allow the body of a dear relation to be kept in a mortuary – not even for the short time it took to do an autopsy. Even after an accident where two buses were in collision and there were many casualties, it was impossible to find even a single corpse at the scene in the aftermath. Wounded people who did not have time to escape or who could not get into safe hiding quickly enough were killed on the spot by the hunters of human flesh. The blood and bodies were sent to these dreadful shops. (Ruhumbika, 2002)[6]

[6] *Pakawa na maduka ya kuuza viungo vya miili ya binadamu, vilivyokaushwa kwa jua au kwa kubanikwa kwenye moto na hali kadhalika vibichi, 'fresh', na ngozi za binadamu, zilizochunwa nzima nzima kabisa utafikiri aliyehunwa ni swala au*

What a dreadful picture this is of a society that literally devours itself in the frantic race for profit. Corruption enables the link between crime and power to be re-established, as the evil of witchcraft already existed. As corruption is widespread and lies deep at the heart of the system, social success is always suspected of being linked to it. The disguised traffic in human organs is a distorted autophagy in such societies, revealing a deep and hideous distortion of life.

A Kenyan novel that has been reprinted several times tells of a doctor who becomes rich by being involved in the traffic of kidneys to Europe (Mbogo, 1996). He involves himself publicly in politics in support of multipartyism. The criminal organization of organ trafficking is exactly parallel to his political organization. Both are power machines that rely on each other. The political field – or at least the politician's own field – is infested with criminality and reduces everything to the getting and spending of money. The very own body of the doctor, Matoga, who is the organizer of the trafficking ends up being dissected by members of his network when he is killed in a car accident and his corpse is taken to a mortuary.

Novels that deal with corruption are driven towards an apocalyptic perspective because corruption is a vector of global social deterioration. This does not mean that the novels of the 1990s are limited to denouncing corruption in the hope of improving the social order. They adopt an apocalyptic vision of the devastating effects of corruption that reaches into the micro-apparatus of the system. The title of Kamugisha's

(contd) *mnyama-pori mwingine au mfugo unaoliwa nyama! Pakawa na maduka mahsusi ya sehemu za siri za binadamu, za kike na za kiume, za wasichana wadogo ambao walikuwa bado bikira, hadi za watoto wachanga, wa kike na wa kiume. Pakawa hata na mahali pa mtu kwenda kutoa oda na kuagiza kiungo kibichi hiki au kile cha mwili wa binadamu cha kwenda kutengezea dawa za ushirikina na kutafutiwa siku ile ile na kuletewa. Biashara ya kuuza maiti na viungo vya miili ya binadamu kwenye vyumba vya maiti vya mahospitali ikakithiri hadi vyumba hivyo vikafungwa vyote na huduma hiyo ikafutwa kabisa mahospitalini kote nchini, kwani hakuna mtu aliyekubali tena maiti ya maheremu wake ipelekwe kwenye chumba cha maiti hospitalini hata kwa muda kidogo tu kwa madhumuni ya kufanyiwa uchunguzi wa kilichomwua pale ulipohitajika. Na ajali za barabarani zikitokea, hata kama ni mabasi yamegongana uso kwa uso na kuua watu chungu nzima, hakuna maiti hata moja inayokutwa mahali pa ajali. Majeruhi ambao hawakuwahi au hawakuweza kulikokota kutoka hapo na kujificha na kujisalimisha nao hapo hapo waliuawa na wawindaji wa binadamu wenzao na miili yao inapelekwa kuuzwa kwenye maduka ya biashara hiyo ya kutisha.*

novel *Kitu kidogo tu!* (*Just a little thing!*) echoes the phrase that the narrator keeps hearing in a Tanzanian society depicted as utterly dissolute. The narrator who returns home after completing his studies in England realizes that contrary to all his expectations, he is unable to put his skills to the service of a country whose people can only survive thanks to this short phrase: 'Just a little thing!' (Kamugisha, 2000).

The initiatory quest for redemption

The framework of the voyage of initiation has become the most appropriate narrative device for this new situation. Kezilahabi's two novels of initiation, published in the early 1990s, do not represent a break from great realist novels of the '70s and '80s, but the natural development from these novels. With *Nagona* and *Mzingile*, Kezilahabi writes against the background of the general collapse of the social order. The realist order is no longer guaranteed by the vigilance of the police in dealing with bribery and corruption. The police are by then only effective in organizing strip-tease performances attended by people from right across the society. In both narratives, society is impelled towards a frantic descent into death. Society looks for a saviour because people no longer believe in anyone who is responsible for their well-being. The voyage of initiation is taken for the redemption of a world that has become unhinged.

Many novels of the 1990s take up the theme of a journey, a wandering or a quest through African society. Kongowea, the narrator of Ken Walibora's *Siku njema* (*A wonderful day*) takes a long journey from Tanga to Kitale in search of his father. He meets many people along the way. He befriends many, but he refuses to become involved or to settle until his search is over. His journey is beset with violence, accident, illness and poverty. However, he distances himself from this harsh reality by an unswerving commitment to his distant goal. Without a source of income, he becomes an artist, making sketches as if to keep reality at a distance.

Kongowea's journey is mirrored in that of Selemani, a kind of evil double sworn to kill the former, and whom he encounters at every stage of the journey until his day of freedom – that is, when he hears that this doppelganger has been shot dead by the police. Through his quest, Kongowea tries to free himself from this pervasive background of violence. His decision to embark on the journey was caused by his aunt's inconspicuous crime of serving him poisoned tea every day because of some obscure issue over an inheritance. Kongowea finally discovers his father at Kitale: he is an ancient who has passed for a madman for years, but is in truth a poet and lover of the Swahili language.

Kufa kuzikana (*Forever*) draws the same African-apocalyptic theme. The novel depicts a region of the continent in the grip of an inter-tribal killing spree. It is narrated by a character who unwillingly becomes a murderer. Akida's journey has no true destination because he is obsessed by the idea of crime. An astonishing sixteenth chapter describes Akida's escape just after the murder. Hiding behind heavy sunglasses, he gets on a bus leaving the city. The bus makes endless twists and turns through different neighbourhoods before really heading out on its main route. Mad with anxiety that he will be caught, he imagines taking refuge in the small town of Sangura where his crime will be forgotten:

> I'll settle down in Sangura to work in the fields, like a nobody. When I get to Sangura I'll forget all about that wretched fool. I'll forget what I did because I did it in a fit of anger. The whole world will forget about it. It was something that had to be done, wasn't it? What's wrong with doing in a killer? Old man Zablon got what was coming to him. People like him have no right to stay alive. (Walibora, 2003: 139-140)[7]

But Akida does not get over what he did as easily as he thinks, and many years later he gives himself up. He learns that the man he thought he had murdered had only been slightly injured. The murder he had hoped he could forget turns out to be nothing, even though it changed his life completely. In

---

[7] *Nitakaa Sangura nifanye kazi ya shamba kwa mtu yeyote Nikifika tu Sangura nitamsahau nduli yule. Nitakisahau kitendo nilichokitenda katika wimbi ka hasira. Dunia nzima itakisahau kitendo hicho. Kitendo chenyewe kilistahili kutendwa au sivyo? Kuna ubaya gani kumwua muuaji? Kwani dawa ya moto si moto? Kifo kilikuwa stahili yake Mzee Zablon. Watu kama yeye hawana haki ya kuishi.*

a country engulfed by massacres and inter-tribal hatred, it is difficult to distinguish killers from their victims, as they are all rooted in a wave of violence that has overwhelmed normal, decent life.

In W. E. Mkufya's *Ziraili na Zirani*, the apocalypse is caused by a rebellion against God that ends with a world-wide nuclear holocaust. Both the human and metaphysical orders are blown away. A nuclear explosion is also at the heart of both Kezilahabi's *Nagona* and *Mzingile*, and represents some sort of final destination in the Swahili novel of the nineties. Metaphysical words are used for the disintegration of the social order. The nuclear explosion is the vehicle for the extension of the socio-political into the mystical. It defines a literature that is explicitly initiatory.

Bina-Adamu! by Wamitila is an implicit reworking of Kezilahabi's two initiation narratives, borrowing the device of an aimless global odyssey. Distances in space and time are done away with in this concoction of the major political issues of the planet. Japan with its competitiveness in technological research, Germany with its Nazi past, the United States of America with its economic superpower and major ecological problems are all thrown in. These elements are contrasted with the real problems of a village at the heart of Africa. The novel is a kind of plane of pure immanence set in motion by the flow of money and technology that drags all human society in its wake. The narrator embarks on a search for the truth of the world but during his journey he learns that to discover this light is to go through the test of darkness: 'Do not love the light before you have known the dark.'[8] It is one of the narrator's guides, the philosopher, who best describes the space through which they are passing:

> It is like the desert, it is a space deprived of any culture. Even truth and illusion have melted away and become one substance. The limits between good and evil have been utterly swept away. The duality that shaped our history has disappeared. This duality, the cause of the CHAOS OF ORIGIN has vanished, and in its place we have been given the CHAOS OF UNITY. (Wamitila, 2002: 123)[9]

[8] *Usipende mwanga kabla ya kulijua giza.*
[9] *Hili ni kama jangwa, yaani ni uwazi mpana wa kitamaduni usiokuwa na chochote. Hapa ukweli na usiokweli vimeunganishwa na kuwa kitu kimoja. Mipaka iliyoko*

This homogeneity and unity of chaos usurp the place of the real in Wamitila's novel. It is the only foundation on which the author can develop his characters. All the troubles of the world are always there; at any time in the story they can burst in with disorder: ecological problems, political problems, social problems, meteorological problems, racial problems and so on. The only guide to the narrator's quest through this chaos is a mysterious giant by the name of 'P.P.', who holds the reins of all calamities plaguing the world. This evil giant is called Peter Pan, a child who will never grow up, a child who is totally unaccountable for his actions and who randomly throws stones at people without an idea of the wrong he is doing. The Heraclitean God, the 'child who plays chess' has a new face in Wamitila's novel but his traits remain the same. This irresponsible child is among us. We can feel his presence everywhere but he is nobody. At the most he is infantile, a figure in a tall story who slips from our grasp.

One must return to the detective novel for themes and plots that preceded the motif of the initiatory voyage, a motif that has been present in the Swahili novel since the 1990s.

(contd) *kati ya wema na ubaya imefutwa kabisa, haipo asilani. Uwili uliokuwako katika historia umetoweka. Uwili uliosababisha FUJO ASILIA umetoweka na nafasi yake kutwaliwa na UMOJA WA FUJO.*

8 Investigations & Enigmas

In 1975, an article by the writer Euphrase Kezilahabi was published in the journal *Kiswahili* condemning the proliferation of the Swahili detective novel. Kezilahabi's main problem with the authors of this genre is that they do not face the problems of Tanzanian society but hide behind the formalism of an abstract investigation. For Kezilahabi this explains why their texts are not very substantial and do not stand up over time:

> Why then are detective novels no longer interesting when read for the second time? Their value diminishes because they float above real life and are not deeply rooted in a given society. (Kezilahabi, 1975b)[1]

Kezilahabi's anxiety comes from his commitment to an aesthetics of fiction that takes social problems seriously. The huge social project of *Ujamaa* is entirely separate from the themes of the detective fiction of the same period. The playwright Ebrahim Hussein also categorically condemns the crime genre as an artificial import which is totally inadequate for any real account of Tanzania's political and social problems (Hussein, 1971). Likewise P. S. Binali concludes his highly critical review of two detective novels by Mohamed Said Abdulla with this comment: 'All in all, all human beings have flaws and there is no human being who can be good through and through' (Binali, 1973).[2] A review in the literary journal of the University of Dar es Salaam[3] reinforces Binali's opinion, in reference to *Duniani kuna watu* (*There are people in the*

---

[1] *Kwa nini basi riwaya za upelelezi hupungua msisimkio tuzisomapo mara ya pili? Zinapungua kwa sababu zinaelea hewani katika maisha na mizizi yake katika jamii inayohusika ni mifupi sana.*

[2] *Kwa jumla hakuna Binadamu ambaye hana udhaifu na hakuna mwanadamu ambaye ni mwema katika maisha yake yote.*

[3] Published in the literary journal of the University of Dar es Salaam.

world), one of the most important detective novels published in Tanzania. Zanzibar society as depicted by Abdulla (1973) has nothing to do with the current state of the island and takes no account of the effects of the 1964 revolution. Moreover, characters are stereotyped, reappearing in one novel after another, and the genre lacks any positive insights for young people and society at large (Kanyalika, 1975). The critic's three objections reflect his passionate support for a literature that expresses direct engagement with Tanzanian political and social realities.

However, there is a kind of investigative fiction that is much appreciated, by anthropologists in particular: witchcraft stories, adapted from oral narrative poetry. In Peter Lienhardt's edited version of Hasani bin Ismail's narrative poem (*utenzi*) *Swifa ya Nguvumali*, he adds a lengthy introduction to 'the peoples of the coast and their culture' (Hasani, 1968). The poem has all the elements of a good detective novel: criminal gangs, the brutal assassination of an innocent man and an official investigation run by the authorities, while the healer Nguvumali who specializes in witch hunting engages in a parallel and successful investigation. Nguvumali's investigative methods are not entirely rational but readers will be intrigued by these traditional elements of witchcraft if they like this genre in general. English anthropologists, for example, relied a great deal on examining the practices of witchcraft in order to develop an understanding of African societies and their cultures. However, the narrative modalities of this kind of investigation into magic have been much less studied. How to flush out a sorcerer is well worth a narrative (Saffari, 1936b).

Eiko Kimura disagrees with Kezilahabi's and Hussein's critiques, as the title of his thesis suggests: 'Social changes and the detective novel in Tanzania' (1991). Chapter Three of this study has suggested that investigations of witchcraft are the precursor of modern detective novels: 'In the past, no-one had the benefit of modern techniques of investigation and had to resort to the old systems of belief, such as witchcraft, healing techniques, clairvoyance, curses, truth by ordeal and so on' (Kimura, 1991: 86). Only one crime novel, *Mbojo: simba-mtu* (*Mbojo: the lion man*) (Kuboja, 1971) brings in this kind of investigation as the background setting. Police Inspector

Kayola investigates the murder of a child applying all modern forensic techniques. He accumulates witness accounts and looks for incriminating evidence. Meanwhile the victim's parents go to a healer who by divination reveals the identity of the murderer and the supernatural methods he used to commit the crime – in other words, sorcery. The police investigation proceeds through the healer who puts them on the right track so that they can identify and arrest the guilty parties.

The hybrid form of Kuboja's novel uses the conventions of the modern detective novel as adopted by the original Swahili novelists in this genre, while respecting all the modalities of the magic quest for truth. In the following pages, I examine the underlying significance of the latter with reference to the novels of the two main writers of detective stories, Muhammed Said Abdulla and Faraji Katalambulla.

The Zanzibarian M. S. Abdulla published six detective novels between 1960 and 1984. They all feature the perspicacious Bwana Mesa, a pipe-smoker who can solve the toughest case.[4]

The detective fiction genre in the West clearly inspired the Swahili novel,[5] while the local context was highly fertile ground for its adaptation. Every aspect of Swahili culture must be considered in this context, because all of it contributes to the convention of the 'investigation' and there is always an interaction between solving the crime and the cultural features of its setting. This very abstraction in the solving of crimes leads to its adaptability in different cultural settings but not without some local features leaving their mark on the narratives. The stories are imbued with a cultural encounter in every case that comes up.

In a tried and tested formula, all investigations by Bwana Mesa run alongside and eventually benefit the official investigation, which in Abdulla's novels, lies in the hands of one Inspector Seif. As a general rule, the inspector is led to the obvious culprit by a trail of clues, whereas Abdulla's

---

[4] The 1964 revolution, during the course of which the whole of the author's family was killed, took place between the publication of the first novel *Mzimu wa watu wa kale* (*Shrine of the ancestors*) [1960] and *Kisima cha Giningi* (*The well of Giningi*) (1968). It seems that this historical and personal drama did not leave any mark on his work. Muhammed Said Abdulla neither writes to confide in, nor to bear witness, to what he saw. He writes to expose enigmas and the solution to these enigmas.

[5] Only Shaaban Robert wrote some prose fiction in the forties.

protagonist, Bwana Msa, dismisses all the evidence apparently arising from the crime.[6]

The two series of novels rest upon this conflict between Bwana Msa and Inspector Seif who approach their investigations from entirely opposite standpoints. In his book on *The Murder of Roger Ackroyd*, Pierre Bayard shows that a clue is a construct of the detective's interpretative project. The clue is never a given, but always a revelation:

> What is evident is that the clue is less a sign that is already present in the case, and more something that constitutes itself in the course of the interpretative, hermeneutic movement. By proposing a definitive explanation, this type of interpretation puts the facts in a hierarchy and works backwards, constructing a plausible textual structure. In so doing, the clue is less of a pre-interpretative event: rather it is its product. (Bayard, 1998)

The clue results from the detective's investigation, and is linked to the detective's vision of the world.

The clue as an indicator of culture

In these circumstances, a police investigation is inseparable from the cultural facts which the detective consciously or unconsciously absorbs, while picking up the clues. A suspected man in *Mwana wa Yungi hulewa* (*The devil's child grows up*) cannot be the murderer because the silk shirt he wears on the day the crime is too fine to be worn by a man holding a knife with intent to kill:

> China silk is not a material for murderers or people with aggressive or murderous intent (...) If he was filled with a deadly fury, he wouldn't wear silk because a shirt like that on his back would have calmed him down – it's a material for gentleness and elegance; for status and display. China silk calms the soul and makes a body feel soft. No, you can't hold a deadly weapon when

---

[6] This scheme is most obviously updated in *Kisima cha Giningi* (*The well of Giningi*) (1968) in which all clues lead to a husband who might have kidnapped and assassinated his wife after they had recently separated. The best clues to his guilt are his recent attempts to bewitch the young woman. Inspector Seif already has the husband locked up while Bwana Msa persists in trying to convince the policeman that some details invalidate the attractive coherence of the clues.

you're wearing silk, because you only put it on when you're being kind and peaceful. (Abdulla, 1976: 108)[7]

It would take a sociological research project on the place of clothing in Swahili society – and moreover, on the importance of luxury fabrics – to understand fully how this observation by Bwana Msa is a valid point.

Bwana Msa's investigations take place on Zanzibar Island. Swahili culture is very much present, but not in itself; it lies behind the discovery of clues or buried mysteries. The investigation in the first novel deals with a beheaded corpse, found deep inside the 'Shrine of the Ancestors', a place haunted by the spirits of seven mysterious, unidentifiable people who were buried there long ago. Bwana Msa has to resist the immediate explanation of the crime – that wandering spirits committed the murders. During a conversation on belief in supernatural possession, Bwana Msa shows how each investigation rests upon a cultural understanding of how clues come to light, as well as how they are rejected, as in the case of witchcraft:

> 'Listen, Seif', he repeated, 'every person can bewitch another person. Think of one thing. Our parents and our contemporaries – all of us, whether we like it or not, we all believe in witchcraft and spirits. The education we got from white people and our modern civilization is just a veneer, and beneath it belief in spirits and a fear of bewitchment is deep-rooted.' (Abdulla, 1968: 56)[8]

Bwana Msa does not exclude himself from this widespread belief in spirits: it lies deep within him while at the same time he believes it is all nonsense. Bwana Msa is both inside and

---

[7] *Hariri ya China si vazi la kikatili, wala hakuna mtu mwenye nia ya kwenda kupigana au kuuana (...). Kama alikuwa na mori wa kutaka kuua, akivaa nguo hizo atavunja mori wake, kwa sababu Hariri ya China ni nguo ya upole na 'wahid-wahid' na maringo; ni nguo ya madaha, ya mtu kuivaa akapita akisowera nayo. Nguo kama Hariri ya China ni nguo inayondosha 'kalbi-kasi', inayondosha ukatili wa moyo, na ni nguo inayoleta ulegevu wa mwili. La, kisu cha ukatili hakivaliwi na nguo hariri, nguo yenye upole na rehema.*

[8] *'Sikiliza Seif ', aliwanza tena, 'mtu ye yote anaweza kufanya uramali kumkusudia mtu mwingine na akapata. Fikiri kitu kimoja. Wazee wetu na watu walio hirimu yetu – wote, tukitaka tusikate, tunaamini uchawi na mashetani. Hiyo elimu ya Kizungu tuliyopata na ustaarabu wa kisasa umekuja kwa juu tu, lakini chini, shinani kwetu, mzizi wetu, ipo fikira na hofu ya mashetani na hivyo hivyo uchawi.'*

outside his culture. More precisely, he has understood the full extent of the ambivalent status of witchcraft in contemporary Swahili society. He knows that all signs or clues convey cultural meanings and that every search for the guilty party is influenced by local culture. In this respect the detective novel is a literary genre prone to cultural changes. One can transpose Sherlock Holmes to Zanzibar but one needs to adapt him to the new context. Sherlock Holmes would have to investigate cases of witchcraft; thus a rotten egg placed in front of someone's door takes on a much more significant meaning.

To Bwana Msa, however, the mechanism of witchcraft is limited. It is entirely dependent on interpretation, yet must be taken into account in an investigation.

The clue is one part of a well-constructed solution. The clue inserts itself in a coherent network of other indices that lead to the culprit. Thus, it acquires all the features of the sign. Pierre Bayard's comment on the clue works on a more general level for the sign:

> (...) Before being a meaningful object, the clue is a process of exclusion. It is all the more subtle because by attracting light to itself it puts all other signs that cannot reach the threshold of critical perception in the shade, since they are inconsistent with the interpretative project. (Abdulla, 1998: 113)

To inscribe any sign is a matter of choice. The clue is influenced by cultural beliefs only so far as it results from the logic of signs. Since Barthes' *Mythologies* at least, it has been accepted that nothing favours semiological analyses more than cultural facts. Every culture chooses its own realities; every culture creates its own view of the world. It is not by chance that Barthes uses the word 'indices' in his 'Structural analysis of narratives' to indicate additional notations to the pure linear unfolding of the plot:

> The second broad class of units, by nature integrative, comprises all the 'indices' or 'indicators' (in the broadest sense of the word), that is, a unity which instead of referring to a complementary and consequential act, refers to a more or less diffuse concept that is essential for an understanding of the story: the traits of personality in various characters, information about their identity, notations of 'atmosphere', and so on. (Barthes, 1977: 20)

Thus, it is impossible to create a story without cramming it with clues, that is to say making no choices about characters' identities, behaviour, the atmosphere, and so on.

The detective's task is to move from clues to functions in order to find the connections between actions from a network of contextual indications. All the conclusions drawn by Pierre Bayard are thus essential: the detective builds a theory from selected clues. This theory is inevitably absurd as it is an attempt to bring order to a bewildering proliferation of clues. There is no 'adequacy of truth' corresponding to the facts in detective fiction but only a 'disclosure of truth' that always depends on the selection of certain clues.[9]

Thus the detective novel seems to be a genre entirely open to relative interpretations. The 'ideal' murderer who gives himself up in the last chapter becomes at the end of the day only one solution that can always be debated by looking at another set of clues. Perhaps Inspector Seif is not defeated forever; he is waiting for a reader to come along and confirm his hypothesis by lifting the veil over the pages, finding all the clues that Bwana Msa deliberately hid.

Bwana Msa seems to hold a superior position thanks to the broad, in-depth and subtle knowledge of Swahili culture that he offers his reader. The detective novel seems to be a means of revealing culture as well as interrogating it.

The trace v. the clue

There seems to be a conflict of interpretation between Inspector Seif and Bwana Msa in each investigation. In this analysis I hope to show that Bwana Msa's superiority does not arise merely from his ability to impose his choice of clues and identify the most likely culprit. For example, during a conversation with a young man who has heard of his great exploits, Bwana Msa insists on distancing himself from Sherlock Holmes. He sees himself as an 'observer of facts' and not as 'a detective'.[10]

---

[9] On the distinction between 'matching truth' and 'unveiling truth' borrowed from Tzvetan Todorov, cf. P. Bayard, ibid., 130-3.

[10] Cf. M.S. Abdulla, *Mwana wa Yungi hulewa*, p. 4: 'Si mpelelezi wa siri, mimi ni mchunguzi wa mambo.'

This distinction is fundamental to an understanding of Bwana Msa's status, and in his refusal to intervene on a personal level in any of the crimes he investigates. In this regard he is much closer to Edgar Poe's Dupin than to Sherlock Holmes, who keeps on creating conflicts in order to expose secrets. Bwana Msa stands back from the plot. He observes facts from the outside, whether they are words or objects, and only then does he draw his conclusions. There is not a single case in which he gets involved in the plot: the length of his pipe comes between him and the facts. Every novel is punctuated by a detailed description of how he handles his pipe. His main actions are emptying the pipe, scrubbing it, filling it with tobacco, lighting it and puffing away. The pipe is the major distraction of a character who refuses to take any action. It is less the metaphor of his brainwork than a concrete object, energizing his body so he can think better. Bwana Msa fiddles with his pipe because he knows it is the only object that will never harbour (in itself) a trace, whatever case he is pursuing. All other objects have to be closely examined because they can lead to the truth. Bwana Msa's pipe equals Dupin's famous green glasses in *The Stolen Letter*. The pipe keeps the world at a distance.

If one adheres to Pierre Bayard's interpretation of 'the clue', there is nothing left out of the detective's interpretation. The clue exists only because it has been manipulated – which makes it radically different from the trace. The detective, in order to follow the trace is not supposed to intervene in the plot. Therefore, Bwana Msa's main action consists of keeping himself free, aloof; making himself foreign to things and words.

For a start, Bwana Msa puts his own culture at a distance. No cultural fact is taken for granted. He is a black Zanzibari of African origin who conducts his investigations in the wealthy setting of Arab society wherein he has to unravel complex inheritance matters. At the beginning of *Mzimu wa watu wa kale* he is shown holding a book entitled *The other side of things*.[11]

His response to Inspector Seif, who is amazed by his investigative talent is: 'I was capable of turning everything head over heels. That's what's called "the other side of things".' On the

---

[11] *Kinyume cha mambo.*

same basis, these are the words he turns upside down:

> Bwana Msa did not overlook any word he read or heard; he liked searching for the truth of all words and things; one of the fastest ways to know the truth was to turn words upside down and to look at them the other way round. According to him, the best people who did this were figurative painters. When a painter finished a work, he would turn it upside down on the easel and look at it from this perspective as if it were in the right position. Before even beginning to paint, other artists put their heads between their knees and look at the landscape they want to reproduce as if for the first time, upside down. (Abdulla, 1974: 9-10)[12]

This is how the trace comes about. It arises from a particular kind of look; the look of one who wants to lose the sense of forms so that he can only see marks or stains. Far from beginning with signs in order to construct clues, it is more about turning signs upside down and stripping them of meaning.

In his last novel entitled *Kosa la Bwana Msa* (*Bwana Msa's mistake*), Abdulla uses Bwana Msa back to front, as if he wants to highlight how unique his approach is. For the first time Bwana Msa intervenes personally in a family drama, causing a separation and a remarriage. At the end of the novel he admits that his meddling was his biggest mistake. It leads him to jeopardize the natural laws in the choice of one's closest relationships and the handing on of a cultural heritage. In the final scene in which all protagonists of the drama are present Bwana Msa explains that to err is human:

> 'Why are human beings always making mistakes?' Bwana Msa continued. 'It's a difficult question but if we think about it carefully, we must realize humans are endowed with brains. Human beings make mistakes because they have a brain. Angels do not make

---

[12] *Bwana Msa alikuwa hapuuzi neno – japo lapata hivi – analoliona na analolisikia; kwani alikuwa akipenda kutafuta ukweli wa kila neno na kila jambo; na njia yake moja iliyokuwa nyepesi kwake kupatia ukweli halisi, ni kulipindua neno juu chini, aangalie kinyume chake. Njia hii ya kupindua juu chini hutumiwa, atakwambia mwenyewe, hata na wataalamu wachoraji sura za witu. Mchoraji akisha kuchora sura ya kitu, huipindua sura hiyo juu chini akaitazama katika hali hiyo, kama imemkalia sawa. Wengine, hata kabla kuchora, huinama wakapitisha nyuso zao baina ya miguu yao wakaitazama mandhari wanayotaka kuichora – kwanza-katika hali ile, kama kwamba wako kichwa chini miguu juu.*

mistakes; they do what they are told – this is what the Koran says. They do not think of this or that; if one of them is told to take the life of a creature, then they do it. They don't ask why they have to do it. The reason is that angels weren't given brains for thinking, like us human beings. We, the ones with brains, when we see or hear things, our spirit leads us to see them just as we like. I'll imagine something this way; you'll see it another way; another person will imagine it differently again – all this, for one single object. Our diversity comes from the fact that we invent multiple versions of one thing. But this difference of opinion is the cause of all our mistakes.' (Abdulla, 1984: 171-172)[13]

It is somewhat odd to hear such words from an experienced detective. It seems as if he is condemning the human faculty of imagining the world. The whole practice of signs is cast in doubt. Bwana Msa makes it totally clear that the link between the sign and the clue is to be found in an interpretation. Bwana Msa blames himself for having fallen for clues when they are pure constructs of the brain. Bwana Msa thought that he had the power to declare a marriage null and void without taking into account the existence of a child (a potential heir).

He puts more trust in a paper chase than in the vicissitudes of blood and money. How could he, the man who spots physical resemblances under fake identities in all other novels, suddenly focus on family inheritances? The man who tracks down traces, who used to believe only in bodies and the traces they leave behind, changes radically in the course of this novel. He lets himself be led by the law of signs, and ends up making a big mistake.

On several occasions in the novels, Bwana Msa finds himself in caves, in dark tunnels that he has to pass through to come

---

[13] *'Kwa nini binadamu anakosa?' Bwana Msa aliendelea na maelezo yake. 'Labda swali hili ni gumu kulijibu. Lakini tukifikiri sana kwa nini binadamu anakosa, tutaona kuwa binadamu kapewa akili. Binadamu anakosa kwa sababu ana akili. Malaika hawakosi; wanafanya jambo lile lile walioambiwa kulifanya – kama inavyosema Kurani tukufu. Hawafikiri nini wala nini; ameambiwa kutoa roho viumbe, anatoa tu; haimpitikii kufikiri kwa nini mimi nitoe roho viumbe? Na hayo ni kwa sababu malaika hawakupewa chombo cha fikira, hawakupewa akili ya kufikiri kama tuliyopewa sisi binadamu. Sisi wenye akili, tukiliona jambo au tukilisikia jambo, akili zetu zinatupelekea kulisawirisha jambo lilie kwa namna inavyotuelekeza akili yetu. Mimi nitalielekeza hivi; wewe utalielekeza vingine; na mwingine atalielekeza vingine – jambi lile lile moja. Tunapotea, maadam zitazuka tafsiri nyingi kwa jambo moja tu. Nakupotea kuna maana ya kukosea.'*

into the daylight. He is not afraid of total darkness. He knows that the key trace is hidden in the depths of caves and holes. The links in a network of clues must be broken so that there is a chance of finding a trace. The man who refuses to involve himself in people's business never baulks at delving into the narrowest places. Caves, obscure holes and underground passages always appear in Abdulla's novels and the truth invariably emerges from these dark places.

In contrast to the clue which leaves him in the dark with its various meanings, the trace reveals all and puts him back in the daylight. The major difference between the clue and the trace is that darkness comes first in the case of the latter. Furthermore, the discovery of a trace is always the result of an initiation. Going into a cave means to extricate oneself from the cultural and social order, to break with the hegemony of signs.

Bwana Msa and his young companion go deep into the sacred forest of the ancestors as if they were entering a cave:

> 'Like we said, it was totally black in there! We couldn't see each other at all. Terrifying! If Najum hadn't been afraid he'd be called a coward he would've gone back. It's no place for human beings, down there.' (Abdulla, 1960: 29)[14]

At the heart of this shrine to the ancestors, Bwana Msa and Najum find the remains of Bwana Ali in a clearing where seven graves are lined up in a row:

> Najum was as awestruck as Robinson Crusoe when he discovered the footprints in the sand on his island; by the fourth grave, by the headstone, there was a man! He was sitting up, leaning his back against the grave, his legs stretched out in front. But there was a detail that made this man much more frightening. His head was not on his shoulders as it should be. The man was holding his head on his thighs! (Abdulla, 1960: 35)[15]

---

[14] *'Ndani, kama tulivyosema, kiza totoro! Hapana mmoja aliyemwona mwenziwe. Kunatisha! Na Najum, kidogo tu, kama asingaliogopa kuambiwa mwoga, angeghairi kwenda mbele. Si mahali pa kupita mtu.'*

[15] *Najum aliruka kwa hofu kama hofu iliyomwingia Robinson Crusoe alipoona unyayo wa mtu juu ya mchanga kule kisiwani kwake; kwani kwenye kburi la nne, kwa upande wa kichwani, alikuwapo mtu! Alikuwa ameketi chini hali ameegemea kaburi lenyewe na miguu yake kainyosha kwa mbele. Lakini mtu huyu alizidi*

It is not the corpse itself that fills Najum with fear, but rather its status as a trace. If there is no good detective novel without a corpse, it is because the corpse is not limited to its role as a clue.[16] Of course, a good detective knows that he should not trust a corpse because it is sometimes used by the killer to leave false clues: this man loads the corpse with false leads that require some expert analysis. But the corpse has another dimension quite separate and beyond the technical skills that the classic detective tends to rely on.

The corpse is the fingerprint of a crime. Long before its agency in solving the crime is revealed, it is the primary evidence that a crime actually took place. In M. S. Abdulla's novels, the corpse is the final trace of a criminal's activities, all of which they still have to uncover. If a corpse turns up in a novel simply to mislead the detective who puts his trust in clues, the clue initiates the course of the action. To look at the corpse rather as a *trace* means it is a primary feature of the novel. The corpse as trace is quintessentially the main character, bringing on that person's destiny. Thus, the detective interprets the corpse like a palm-reader. If there are signs on the corpse, they no longer belong to semiotics, but to divination. The corpses in Abdulla's stories have an aura about them, revealing their past. A quick examination of the marks on the corpse makes it possible to reconstruct the route that brought it to a given place and left it in a specific pose. The trail is not found by virtue of clues but through the body's imprints. Bwana Msa explains that Bwana Ali was decapitated somewhere else; that the headless corpse decomposed before it fell apart and was dragged to the sacred forest of the ancestors, to be found much later. The whole process is written in the sand: Bwana Msa is also a geomancer: before he interprets the signs, he reads the traces.

The corpse brings a touch of romance to the novel. The thrill caused by the finding of the body provokes another solution to the mystery. The way the body is laid out tells its own story. What is peculiar about the corpse in *Mzimu wa watu wa kale*

(contd) *kutisha kwa jambo moja. Kichwa chake badala ya kuwapo mahali panapohusu, juu ya mbega yake, hakikuwapo hapo. Mtu huyo alikuwa amekipakata kichwa chake mapajani hali amekiwekea mikono yake yote miwili!*

[16] This is Van Dine's first principle (Van Dine, 1928).

is the strange position it was found in: it was obviously laid out in a ritualistic way, as Bwana Msa works out so cleverly. There are similar examples in other novels of discovering how a crime took place. In the final brilliant summing up in *Mwana wa Yungi hulewa* (The devil's child grows up) (1976), Bwana Msa uses a police photo of this particular body and from this one image, proceeds to reconstruct the chain of events:

> It's obvious that Sichana got hold of Amanullah's knife, which she'd hidden in her box [...] she held it with the right hand, and with her left, managed to haul herself upright. With all the force left in her wounded body she threw the knife at Jeejee – a final stroke of luck. When she'd thrown it, her left hand, the one she was leaning on, gave way and she fell forward on her stomach. Thus, the parts of her body that she had straightened up to give her the power to throw the knife – the head, the chest, the belly – suddenly collapsed, but the hand that threw the knife stayed fully extended, in the same position, straight, as it had to be for her to throw the knife. (Abdulla, 1976: 119)[17]

The police photograph had caught the corpse exactly as needed for Bwana Msa to be able to reconstruct the event. Here, we are at the heart of the fictional process. It is all about movements: the stretching and shrinking of bodies. Unlike objects, corpses bear all the marks of movements: it is all in the posture. The art of of the detective consists in putting his trust in the dynamism of the trace.

This way of hooking the plot into the corpse is one of the devices used by Faraji Katalambulla, author of some of the most puzzling detective novels in Tanzania. His first novel *Simu ya kifo* (*The phone call of death*) (1965) features an Inspector Wingo, in a case where he cannot make sense of any clues in a shocking series of corpses. A mysterious phone call

---

[17] *Ni dhahiri kuwa Sichana alikitoka kisu cha Amanullah alichokuwa nacho yeye kakificha sandukuni mwake [...] akakishika kwa mkono wake wa kulia, na kwa mkono wake wa kuo, alijinyanyua, akamrushia Jeejee kile kisu kwa ukomo wa nguvu alizokuwa nazo wkati ule wa kufa – bahatinasibu, kikimpata au kisimpate. Kwisha kukirudusha kisu tu, mkono wa kuo uliofanya kazi ya mwega au mhimili ulijiacha, ukafyatuka chini yake kwa kujikunja chini ya tumbo, na hapo hapo sehemu zilizokuwa zimenyanyuka kwa kutaka nguvu za kurushia kisu – kichwa, kifua, tumbo – zilibwaga kwa ghafla chini, bali mkono uliorusha kisu ulibakia vile vile umenyoka kwa ukomo wa kunyoka kwake, kama ulivyohitaji kunyoshwa wakati ulipokirusha kisu.*

leads him each time to discover yet another, which ruins all the trails he was following before. Detective Wingo is bounced around from one corpse to the next, without any purposeful direction on his part. He goes through a dark tunnel which, in spite of himself, leads him to the truth. He is driven by a wave of killings beyond his control, but relentlessly, the bodies lead him to solve the case. His success is achieved through dispossession.

Katalambulla's first novel which was a bestseller in Tanzania is a direct development of the economic narrative style that was introduced by Abdulla. The same process works in Ben Mtobwa's novel *Najisikia kuua tena* (*I feel like killing again*) [1984] in which the murderer announces his desire to kill before he does anything else.

The plot of Katalambulla's *Buriani* begins with a particularly upsetting mise-en-scène. The narrator takes a seat in a train after bidding farewell to his wife but then he finds her body, stabbed to death, lying at his side in the railway carriage. Wrapped in a shawl, the corpse had been put on the train at its first stop by murderers who got off and vanished before the train departed. The detectives on this case no longer need to go to the crime scenes, because the dead follow them; bodies turn up right next to them. The narrator (husband) begins his investigation in the dark, with only a slip of paper he finds in the compartment where he was sitting. Step by step, he uncovers the truth about his wife's murder, building from one coincidence to the next and from one false start to the next.

The flow of traces

To Inspector Seif, a woman who has been strangled and a man whose eyes have been gouged out are clear evidence of a case of jealousy in *Mwana wa Yungi hulewa* (*The devil's child grows up*). Bwana Msa needs to apply all his skills to trace the story back from these corpses to the revelation of a theft committed by two sisters – the owners of the house in which the murders took place. The bedrock of the plot thus comes to light. Fake identities are revealed. Someone who believed his name was Amanullah discovers that he is really called Emmanuel, and a woman called Sishana turns out to be Shannon. Behind these name-changes, there is a confusion of racial identities. It turns out that Emmanuel and Shannon are the secret children of an Indian from Goa and a young girl of Arab origin. Behind these concealed births and other family secrets, there are many crosscurrents of money, race and culture.

At the heart or Bwana Msa's investigations there is always a narrative thread on the transmission of cultures. The themes of money, disappearance, theft or murder that set off an investigation are often side-effects of more serious issues around the embezzlement of inheritances, or the diversion of wealth from the proper family line. Bwana Msa acts at this level. Thus, there are always two levels of investigation in Muhammed Said Abdulla's novels. The investigation is triggered by a crime that needs to be solved, and the expert Inspector Seif, is the man for the job. Seif starts from the crime in order to find the criminal. He looks for a thief in the case of a theft and in the case of a murder he looks for a murderer. At this surface level, the crime opens a space for investigation that closes when the guilty person is discovered.[18]

However, besides this meticulous crime solving Bwana Msa embarks on another task: a genealogical investigation that starts from 'what's in the air'. Bwana Msa can spot incon-

[18] The double level of investigation is explicit in a novel such as *Siri ya sifuri* (*The secret of the zero*) (1974) in which Inspector Seif is summoned by a crook who has cooked up the story of a theft in order to compromise a rival. The Inspector looks for someone who stole an important amount of money at Bwana Wasiwasi Malifedha's house. The presumed thief is Saidi, the secretary and lover of the young Mwanatenga who is regarded as the future heir. Seif could have concluded the case quickly if Mwanatenga, who saw things differently, had not called Bwana Msa. Msa reveals that Mwanatenga is the daughter of Bwana Hafifu, a pauper who lives in a hut near the family home. Bwana Hafifu is the real inheritor of Bwana Malifedha's money. Mwanatenga's inheritance will thus not come from Bwana Malifedha. In *Mzima wa watu wa Kale* (1960) Bwana Msa investigates the disappearance of Bwana Ali, a wealthy man, but a miser. His beheaded corpse, as well as a certificate proving that his assets were sold to an Indian trader from the village, are finally found at the heart of the shrine of the ancestors. Questions soon multiply: why did Bwana Ali suddenly sell everything he owned? Where is the money he got from selling all these assets? Who killed him? The theft and the murder belong to two different logical patterns. If one could hold the spirits as responsible for the crime, this seems to be more difficult in the case of the theft. Bwana Msa's expertise consists in revealing that Bwana Ali was a swindler who tried to stop the real heir (Ahmed) from getting the wealth he was entitled to. The conditions under which the theft and the murder happened are clarified but, more importantly, the victim is not the miser, as everyone thought, but an honest and poor man.

gruities in a family even when he meets them for the first time, as in the case of a girl who has no resemblance to the man who is said to be her father (*Siri ya sifuri*). In another novel, a brother looks completely different from his sister (*Duniani kuna watu*). Then in contrast, some children look so alike that it is impossible that they are not related (*Mwana wa Yungi hulewa*). Bwana Msa is an expert in 'family resemblances'. This explains why he gives much credit to photographs; they play a crucial part in solving mysteries because they reveal the essential 'aura' of an individual. The photograph captures family resemblances, but also the atmosphere. Thus, in the course of his investigations, Bwana Msa pays close attention to all the photographs he finds so that he can use them when it is time for the final explanation. Showing the photos has as much value as producing a birth certificate. Very often the family's atmosphere belies the declared, named relationships, so mistrust is introduced, as Bwana Msa explains to his friend Najum:

> 'Listen, many people know Ahmed under the name Ahmed bin Ali which means Ahmed, son of Ali. But look at Ahmed, and then look at Bwana Ali. For Heaven's sake! Do you see any resemblance between them? There's no similarity, whether it's in the nose, the eyes, the mouth, or in their whole look or behaviour. Ahmed is the complete opposite of his father.' (Abdulla, 1960: 33)[19]

A family's resemblance is directly linked with the surname which means that it must be put aside in order to identify the truth of their relationships. In this specific case, Bwana Msa notices that the boy and the girl have an identical birthmark on their faces even though their names are quite different.

In general, Bwana Msa is a collector of material details. Signatures on declarations of bankruptcy, proof of identity, wills, as well as fingerprints themselves provide just as much evidence as photographs. The detective's task is to gather as much physical evidence as possible and to draw conclusions

---

[19] 'Sikiliza, kuna watu wengi wanaomjua Ahmed kwa jina la Ahmed bin Ali, yaani Ahmed mtoto wa Ali. Lakini wewe mtazame Ahmed, kisha mtazame Bwana Ali. Haki ya Mungu, waweza kugundua mshahaba wo wote baina yao tuseme, katika sura zao? Si pua, si macho, si mdomo, si umbo wala si tabia. Ahmed ni kinyume kabisa na baba yake.'

from all of it. Clues on the other hand, always result from the detective's interpretation, while evidence turns up before his eyes and provides direct proof – as long as the detective knows how to perceive it.

In *Duniani kuna watu* (*There are people in the world*) Bwana Msa gets hold of a copy of the Koran, not meant for him, but which contains coded clues that lead him to find some stolen money. The Koran was a posthumous present of the late father to his bastard child who should inherit his wealth. Once again Bwana Msa produces photographic evidence and a complex play on physical resemblances in order to establish the family ties between the sender and the receiver of the Koran. The holy book thus becomes a key element of the investigation since it belongs to the normal genealogical pattern of inheritance. The father leaves clear evidence, by chance and yet on purpose, so the true inheritor is found. Unintentionally he leaves his traces all over the holy book, which leads to the discovery of the money, while intentionally, his features are clearly seen on the face of his real son, identifying him as the heir. There is a complex interplay between these two levels of investigation.

Thus, there are often two lines of investigation running concurrently, the one defined by the other. In all the Inspector Seif novels, he only has access to one of these lines in each case. He is totally at liberty to pick up clues and provide their most plausible interpretation. But at the same time, Bwana Msa has the ability to follow not only clues but also traces and sworn statements. The great difference between Bwana Msa and the other detectives who are considered to be the models for this character is the fact that he does not regard traces as signs. To Bwana Msa, the world of signs is limited.

From the trace to the revelation

There are three racially weighted spheres on the horizon of Abdulla's storylines: Blacks, Arabs and Indians. The solution to any mystery calls for a clarification of the state of affairs between them. Matters of inheritance often conceal racial conflicts. Money should flow according to blood ties but there are other great fortunes to be passed on that were made where the races meet, via maritime trade around the Indian Ocean and continental commerce in Mozambique and Congo.

In the novel *Siri ya sifuri*, such a fortune comes from a hoard buried at the foot of a baobab tree on Zanzibar Island by the Portuguese. The money is lifted out of a yawning hole which is quite evident throughout the novel. Bwana Msa investigates the case of a man who falls into this chasm. Bwana O, who dug up the treasure, is the fictional hero character *par excellence*. He embodies the family secret. During the conversation about contradictory words that opens the first chapter, Bwana Msa recalls a remark made by a knowledgeable acquaintance:

> 'Maalim Hafidh said that zero is a number full of secrets and surprises; he said that zero in itself is nothing; but!.. It can significantly expand a number, it can multiply any number by ten. It all depends on what side of the zero the number is placed.' (Abdulla, 1974: 18)[20]

Bwana Msa's task is to reveal the identity of Bwana O who holds on to the wealth at stake, but is also the biological father of the young Mwanatenga, who lives in poverty in a hut at the edge of a chasm. Family secrets around which Abdulla weaves his plot are gaps in the narrative: they are like the dark caves that Bwana Msa eventually penetrates and finds the light. The secret is meaningless as long as it works as a secret but it becomes crucial as soon as it is brought to light. The trace, which I distinguish from the clue, is merely the trace left by the secret. The trace always fades away on a dark background.

Thus, it is clear that a secret will leave a trace. Bits of reality cannot be swept away so easily. One needs to read Abraham and Torok's work on family secrets and their link to the process of incorporation, the constitution of the self, in order to understand why a secret cannot be manifested in a sign. A secret is angular, not part of any system. It is the blind spot of systems. At best, the inconsistencies of the system and the

---

[20] 'Maalim Hafidh kasema kwamba sifuri ni siri yenye viling na vituko; akasema kwamba kwa nafsi yake tu, sifuri haina kitu; lakini, lo!... Inaweza kuifanya idadi kubwa kabisa ikawa haina thamani yo yote, kama inavyoweza kuikuza idadi hiyo au nyingineyo mara kumi zaidi, kutegemea upande gani wa sifuri idadi hizo zimekaa.'

dissonance of clues may direct attention to the secret but one always needs to adjust one's way of looking in order to see the trace. Bwana Msa also believes in dreams, intuitions, trances and other absences that will enable him to discover the trace.

Trains occupy a special place in Katalambulla's narratives. Their continuous movement on fast tracks parallels the way an investigation unfolds. *Pili pilipili*, a short novel without a murder mostly takes place on a train between Dar es Salaam and Mwanza. The narrator, who had planned to get off at Igalula to meet his family and to organize his marriage, is cast under the spell of a young girl (Pili) and stays on the train till the end of the line. The romantic interlude turns to an investigation when the narrator notices that his wallet has been stolen on the train. Pili convinces him to stay on the train and caters to his every need. It is only at the end of the novel that the narrator understands that Pili is the thief and that she looked after him with his own money. This amusing story takes the reader to the heart of the initiatory logic of the trace. In place of the corpse we have a beautiful young woman who diverts the narrator from his regular life and sets him on a journey well beyond his control. For the narrator, Pili is both thief and guide to the truth. In the logic of initiation, all criminals behave in the same way.

One of the most notable features of Katalambulla's writing is the use of an internalized focus, so that readers are made aware of all the thoughts of the detective. Thus the reader slips into the twists and turns of an investigation. At each stage of the story, the character is in a precise situation and must act in the most appropriate way. The character considers many alternative options. The calculation is inevitably fast but it is done systematically. Katalambulla's characters keep on developing many small scenarios before selecting out one. The story always moves forward in a fog of possibilities that gradually disperse. The detectives in Katalambulla's stories are at the same time very aware of facts and fully part of a reality beyond their control. They are on this train that takes them to another place in spite of their wishes. In a way, the world is made ready for them because the truth about the crime has to come out. They are merely the instrument for revealing the truth just as the train rolls on to its final destination.

A number of articles published about the character Bwana Msa question in a somewhat contradictory fashion the duality of the detective's rationality and his supernatural powers of divination. An analysis of *Mzimu wa watu wa kale* published in *Mulika* (1973) presents the character as a kind of soothsayer with supernatural powers (Williams, 1973).

Later in the same journal, S. A. Mohamed argues against this interpretation and tries to demonstrate that Bwana Msa's method is a work of analysis and reasoning (Mohamed, 1973). Following the trace there is no contradiction between analysis and divination: Bwana Msa merely interprets the signs that come to him without him having any choice in the matter. To interpret signs is fully rational. His ability comes into play at the level of choosing the signs he works with. Yet in a way, Bwana Msa does not choose them: he merely makes himself available and lets the signs impose themselves on his thoughts.

This explains why coincidences occur so frequently in Bwana Msa's investigations. Sherlock Holmes proceeds by cross-checking the evidence. He provokes situations and tries to force the truth out of its lair. Bwana Msa waits for chance events to lead him to the solution. The mere mention of the name of a suspect during a conversation leads to Bwana Msa's sitting next to this person in a train filled with people, and conversing with him without realizing with whom he is talking.[21] The proliferation of coincidences has nothing to do with the author's awkward style; rather, it follows a deep logic in Abdulla's fiction. The notion of coincidence only exists for the one who believes in clues. One trace leads to the next in the logic of traces. It is easier to go along with the discovery of physical traces in those cases where it is difficult to believe in a series of random clues.

Needless to say, the logic of the trace is totally irrational but Pierre Bayard has convincingly argued that to unravel mysteries by using clues also results from a rambling, even delusional process. Therefore, it seems that we are dealing with two different types of 'delirium'. On the one hand, there is the theory analysed by Pierre Bayard. On the other, there

---

[21] This is how he meets Jamila who is suspected of having torn a page from the marriage registrar in *Kosa la Bwana Msa*. One could give many examples of this device.

is the delirium of the mystic, as is the case here. If Sherlock Holmes (or Hercule Poirot) is a theoretician, then Bwana Msa is a kind of mystic. Each one operates on one or other side of this distinction. The enigma is solved by using signs in the first case and by looking behind the signs in the second. The 'revelatory truth' supersedes the 'revealed truth'. The migrations of peoples, the flow of blood or money and the dynamics of family growth are the silent movements of the world to which Bwana Msa pays great attention. Clues, as well as the cultural context in which they occur, are set adrift by these great background movements. The limited sphere of all the protagonists involved in an investigation is blown open by the great revelations that Bwana Msa brings forth in the final chapters of Abdulla's novels. A sudden and brutal enlargement of their world destroys the enigma. The unlimited fiction of this world and its intrigues unravel in the plot so that all the elements can then be reconstructed. The powerful flow of the subjective experience of reading blows apart the meticulous gathering of clues.

9 Said Ahmed Mohamed
The Dark Side of Images

Most novels by Said Ahmed Mohamed end badly, in some kind of catastrophe. However, nothing is further from his world-view than the concept of fate. His disasters are always the outcome of a build-up of conflicts, set out in the novel in minute detail. Any two characters, no matter what they are like, never meet in a neutral way; there is no such thing as an encounter without some imminent conflict. The basis of these conflicts is the animal hostility of human beings. As the narrative unfolds, it becomes clear that this hostility is rooted in either their familial or social background. Men and women do not find it easy to live together.

The second chapter of the novel *Dunia mti mkavu* (*The world is a dry tree*) opens with a lengthy account of the problems in a courtyard, where Bakari Jaku lives. A couple get into a fight in their living room. Disputes arise about the use of toilets or about queue-jumping at the communal water hydrant (Mohamed, 1980a). Relationships tend to be promiscuous so of course this leads to fights. However, the battle is less about the war of the sexes and more about infidelity. When people live crammed together, they are going to come to blows. When a woman is stronger than a man, she dominates. The way to avoid this conflict is to have more space. It becomes clear that people want to get rich so they can live with more personal space around them:

> 'Oh, you're so right. It's high time we left. We'll move as soon as we find somewhere else. It's impossible to go on living with such brutes. It's nothing but shouting, fighting, swearing and chaos – every day God gives us. Oh yes, we'll move out somewhere. I've had enough. Today it's okay to have an argument, tomorrow we'll be arrested for nothing, and the day after that, God knows who'll be slaughtered and we'll be called up as witnesses. What kind of

life is this! Those people will land us at the police station. I've never gone to a police station, my whole life. What a mess! If we find a... Even if we don't find another place we'll move. And don't talk to me about just a room! It'll be just the same somewhere else! It's like being trapped between Scylla and Charibdys.

– Don't talk that way about bad luck! After the rain, always the sun... But you know, I don't have the money to rent a whole house...' (Mohamed, 1980a: 31)[1]

The best way to avoid contact with unsuitable people is to have a house surrounded by a garden. All wealthy people acquire one. They live in palaces (*kasri*), not houses (*nyumba*). In these novels, the interiors of these grand homes are always described down to the last detail; not just the furnishings, but how big the house is, how the walls and windows are decorated.[2] Characters in these novels go from room to room, floor to floor, just to show you exactly how huge these places are.

Image as the external sign of wealth

These residences have the ability to transform the world into images, which is why windows, pictures, photographs and the TV set are quite relevant. In a fairly long scene of *Kiza katika nuru* (*Darkness within light*), Bwaba Juba's wife, Bi Khaltiyy, is bored all alone in her house and she goes back and forth, television to window, until she eventually immerses herself in a photo album (Mohamed, 1988a). Rich wives, like her, all alone in their houses, spend most of their time quite happily browsing through photographs. They live in a world dominated

[1] 'Ah, wachilia mbali, tukipata nyumba tutahama, taabu kukaa na washenzi hawa; kelele, ghasia, matusi, zogo kila siku ya Mungu, lo... a-a...he, tutahama. Mashaka gani haya; leo ugomvi, kesho tukamatwe bure, kesho-kutwa nani kachinjwa na sisi ndio tuwe mashahidi. Maisha gani haya! Hawa kutupeleka sisi polisi! Maisha yangu yote toka kuzaliwa sijafika polisi; maisha gani haya! Tukipata...
—Wala hatupati tukahama. Na tena unasema chumba; ikiwa chumba si itakuwa hayo hayo kila siku? Kutoka kwa Mussa kwenda kwa Firauni?
—Kheri apendayo Mungu bibiye, kenda karibu na kumi, lakini sijui kama tutapata nyumba nzima, maana unajua sina uwezo wa kukodi nyumba nzima, mshahara wenyewe...'

[2] See Bwana Zuberi's house in *Asali chungu* (Mohamed, 1977: 7-8), Bwana Maksuudi's in *Utengano* (Mohamed, 1980: 19) and Bwana Juba's in *Kiza katika nuru* (Mohamed, 1988: 165-168).

by images. The young wife of Bwana Zuberi in *Asali chungu* (*Bitter honey*) by the name of Bi Amina falls in love with the image of a young man, Dude, whom she sees passing by in the street. Her subsequent relationship with this young man is constantly reinforced by photographs. The two lovers often go out in her car, visiting one beautiful house after another.

A car is an indispensable marker of material wealth, which is why Said Ahmed Mohamed pays special attention to chauffeurs. Bashiri in *Asali chungu* (*Bitter honey*), Rashidi in *Utengano* (*Separation*) and Kitwana in *Kiza katika nuru* (*Darkness within light*) are pivotal characters. They allow the wealthy figures in the novel to develop in the world without direct contact with it. To some extent, the car is a walking window. In the short story entitled *Tumba iliyovia*, Saada, a young woman returns to her village after five years' study in Europe, but she prefers spending the night in her car rather than getting dirty in the huts she now despises.

The distancing effect of the car is evident in the tenth chapter of *Asali chungu*: Bi Amina and her lover, Dude, are driving back from a day out in the the countryside when they are flagged down by a group of people at the side of the road. Dude pulls over, although Amina does not want him to. He discovers his childhood girlfriend, Baya, in a state of hysteria. She accuses him of turning his back on the real world, and of selling his soul to a wealthy woman. This scene brings the love affair to an end. Amina is driven home, and she asks Dude to give her back the car keys:

> Anger and sadness choked him, but he did not cry. He felt the weight of his hand as he tried to take the keys out of the ignition. He held them up and dropped them in Bi Amina's hand. When the keys touched her palm he felt as if something inside him was torn apart [...] She closed her fist over the keys, pushed the door open and rushed in, letting the door slam behind her! Eventually, Dude managed to open his mouth. He tried to call her back: 'Ma... ma... ma...mama, Mama Amina.' But Bi Amina, so swept up in her feelings, didn't want to listen to him. Dude looked on in total amazement as Amina ran inside the house and the door closed behind her. (Mohamed, 1977: 129) [3]

---

[3] *Sauti yake ilichanganyika na ghadabu na kekefu za kilio, lakini chozi halikumtoka. Pale alipokuwa akiinua kufikia ufunguo wa gari kwenye swichi, Dude aliuhisi*

The unforgivable mistake Dude made was to stop on the road, to respond to a call instead of clinging to an image. The young man is rejected by the world of the rich because he did not know how to be happy with only images. He did not know how to keep himself as superficial as an image and he questioned moral solidarity: 'Maybe those people really need help; maybe it's a matter of life or death' (Mohamed, 1977: 124).[4] Dude sees people speaking to him whereas Bi Amina only sees figures waving their arms. The same theme occurs in *Kiza katika nuru* when the driver, Kitwana, swerves to avoid running over a dog, much to the displeasure of his employer, Bwana Juba (Mohamed, 1988b: 216-217).

One could argue that there are two worlds in Said Ahmed Mohamed's novels: the world of images and the other world of darkness, of hard labour and misery. The gap between the rich and the poor goes beyond the simple issue of money. To belong to the rich people is to adopt a particular mentality – to never look below the surface. Rich people live above reality and transform the world around them into an appropriate setting for how they want to be.

This explains why the careful regulation of being allowed in or being kept out of their exclusive settings is so important. To maintain their value, such enclaves must be impenetrable. In *Utengano*, Bwana Maksuudi rejects his wife because he suspects her of having allowed a complete stranger into his home to help deliver her baby. Maksuudi flies into a terrible rage because he is aware of the risks in letting anyone walk in or out of his property. It might lead poor people to hatch a plot against him. In contrast to poor people's houses that are open to the four winds, the main function of rich people's houses is to keep the world at bay.

Therefore, to move into wealthy society means leaving the real world behind. The problem with rich people is that

(contd) *mkono wake mzito. Lakini aliufikisha hapo na kuutoa; akaondosha kiganjani pa Bi Amina. Kama vile ufunguo ulivyoanguka kiganjani pake, ndivyo mpasuko fulani katika kichwa chake alivyouhisi [...]. Kwani baada ya kuudhibiti ule ufunguo kiganjani pake, Bi Amina aliusukuma mlango wa gari akatoweka na kuuacha ukigonga nyuma yake! Hatimaye Dude mdomo wake ukafumbuka. Akajaribu kuita: 'Ma...ma...ma...mama, Mama Amina.' Lakini Bi Amina, kama mwenye pepo, hakutaka kusikia kitu wala kugeuka. Dude alishangaa na kumwangalia Amina akiingia ndani, na hatimaye mlango kukomewa.*

[4] '*Labda watu wale wana haja muhimu sana; pengine ya uhai na mauti.*'

The Dark Side of Images 167

they cannot forget the have-nots. That other side of life can overwhelm their world at any moment. Wealthy people have two great fears: first, that the cosy stability provided by their world is just a dream; second, that truth thrives in movement:

> Change is natural. This is the rule of the world. But there are some people who are amazed that things change. The power of change manifests itself at every hour, at every moment, in sunrise and in sunset, in the tides, when there is light and when it becomes dark, when it is windy and raining, or when the snow melts in rivers and lakes. It is this power of change that destroys mountains and rocks so that the face of the earth is transformed. A new landscape emerges. Seconds becomes minutes; minutes become hours; hours become days, then days the weeks, the months, the years, and... with all the more reason, the human being, that weak creature, is tossed about and transformed every day of his life. Today a human being is young, tomorrow old. Yesterday in good health, today in sickness and then death. People complain, 'The days go by...'
>
> Days go by while human beings decay. Days come, disappear and come again. Every day is new but very old. Human beings go straight forward, without stopping. They tend to forget that there is a finite point, and that with the passing of the days they are using up their allotted time. They only think about their health, their work, their status and position in society. Then at the end, those who were the first become the last. Human beings remember that the world is in constant motion, and that, inevitably, there comes a time when the poorest take their turn. (Mohamed, 1980b: 97)

Such thoughts plague Maksuudi after he has lost all his money and spent two years in jail because he was involved in corruption. The fundamental law of change makes wealthy people vulnerable and finds its best course of action in the world of poverty. The rebellion of the poor is as natural a law as the passing of the days. A chain reaction to injustice occurs, sparked off by misery. If luxury can be equated with living in, by, and for an image, misery is the action of keeping people and objects bogged down in the depths. Characteristically, poor people's huts, even those of people living in the countryside, never give a view of the landscape. Instead they face in towards other poor shacks where the daily dramas of life are played out.

Poor people are denied access to images. There is always someone or something that gets in the way. Money gives human beings the power to free themselves from the snares of the world. Bakari Jaku, one of the protagonists in *Dunia mti mkavu* regards the world as

> a web of nets, a million nets, in which human beings are trapped and struggle to find the way out. Money is the way to get free: the more money you have, the quicker the escape. Without money there's no chance. The poor man has to struggle for a very long time to get out of each net and he will probably die before he is totally free. (Mohamed, 1980a: 36)[5]

This metaphor of the world as a muddle of nets is very telling. The world is the net from which we all try to escape. By implication, rich people are those who have succeeded in 'finding the way out' that is, to get into the apparently stable and serene world of the image. For Said Ahmed Mohamed, the dualism of rich versus poor does not divide a unique world but corresponds to a radical dualism between two worlds. On the one hand, there is the world of images that is superficial and static. On the other, there is a world of actions dedicated to depth and movement.

Potentially violent women and the crisis of image

These two worlds could ignore each other if it were not for certain zones of contact through which the flux of movement penetrates the world of the rich. The weakness of this world of images is its non-productivity. It does not look for ways to ripen the fruits that could enrich its surroundings. Rich people get there first, to whatever the world of darkness produces. *Dunia mti mkavu* opens with a conflict between Fauz, a rich man, and Fumu Juku, a farmer, about the fruits of his labour. Fauz cannot bear watching Fumu living off what he grows for himself on his own patch. According to Fauz, Fumu has no right to look so happy. He decides to forbid him from cultivating the land.

---

[5] Quotation from Mohamed, 1980a: 36.

The conflict between Fauz and Fumu is made much worse when a woman comes on the scene. The wealthy Fauz has stolen Fumu's fiancée by buying her off her parents. Here are the words used by Masika's father to try to convince his daughter to agree with this heaven-sent marriage proposal: 'Masika, we are poor. I'm not on the same level as these people. Can't you see that this marriage will bring us wealth? I'd never allow my daughter to marry a pauper while a stroke of good luck falls to me' (Mohamed, 1980a: 21).[6] Masika is snatched away into the world of the rich. Fauz poaches her like a ripe fruit. What Fauz does not know is that ripe fruits remember how long it takes to mature... Fauz is eventually murdered by his wife, in his very own home. Rich people can keep on building great walls between themselves and the poor, but danger always comes from the inside.

Women play a decisive role in Said Ahmed Mohamed's plots. They establish the link between the two worlds. They give birth to a third, transverse space through the biological family. Women have children who can belong, following their individual development, to the worlds of the rich or of the poor. This rule also applies to natural brothers. For example, *Dunia mti mkavu* describes the fragmentation of Mr Jaku's family with his four sons spread across all levels of society: three of them stay poor (a farmer, a docker and a thief) and the fourth moves up in the world, after he is adopted. They will all die during the 1948 general strike and their blood flows into the same stream, as the old Jaku witnesses:

> Mzee Jaku finally reached the place where the bodies were. He was stupefied: covered in sweat, his hair standing on end, and his heart now beating wildly. He looked at Pandu's corpse, then at Fumu's, then Bakari's, then finally at Kibwana's – Farouk, as everyone used to call him. They were all his children. Fumu was stretched out on his back, his eyes staring at the dark sky, washed out by rain. Bakari was lying on his stomach. He refused to show his face to a world that had got the upper hand over him when he was still a boy. Pandu's corpse was huddled up as if he was begging the world to stop oppressing him. As far as Kibwana

---

[6] *'Masika, sisi tu masikini. Mimi ni nokowa tu wa mabwana hawa; huoni kwamba ndoa hii itafungulia milango ya heri. Mimi sikubali mwanangu aolewe na masikini maadamu imemwangukia nyota ya jaha.'*

was concerned, his corpse bit the earth as if he was apologizing for trampling over it in violence and contempt. Mzee Jaku [...] collapsed and wallowed in the blood of his children as it mingled with the flowing stream. (Mohamed, 1980: 120) [7]

The key figure missing from this scene is the boys' mother, Bipole. She died of sorrow long ago after she was forced to give up her children, because she could not feed them. She knows that beneath social appearances, the ties of blood bind everyone. The general strike and the consequent repression of the workers will pull all family members together in a time of extreme crisis.

The structure of *Dunia mti mkavu* reveals two levels of narrative. On the one hand, there is the principle of dichotomy. This is characteristic of the social order and its main disruption is the distinction between the rich and the poor. This line also regulates the life of the poor according to different jobs: there is a world of fishermen, a world of dockers, of farmers, of jobless people and so on. These underworlds within the world of the poor struggle to survive against the same issues and may occasionally become rivals. The activists' task is to create a solidarity among the poor in a fight against the common enemy: rich people. Kumba takes up this task in *Dunia mti mkavu*, while Mvita does the same in *Kiza katika nuru*.[8] The big issue is how to flag up the differences between a rich man and a poor one, to reveal exactly what is going on in that great divide. What matters most is not the law, but life itself. Thus Kumba can explain to the thief Pandu Juku that he should join workers in the fight against the rich, because, like them, he has to scratch a living at the bottom of the pile.

The activist's task is to reduce the code of social differentia-

[7] *Mzee Jaku sasa alikuwa keshafika chini ya wale maiti. Mughma umemwaa; kijjasho kinamkatika, malaika yamemsimama, moyo unamwenda mbio. Alitazama maiti ya Pandu, tena ya Fumu, halafu ya Bakari na mwisho ya Kibwana au kama ulimwengu ulivyozowea kumwita, Farouk. Wale wote ni mwanawe. Kabisa hakuweza kupotewa na damu yake. Maiti ya Fumu ililala kichalichali ikitazama mbingu nyeusi na kukoga mvua iliyomwaika; ya Bakari imelala kifudifudi, kabisa imekataa kuipa uso dunia iliyomcheza toka kuzaliwa. Maiti ya Pandu imejipeta kwa unyonge kuilalamikia dunia iliyomdhulumu, na Kibwana, maiti yake iliuma ardhi na kuiomba msamaha kwa vile alivyokuwa akiikanyaga kwa matakuro na dharau. Mzee Jaku [...] alianguka na kuitapakaa damu ya watoto wake iliyokuwa ikichanganyika kwenye mkondo wa maji.*
[8] See the message to the farmers, ibid.: 189.

tion to a simple dualism: rich versus poor. It provides the basic structure of the novels discussed here. All the Jaku brothers who have stayed amongst the poor meet up again during the build-up to the strike, although they do not recognize each other. However, their militant activity never puts these brothers in contact with the one who crossed over the line, into the class of the wealthy. Only women can make that crossing, and even then only with great difficulty.

Women echo the effects of social activism at the family level through some moment or other of crisis. They reveal the most extreme forms of social tension. Whether they are the partners of rich men (see Masika in *Dunia mti mkavu*), abandoned wives (see Kudura in *Kiza katika nuru*), or women who are shut out of the world of the wealthy when they are wholly rejected, as is the case with Bi Tamina and her daughter Maimuna in *Utengano* – they all take part in crises of extreme violence. Masika kills her husband but she succeeds in outrunning the police and murders Kibwana at the very place where he has just executed his three brothers. In the same vein, Kudura also murders her husband at the end of the novel. Maimuna, out of her mind, threatens her brother and her father with a broken bottle.

Female characters are much more unstable than their male counterparts in Said Ahmed Mohamed's novels, thus forming a key element in the dynamic nature of the narrative. Without women, these works would simply be an account of the interaction between the two classes, in socio-political terms. The narrative would be locked into a never-ending cycle of revolution and repression. Madwomen and murderesses are linked to political action although they never throw a direct light on that sphere. Kudura murders her husband in revenge for the killing of her son Mvita. She acts in a fit of personal vengeance. Because women are entrammelled both in the world of the rich and that of the poor, they can only find a way out through explosive action.

Tata za Asumini (*Asumini's doubts*) (1990) moves away from the socio-political sphere in fiction to explore the sexual problems of a young girl who loves purity more than anything else, and therefore guards her virginity. The change of orientation in this novel is dramatic. It conveys the gradual deepening of the girl's crisis, eventually leading to her suicide. The character of Asumini is like a serial time-bomb: she experiences one explosion after another and ultimately breaks down completely. Neither her female friends nor the man she loves can reason with her, no matter how psychologically attuned they are. A description of Asumini could be summarized as follows: 'Asumini or rather "her life" was a coin with two faces: one of light and one of darkness!' (Mohamed, 1990: 101)[9] The whole novel is a portrait of Asumini, who is never satisfactorily drawn.

The young girl tries to establish contact with the world, especially with men, but only in a manner that keeps her pure and untouched. Her ideal of purity, which is perhaps the shining light of her inner self, is associated with childhood memories. Asumini contents herself with images and memories. She spends hours looking at herself in the mirror, as if trying to capture her image. Meanwhile her body is tied to her, and unknown to her it makes all kinds of connections with the world from which she cannot escape. Despite her efforts Asumini lives in an impure world dominated by desires and distastes. She does not want to acknowledge that the world is constantly caressing her and that she is just like many other woman, subject to male domination. Sewa who shows her respect and loves her, succeeds in making her confront and make contact with the world. She does not survive the ordeal.

It is obvious that a political issue plays a role in her destiny. Asumini's fits of madness are key moments in the narrative, where the fabric of her self-image is torn apart. Said Ahmed Mohamed's novels are a reflection of the political status of images, that is, the capacity of imagery to form a connection with the world. The tenth chapter ends with a powerful scene in which Asumini visits her native village where she meets her childhood friend, the boy Jazume. After playing together as they used to do in the past, in their childhood secret corner, she makes direct advances towards him. Jazume is alarmed and runs away. It is a bitter defeat for Asumini. She realizes that her life as a woman cannot take place in her world of memories and that she needs to face the external world. She was prepared to let Jazume touch her because he is part of her

---

[9] See quotation from Mohamed (1990: 101).

memory. Jazume is not afraid because he felt ashamed of what happened but because he is shocked at how inappropriately Asumini had behaved:[10]

> It was the first time he had seen anything like it and would never have believed Asumini would do such a thing. She had acted so suddenly, without any explanation of what she was doing, without letting things happen in the natural way; just crudely, like that! (Mohamed, 1990: 136)[11]

Jazume has correctly judged Asumini's problem. She is totally incapable of letting things happen with all nuances of reality. She is a split personality. She has a sunny side and a dark side; there are no shades or hues in her makeup. Her shining side is full of pure but rigid images that cling to reality and do not allow for any negotiation with that reality. Her dark side is caught up a swirl of contradictory feelings, beyond her control, threatening to tear her very self apart.

A stable to a shifting self-image

Said Ahmed Mohamed's characters are always delivered into forces over which they have virtually no control. They come through in nightmares that are often retold in his novels. In the play *Pungwa* (*Exorcism*, 1988), a character is possessed by a spirit who speaks through his mouth. He is inhabited by 'a voice that lives in his blood'.[12] Characters' anxieties are always manifested in haunting words that take over their very being. They become puppet figures, caught up in the turmoil and stress that courses through their veins. The sea is omnipresent in Said Ahmed Mohamed's novels, less as an essential element in the twists and turns of the plots on Zanzibar Island but because of its incessant movement and change of mood: 'The sea was calm. The little canoes and boats swung gently on their moorings. One could see them

---

[10] See quotation from Mohamed (1990: 136).
[11] *Hajapata kuona mandhari hii tangu kuzaliwa, na wala leo hakutarajia kabisa kama jambo lile angalifanya Asumini. Kalifanya bila mwanzo, bila ya kuonyesha dhamiri na ishara bila ya kwenda hatua kwa hatua: ghafla tu namna ile!*
[12] See quotation from Mohamed (1988b: 21-22).

diving and rising, tossed about, right and left' (Mohamed, 1980a: 80).[13]

The unremitting movement of the sea mirrors the dark reality of human life. At the end of the novel Asumini becomes aware of it as she stands on the shore, watching the waves, 'feeling the whole sea penetrating her'.[14] The sea symbolizes a peaceful synthesis of billions of conflicting currents, subsumed below its unified surface. This is in contrast to Said Ahmed Mohamed's characters, who are often locked inside a fixed image that is always threatened with disintegration.

Thus there seem to be two types of image of a quite different nature. On the one hand, there is a fixed, exclusive image, always threatened with disintegration by powers that it has externalized. On the other hand, there is a dynamic, integrative image that achieves the synthesis of millions of contradictory natural powers. The idle and superficial life of the rich people of Zanzibar belongs to the first category of images. Their life is unjust because it is discriminatory. It is also fragile because it breeds powerful and external opposing forces. Rich people are constantly threatened by the resentment they breed in the poor. They live in an artificial and rigid world on the point of disintegration. In many of Mohamed's novels, houses are burnt to the ground when rioters set them on fire.[15]

Nevertheless, scenes depicting crises where image is torn apart are not the end of the process. A redistribution of light and darkness must take place; as if one could melt into the other. Then another kind of image could come into being.

There is a light that is not the polar opposite of darkness, but takes its substance from it. This is the kind of light that the characters in Mohamed's novels search for. *Kiza katika nuru* takes the theme of opposition between light and darkness to a new level. Mvita, the son of the rich Bwana Juba chooses the dark side. He fights alongside the poor and he tries to

---

[13] *Bahari shwari — vijiwimbi vinatingisha vigawala na boti za wapenda-bahari; hizi zote zilikuwa na mchezo katika mtingisho, zitaonekana zinafanya kupiga mbizi, lakini kwa ghafla ziliinukia nyuma, halafu zikapigwa kofi kwenye mbavu zao za kulia na tena kushoto.*

[14] *Alihisi ile bahari yote imeingia ndani ya moyo wake.*

[15] This is the case of Zuberi's house at the end of *Asali chungu*. See also Maksuudi's house in *Utengano*.

encourage signs of light.[16] In a very intimate moment between Mvita and Salma, the moon rises up:

> 'Look, Mvita' said Salma, pointing to the sky. 'The moon is coming out, and here we are, standing in its light...this beautiful moon, this old moon, this moon we have always seen, time after time, is also always being born, like the baby who is coming to us soon...' Mvita looked up at the moon – majestic and gentle. It was a new moon, not a full one, but it shone like a huge silver ring.[17] (Mohamed, 1998a: 244)

These happy meetings between Maimuna and Kabi, the disabled fisherman, take place on the bank of a river, after sunset, in the twilight.

Fire is also an important element in Mohamed's novels. It has already been noted that rich people's houses are often devastated by the break-out of fires when poor people go on the rampage. However, the destructive nature of fire is balanced by the light it produces. The intimate conversation between Mvita and Salma takes place around a fire; Mvita admires the body of his beloved rosily illuminated by the flames. In *Dunia mti mkavu*, the aged man, Gae, who is half-crazy, stirs Fumu Jaku to political consciousness as they sit beside a fire. Fire has this special attribute, destroying everything while giving out light that brings its own shadows. This same idea is expressed by the old man Gae:

> At first, he did not follow what old Gae said. His words were like an enigma that kept increasing in depth. But gradually a feeble light started to penetrate the opacity of the old man's words. Little by little, this light revealed the important secret buried in this darkness and Fumu began to see clearly. He understood. (Mohamed, 1980a: 3)[18]

---

[16] See Mvita's thought on darkness (Mohamed, 1988a: 180-181).

[17] *'Tazama Mvita, Salma alionyesha juu. Mwezi unachomoza, sasa hivi tutakuwa na nuru, mwezi utaleta nuru utakapochomoza. Mwezi mpevu, mwezi mkongwe, mwezi ulioona yote tanu kale, lakini mwezi mchanga kama moto wetu...' Mvita liinua kichwa juu na kuutazama mwezi – mtukufu, mpole, upinde wa mwezi, si mwezi kamili, lakini uling'ara kama pete kubwa ya fedha.*

[18] *Mwanzo, kiini cha maneno ya Mzee Gae hakukigundua. Kilikuwa kama fumbo gumu lililomzidi kimo. Lakini baadaye nuru hafifu ilianza kupenya katika kiza alichokiweka Mzee huyo. Kidogo kidogo nuru hiyo ilifunua siri kubwa iliyofichama, na baadaye Fumu alianza kubaini mambo. Aligundua.*

In this novel on anger, *Dunia mti mkavu*, old Gae's role is as the one who reveals the truth, a role that is vested in love itself in other works by Mohamed. This moment of incandescence must occur so that light and darkness may interpenetrate, giving birth to a new image of the world. Disasters are necessary in Said Khamed Mohamed's novels. They are the only means of doing away with a particular mode of an image's existence that is not drawn to the light. This sterile image is bound to be torn apart, or better, to be consumed by fire. The old man Gae criticizes Fumu for using all his energy in production and for being 'unable to get a match to light a fire'.[19] What Fumu produces only serves an image of the world that seeks the very destruction of that world.

If the possibility of happiness truly exists, it is to be found in the accord between the world and reality. The world 'is a dead tree' as soon as it cuts itself off from the dark roots of reality in which poor people, who are excluded from the world, keep struggling on. This unseen reality searches for a spark that will help it destroy this world and create a new one in the image of these truths.

The most recent novel by Said Ahmed Mohamed,[20] *Babu aipopofuka* (*When grandfather rises from the dead*) continues this political theme on the image through a reversal of parameters. 'K', the main character of the novel, belongs to the profiteering class. He lives in a luxurious world totally adapted to the construction of images, such as a beautiful house, a nice car, a circle of friends and a harmonious family. There is only one problem in this perfect scene: the dog, who devours his food with such frightening speed that it is impossible to see his plate full. 'Doggy' the dog is like a black hole, just about to wolf down the whole world.

We soon realize that the glutton in this story is not the dog but the ghost of K's grandfather, who comes back to meddle in his life. Throughout this novel, Mohamed introduces a new aspect in his system of images: the invisible. The grandfather's ghost takes K to the other side of image. K learns to reject

---

[19] *'Kwa nini unashindwa kupata kijiti cha kibiriti kuwashia moto?'*
[20] At the time the original French edition of this book was published (2006). Later novels by Said Ahmed Mohamed are: *Dunia yao* (*I am not of their world*) (2006) and *Uso za Mwanamke* (*Faces of a woman*) (2010).

images in order to see the reality of the world more clearly. K loses his job, his house, his car and his family. This complete loss is the price he has to pay for getting in touch with reality. He drifts away into invisibility and finally commits suicide, the only witness to this event being his dog. Furthermore, his total dispossession is the outcome of the devastating work of a reality engendered by the political situation.

K's initiatory trip is destructive because the reality he discovers is a desert. The world of image has wiped out everything. Only the desert remains. The appalling political observation that Said Ahmed Mohamed makes in this novel is that there is no alternative to the image except for the desert and death. This observation would be a cause for despair if there were no ghosts left behind. These are activists of another sort. Their mode of intervention is not action. They stand for the return of what reality rejected. They are the unmanageable result of the process of disintegrating reality. They are no longer flesh and bones in a world that has become spectral; they are only 'signs of skin, flesh and bones' (Mohamed, 2001: 168).[21]

Babu alipofufuka reveals the dramatic consequence of the vampire-like gobbling of the world by the wealthy. In its turn, this world, entirely devoted to images, finds itself trapped in the void it has created, with no other future but to dive into, if not drown, in invisibility.

[21] *Sasa alikuwa kabaki alama tu ya ngozi, nyama na mifupa.*

Conclusion

The development of the Swahili novel has proceeded hand in hand with a significant amount of critical and sometimes polemical commentary on the role of the novel in modern society. The summary of the trends in fiction writing in this book points to a widening scope. Looking at the polemics of the nature and purpose of fiction, it is evident that this debate takes place in the political rather than the literary arena. When a novelist's work is considered to be based on social issues, it is clear that a grand political vision of society lies behind that judgement. The great value given to fictional texts in the Swahili literary field relies on this interconnection between literature and politics. The literary world is fragile, yet it is this quality of involvement that sustains its political impact. Each new Swahili novel is expected to provoke a public debate from this socio-political perspective because there is no other platform for an artistic or literary appreciation of new fiction.

The first consequence of this absence is the powerful influence of popular fiction in the broader field of literature. Crime and sex are the preferred themes for the general readership. The majority of Swahili novelists, including those whose works are the most impenetrable, are to all intents and purposes compelled to employ themes imposed by the popular novel. The fact that the Swahili novel is oriented towards the popular novel has required a change in perspective when assessing their value. The popular novel cannot be regarded as a peripheral and trivial phenomenon. For example, the popular author Ben Mtobwa (one of the Swahili writers whose works have largely been translated into other languages) is a must-read of Swahili literature although he has avoided being a part of academic or cultured circles with ambitions to set the criteria for a significant and serious modern literature.

The interplay between serious and popular literature has

steadily grown alongside the changes in Swahili society. In the Marxist context, literature was characterized by its attempt to communicate with ordinary people about their concerns, but this approach was less successful than popular literature, which increased its market share. More serious writers found themselves in the paradoxical situation of writing elitist works for the people but this elitism had nothing to do with issues of class or a caste.

Shaaban Robert was the first to turn elitism into a strictly individual concern, in which there is no distinction other than personal glory. Much more significant than the divide between popular and serious literature is the growing tendency for novelists to challenge all criteria of aesthetic judgements of their works. Whether it is raucous or refined, Swahili literature is written beyond given boundaries with the aim of making a direct and authentic appeal to its readers.

The second consequence of this autonomous literary development is the status of writers.

It is typical that not one of the most talented Swahili novelists discussed, Shaaban Robert, Muhammed Abdulla, Mohamed Suleiman, Euphrase Kezilahabi or Said Ahmed Mohamed, represent a reference point or model for the next generation. Swahili literature is not in the hands of a select group of 'major writers'. There are no literary giants to challenge or debunk so that an avant-garde can take over. Most significant Swahili writers are not considered 'major writers'.

Even Shaaban Robert, who did indeed write in the colonial period when attempts were being made to establish a classic Swahili literature, was barely published in his lifetime. Moreover, those that were published were used more as *historical* points of reference than as a model or reference point for future writers. Therefore, strictly speaking, there are no schools of fiction, as such, but rather trends whose subsequent recognition has provided the basis for this study. In his *Diaries*, which provided the basis for the analyses of Deleuze and Guattari on 'minor literatures', Kafka (1948) makes the point that in the presence of major literary figures, minor writers can only operate in niche markets. 'The lack of compelling national [literary] figures denies any outlet for those who are completely devoid of talent.' Kafka goes on to explain that the presence of great masters enables inferior writers to find some small place in the shade of great works. There were numberless hacks writing novels in the style of Balzac. Such a phenomenon does not exist in the field of Swahili fiction, because there are no local models to imitate. Thus every writer has to become his own master and make his own name. To this date, there is no major exponent in any genre, be it romance, espionage or crime fiction, who stands out as the master of his craft. Popular novels come from a broad and diverse range of authors.

The fact that the Swahili novel lacks its own role models does not affect its recourse to various external influences. Kafka remarked on the precise opposite in 'minor literatures':

> The liveliness of such a literature exceeds even that of one rich in talent, for, as it has no writer whose great gifts could silence at least the majority of cavillers, literary competition on the greatest scale has a real justification. (Kafka, 1948: 149)

The widest possible scope that Kafka refers to is of necessity international. The lack of indisputable masters in any one country opens up its literary field to international influences from all over the world.

Swahili literature is lively and in direct touch with the most vibrant part of world literary creativity despite the fact that only a few writers are published, their print-runs are tiny, and that distribution is less than efficient. There is a direct link between the economic and the institutional fragility of a literary sphere and the extent to which it is engaged in the international market. More precisely, the boundary between the national and international market vanishes.

The third consequence of this fragility in the literary sphere is how the 'people' are represented in the literary process. To quote Kafka again, for the last time:

> There are, to be sure, fewer experts in literary history employed, but literature is less a concern of literary history than of the people, and thus, if not purely, it is at least reliably preserved. For the claim that the national consciousness of a small people makes on the individual is such that everyone must always be prepared to know that part of the literature which has come down to him, to support it, to defend it – to defend it even if he does not know it and support it. (Kafka, 1948: 149)

In sociological terms, in a situation where the independence of a literary field is not established, literary works can only survive if people read them. Swahili literature as a whole, including the popular novel, is characterized by this obsession with the social sphere which is to be understood in relation to the wider political debate about social change. It features in newspapers, on street-corners, and in all public and private settings in East Africa. Novels serve as both repositories and agents of these debates. They become embedded in a society, making the space for this debate to flourish. Through this desire for a constant public dialogue, novels find their place in the political dimension.

Quantitative questions have nothing to do with 'minor literature'. It is of little significance whether Kezilahabi's novels are read more or less than Ben Mtobwa's. To judge literature on the basis of sales figures takes us in the direction of novels written to order, for world-wide markets with no relevance to a living culture, such as the Swahili. Beyond literature that offers nothing more to the world than its own self-image, what we all need is literature that bears witness to the ever-present and crucial debate about the future, even if some would like us to believe that the subject is closed.

Bibliography

Literary Works

Abbreviations:
EAEP: East African Educational Publishers
EALB: East African Literature Bureau
EAPH: East African Publishing House
KLB: Kenya Literature Bureau
TPH: Tanzania Publishing House

Abdulla M. S. (1960) *Mzimu wa watu wa kale*, Nairobi: EALB
____(1968) *Kisima cha Giningi*, London: Evans Brothers Ltd
____(1973) *Duniani kuna watu*, Dar es Salaam: EAPH
____(1974) *Siri ya sifuri*, Dar es Salaam: EAPH
____(1975) *Mke mmoja waume watatu*, Dar es Salaam: EAPH
____(1976) *Mwana wa Yungi hulewa*, Dar es Salaam: EAPH
____(1984) *Kosa la Bwana Msa*, Accra: Africana Publishers
Abdul-Wahab Z. B. (1975) *Ulimbo*, Nairobi/Dar es Salaam/Kampala: EALB
Akwilombe R. (1988) *Dar imenihadaa*, Dar es Salaam: Akajase Enterprises
Anduru A. (1983) *Kukosa radhi*, Dar es Salaam: Press and Publicity Centre
Baalawy S. O. S. (1968a) *Bibi Maahira tena*, London: Evans Brothers Ltd
____(1968b) *Hadithi za Bibi Maahira*, London: Evans Brothers Ltd
Baka A. (1969) *Haifai*, Nairobi: Evans Brothers Ltd
Balisidya N. (1975) *Shida*, Nairobi: Foundation Book Ltd
Banzi A. (1972) *Titi la mkwe*, Dar es Salaam: TPH
Block H. P. (1948) *A Swahili Anthology*, Leiden: A. W. Sijthoff's uitgeversmaatschappij n. v.
Burhani Z. (1981) *Mali ya maskini*, Nairobi: Longman Kenya
____(1987) *Mwisho wa kosa*, Nairobi: Longman Kenya
Büttner C. G. (1894) *Anthologie aus der Suaheli-Litteratur*, Berlin: Verlag von Emil Felber

Buyu J. (1971) *Mtugeni*, Nairobi: Longman Kenya
Chachage C. S. L. (1981a) *Kivuli*, Dar es Salaam: BCI Publishers
____(1981b) *Sudi ya Yohana*, Dar es Salaam: Dar es Salaam University Press
____(1991) *Almasi za bandia*, Dar es Salaam: Dar es Salaam University Press
____(2002) *Makuadi wa soko huria*, Dar es Salaam: E & D Ltd
Charo K. m. (1976) *Toka kizazi hadi kizazi*, Nairobi/Kampala/Dar es Salaam: EALB
Chimerah R. (1995) *Nyongo mkalia ini*, Nairobi: Oxford University Press
Chiume M. W. K. (1980) *Gongo la umma*, Dar es Salaam: Black Star Agencies
Dumila F. (1972) *Upekuzi wa busara*, Nairobi: Equatorial Publishers
____(1979) *Insha za hekima*, Nairobi: KLB Literature Bureau
Farsy M. S. (1982) *Kurwa na Doto*, Nairobi: KLB
Ganzel E. (1971) *Ndoto ya mwendawazimu*, Nairobi/Dar es Salaam: EALB
Geranija P. C. and Muwanga A. S. (1976) *Doa la mauti*, Nairobi: Heinemann
Habwe J. (1995) *Maumbile si huja*, Nairobi: Jomo Kenyatta Foundation
____(2000) *Maisha kitendawili*, Nairobi: Jomo Kenyatta Foundation
Haj M. (1990) *Umleavyo*. Nairobi/Dar es Salaam: Oxford University Press
Harries L. (1965) *Swahili Prose Texts*, London/Nairobi: Oxford University Press
Hasani b. I. (1968) *The Medecine Man. Swifa ya nguvumali*, Oxford: Clarendon Press
Kalindimya J. E. (1988) *Wimbi la huzuni*, Dar es Salaam: Tajack Industries Ltd
____(1989) *Mtafutano*, Dar es Salaam: Tajack Industries Ltd
Kamugisha T. A. R. (2000) *Kitu kidogo tu!* Dar es Salaam: MPB Enterprises
Kareithi P. M. (1969) *Kaburi bila msalaba*, Nairobi: Phoenix Publishers
Katalambulla F. H. H. (1965) *Simu ya kifo*, Nairobi: KLB
____(1975) *Buriani*, Dar es Salaam: EALB
____(1977) *Pili Pilipili*, Kampala: EALB
Kezilahabi E. (1971) *Rosa Mistika*, Nairobi: EALB
____(1974) *Kichwa maji*, Dar es Salaam: EAPH
____(1975) *Dunia uwanja wa fujo*. Kampala: EALB
____(1979) *Gamba la nyoka*, Arusha Tanzania: Africa Publications

____(1990) *Nagona*, Dar es Salaam: Dar es Salaam University Press
____(1991) *Mzingile*, Dar es Salaam: Dar es Salaam University Press
Kharusi N. S. (1966) 'Usinisahau', *Swahili* 36: 56-80
Kiango S. D. (1974) *Jeraha la moyo*, Nairobi: Foundation Books
Kibao S. A. (1975) *Matatu ya thamani*, Nairobi: Heinemann
Kiimbila J. K. (1966) *Lila na Fila*, Dar es Salaam: Longman
____(1971) *Ubeberu utashindwa*, Dar es Salaam: Chuo cha Uchunguzi wa Kiswahili
King'ala Y. M. (1984) *Anasa*, Nairobi: Heinemann
Kirumbi P. S. (1971) *Nataka iwe siri*, Dar es Salaam: Chuo Kikuu cha Dar es Salaam
Kitereza A. (1980) *Bwana Myombekere na Bibi Bugonoka na Ntulanalwo na Bulihwali*, Dar es Salaam: TPH
____(1996) *Les enfants du faiseur de pluie*, Paris: Unesco/L'Harmattan
____(1999) *Le tueur de serpents*, Paris: Unesco/L'Harmattan
Kitogo S. (1984) *Cha moto atakiona*. Dar es Salaam: G. J. Publishers and Artist
Komba S. M. (1978) *Pete*, Dar es Salaam: TUKI
Kondo I. G. (1985) *Ashura*, Peramilho: Benedictine Publication Ndanda
Kuboja N. J. (1971) *Mbojo: simba-mtu*, Nairobi/Kampala/Dar es Salaam: EALB
Levi G. (1975) *Mpelelezi hodari na genge la wahalifu*, Nairobi: KLB
____(1981) *Mbegu za chuki*, Nairobi: KLB
Levi Shimanyula G. (1981) *Fedheha ya fedha*, Nairobi: KLB
Liwenga G. (1981) *Nyota ya huzuni*, Dar es Salaam: TPH
Mbatiah A. M. (1999b) *Upotevu*, Nairobi: Standard Textbooks Graphics and Publishing
Mbega O. (1982) *Ndoto kivulini*, Dar es Salaam: International Publisher Agencies
Mbelwa H. C. M. (1973) *Donda ndugu*, Dar es Salaam: TPH
____(1974) *Mfu aliyefufuka*, Nairobi/Dar es Salaam/Kampala: EALB
Mbogo E. (1996) *Vipuli vya figo*, Nairobi/Kampala/Dar es Salaam: EAEP
Mbotela J. (1959) *Uhuru wa watumwa*, London/Edinburgh/Melbourne/Johannesburg: Thomas Nelson and Sons Ltd
Mcharo P. A. (1988) *Mkumba vana mwamba wa mauti*, Dar es Salaam: Nyota Publishers Ltd
Merinyo C. (1988) *Kifo cha AIDS*, Dar es Salaam: Grand Arts Promotion
Mfaume B. (1993) *Tufani*, Dar es Salaam: Heko Publishers
Mhina G. (1996) 'Safari ya ndoa saba', *Swahili* 36: 15-42
____(1971) *Mtu ni utu*, Dar es Salaam: TPH

_____ (1986) *Kovu*, Dar es Salaam: Press and Publicity Centre
Mkangi K. (1984) *Mafuta*, Nairobi: Heinemann
_____(1994) *Ukiwa*, Nairobi: EAEP
_____(1995) *Walenisi*, Nairobi: EAEP
Mkufya W. E. (1999) *Ziraili na Zirani*, Dar es Salaam: EAPH,
Mohamed S. A. (1977) *Asali chungu*, Nairobi: Shungwaya Publishers
_____(1980a) *Dunia mti mkavu*, Nairobi: Longman Kenya
_____(1980b) *Utengano*, Nairobi: Longman Kenya
_____(1985) *Si shetani si wazimu*, Zanzibar: Zanzibar Publishers Ltd
_____(1988a) *Kiza katika nuru*, Nairobi: Oxford University Press
_____(1988b) *Pungwa*, Nairobi: Longman Kenya
_____(1990) *Tata za Asumini*, Nairobi: Longman Kenya
_____(2001) *Babu alipofufuka*, Nairobi: Jomo Kenyatta Foundation
Moyo S. B. (1990) *Daima nitaheshimu polisi*, Ndanda-Peramilho: Benedictine Publications
Mtobwa B. R. (1986) *Pesa zako zinanuka*, Dar es Salaam: Heko Publishers
_____(1987a) *Salamu toka kuzimu*, Dar es Salaam: Heko Publishers
_____(1987b) *Tutarudi na roho zetu?* Dar es Salaam: Heko Publishers
_____(1988) *Malaika wa shetani*, Dar es Salaam: Heko Publishers
_____(1989) *Dar es Salaam usiku*, Dar es Salaam: Heko Publishers
_____(1989) *Zawadi ya ushindi*, Dar es Salaam: Heko Publishers
_____(1994) *Roho ya paka*, Dar es Salaam: Heko Publishers
_____(1995) *Nyuma ya mapazia*, Dar es Salaam: Heko Publishers
_____(1998) *Kipofu mwenye miwani myeusi*, Dar es Salaam: Heko Publishers
_____(2000) *Mhariri msalabani: siku mia moja na hamsini za mateso katika maisha yangu*, Dar es Salaam: Heko Publishers
_____(2003) *Najisikia kuua tena*, Nairobi/Kampala/Dar es Salaam: Mkuki Books
_____ (n.d.) *Mikononi mwa nunda*, Dar es Salaam: Heko Publishers
Mukajanga K. D. (1982) *Kitanda cha mauti*, Dar es Salaam: Grand Arts Promotion
_____(1985) *Mpenzi*, Dar es Salaam: Grand Arts Promotion
Mung'ong'o C. G. M. (1977) *Mirathi ya hatari*, Dar es Salaam: TPH
_____(1980) *Njozi iliyopotea*, Dar es Salaam: TPH
Muridhania K. *Damu ya ulimi*, Dar es Salaam: TPH , n.d.
Mushi J. S. (1969) *Baadha ya dhiki faraja*, Dar es Salaam: TPH
Musiba A. E. (1979) *Kikosi cha kikasi*, Dar es Salaam: G.C.E. Ltd
_____(1988) *Hofu*, Dar es Salaam: M & K Publishers & Agencies Ltd
_____(2000) *Uchu*, Dar es Salaam: Dachi Investment Co. Ltd
Mvungi M. (1975) *Hana hatia*, Dar es Salaam: TPH na TUKI
Mwaduma S. Z. (1974) *Simbayavene*, London: University of London Press

Ndibalema C. (1974) *Fimbo ya ulimwengu*, Nairobi: Heinemann
Ndumbu A. (1976) *Mbio za sakafuni*, Kampala/Nairobi/Dar es Salaam: EALB
Ngare P. (1975) *Kikulacho ki nguoni mwako*, Nairobi: EAPH
Ngomoi J. (1977) *Ndoto ya Ndaria*, Dar es Salaam: TPH
Njama A. H. (1995) *Haki haizami*, Nairobi: Jomo Kenyatta Foundation
_____(2000) *Mkondo wa maisha*, Nairobi: Jomo Kenyatta Foundation
Nkussa H. (2001) *Kikulacho*, Dar es Salaam: Ruvu Publishers
Nkwera F. V. (1967) *Mzishi wa baba ana radhi*, Dar es Salaam/Kampala/Nairobi: EALB
Nshiko T. (1978) *Fimbo ya mnyonge*, Dar es Salaam: TPH
Nurru S. M. (1974) *Ndoa ya mzimuni*, Nairobi: KLB
Nyandindi M. Y. (1991) *Kanyago la maisha*, Ndanda-Peramilho: Benedictine Publications
Nyaruba S. M. [1987] *Bado aziri* (Self published)
Nyasulu G. (1974) *Laana ya Pandu*, Nairobi/Kampala/Dar es Salaam: EALB
Nyerere J. K. (1973) *Ujamaa*, Oxford: OUP
Ole Kulet H. R. (1990) *Maisha ya hatari*, Nairobi: Longman Kenya
Omari C. K. (1971) *Mwenda kwao*, Dar es Salaam: Chuo che Uchunguzi wa Kiswahili
_____1976) *Kuanguliwa kwa kifaranga*, Nairobi: Heinemann
Riwa N. L. (1964) *Kisa cha sultani Hatibu*, Nairobi: Oxford University Press
Robert S. (1966) *Kusadikika*, Dar es Salaam: Nelson East Africa
_____(1967a) *Masomo yenye Adili*, Nairobi: Nelson East Africa
_____(1967b) *Wasifu wa Binti Saad*, Nairobi: Nelson East Africa
_____(1968a) *Adili na nduguze*, London: Macmillan
_____(1968b) *Kielezo cha fasihi*, Dar es Salaam: Nelson
_____(1968c) *Kufikirika*, Nairobi: Oxford University Press
_____(1968d) *Siku ya watenzi wote*, Nairobi: Nelson
_____(1968e) *Utubora mkulima*, Dar es Salaam: Nelson East Africa
_____(1971) *Insha na mashairi*, Dar es Salaam: Nelson East Africa
_____(1991) *Maisha yangu na Baada ya miaka hamsini*, Dar es Salaam: Mkuki na Nyota Publishers
Ruhumbika G. (1978) *Uwike usiwike kutakucha*, Arusha/Dar es Salaam: EAP
_____(1992) *Miradi Bubu ya wazalendo*, Dar es Salaam: TPH
_____(2002) *Janga sugu la wazawa*, Dar es Salaam: E & D Ltd
Saffari A. J. *Harusi*, (1993a) Dar es Salaam: Dar es Salaam University Press
Shafi S. A. (1978) *Kasri ya Mwinyi Fuad*, Dar es Salaam: TPH
_____1979) *Kuli*, Dar es Salaam: Tanzani Publishing House
_____(1986) *Les girofliers de Zanzibar*, Paris: Karthala

____(1999) *Vuta n'kuvute*, Dar es Salaam: Mkuki na Nyota Publishers
____(2003) *Haini*, Nairobi: Longhorn Publishers
Simani E. M. (2002) *Malimwengu msumeno*, Nairobi: Licars Enterprises
Simbamwene J. M. S. (1971) *Mwisho wa mapenzi*, Dar es Salaam: Longman Tanzania
____1972) *Kwa sababu ya pesa*, Nairobi: Longman
____(1978) *Kivumbi uwanjani*, London: Transafrica/TLS
____(1988) *Sikutaki umefilisika*, Dar es Salaam: Jomssi Publications
Somba J. N. (1968) *Kuishi kwingi ni kuona mengi*, Nairobi: EAPH
Suleiman M. (1972) *Kiu*, Dar es Salaam: EAPH
____(1976) *Nyota ya Rehema*, Nairobi: Oxford University Press
____(1978) *Kicheko cha ushindi*, Nairobi: Shungwaya Publishers
Ugula P. (1969) *Ufunguo wenye hazina*, London: Evans Brothers Limited
Velten C. (1901) *Safari za Wasuaheli*, Göttingen: Vandenhoeck und Ruprecht
____(1903) *Desturi za Wasuaheli*, Göttingen: Vandenhoeck und Ruprecht
Wahab Z. B. A. (1985) *Kikulacho*, Nairobi: KLB
Walibora K. (1996) *Siku njema*, Nairobi: Longhorn Publishers
____(2003) *Kufa kuzikana*, Nairobi: Longhorn Publishers
Wambura S. K. (1990) *Nuru ya Bhoke Gesimba*, Dar es Salaam: Ruvu Publishers Ltd
Wambura S. P. (1980) *Atafutaye hakosi*, Nairobi: KLB
Wamitila K. W. (2002) *Bina-Adamu!* Nairobi: Phoenix Publishers
____(2003) *Nguvu ya sala*, Nairobi/Kampala: Longhorn Publishers
Whiteley W. H. (1971) *Maisha ya Hamed bin Muhammed El-Murjebi yaani Tippu Tip*, Kampala/Nairobi/Dar es Salaam: EALB

Articles and Critical Studies

Aiello F. (1999) 'Mabadiliko ni maumbile yenyewe: the thematic and stylistic dynamism in S.A. Mohamed's novel *Utengano*', *Afrikanistiches Arbeitspapiere* [*AAP*] 60: 59-65
Allen J. W. T. (1971) *The Customs of the Swahili People. The Desturi za Waswahili of Mtoro bin Mwinyi Bakari and other Swahili Persons*, Berkeley/London: University of California Press
Arnold R. (1973) 'Swahili literature and modern history: a necessary remark on literary criticism', *Kiswahili* 42/43: 68-73
____(1977) *Afrikanische Literatur und nationale Befreiung: Menschenbildung, Gesellschaftskonzeption im Prosawerk Shaaban*

Roberts, Berlin: Akademie-Verlag
Barthes R. (1977) 'Introduction à l'analyse structurale des récits', in *Poétique du récit*, Paris: Editions du Seuil, 7-57
Bayard P. (1998) *Qui a tué Roger Ackroyd*, Paris: Editions de Minuit
Beckerleg S. E. (1990) *Maintaining order, creating chaos: Swahili medicine in Kenya*, SOAS, London
Bernander L. (1977) 'Interview with E. Kezilahabi', *Lugha* 1: 46-50
Bertoncini-Zúbkova, E. (1993) 'La littérature swahili entre l'Ujamaa et la démocratie', in *Colloque APELA: Littératures africaines et démocraties*, Université Paris IV (unpublished paper)
____(1994) 'La maladie et la mort dans les oeuvres de Kezilahabi', *Littérature et maladie en Afrique*. Actes du Congrés de l'*APELA*, Paris: L'Harmattan, 49-55
____(1995) 'Tabous et transgressions dans le roman swahili *Mafuta* par Kamata Mkangi', in *Colloque APELA: Tabous et transgressions*, Université Internationale de Lisbonne (unpublished paper)
____(1992) 'Stylistic Approaches to E. Kezilahabi's Novels and Poetry', *Afrikanistische Arbeitspapiere* 31, 5-67
____et al., eds, (1989) *Outline of Swahili Literature. Prose Fiction and Drama*, Leiden: E. J. Brill (second edition, revised and enlarged, 2009)
Berwouts K. (1991) *Le sein de la mère. Introduction à la littérature classique et moderne en Swahili*, Bruxelles: ASDOC/CEDAF
Binali P. S. (1973) 'Mizimu wa watu wa kale na Kisima cha Giningi', *Kioo cha Lugha* 3, 12-31
Blommaert J. (1997) 'The impact of state ideology on language: Ujamaa and Swahili literature in Tanzania', in *Human Contact through Language and Linguistics*, Frankfurt: Peter Lang, 253-270
Broomfield G. W. (1930) 'The development of the Swahili language', *Africa* III: 516-522
Deleuze G. and Guattari F. (1975) *Kafka. Pour une littérature mineure*, Paris: Minuit
Eastman C. M. (1972) 'The theme of mistaken identity and the trend of modern Swahili literature', paper delivered at the Fifteenth Annual Meeting of the African Studies Association, Philadelphia
Gatare J. K. (1993) 'Dini katika Riwaya za Euphrase Kezilahabi', University of Nairobi, Nairobi, unpublished MA dissertation
Gibbe A. G. N. M. (1978), 'Dhima ya Mhakiki', *Mulika* 12, 2-8
____(1982) 'Baadhi ya Taswira katika *Gamba la Nyoka*', *Kiswahili* 49: 9-14
Harries L. (1967) 'Style in swahili', *Swahili* 37: 47-51
Hussein E. N. (1971) Ufundi wa Muhammed Said Abdulla, in F. M. Topan, ed., *Uchambuzi ya maandishi wa Kiswahili*, London: Oxford University Press, 21-26

Kafka F. (1948) *The Diaries of Franz Kafka 1914-1923*, New York: Schocken Books
____([1912] 1994) Discours sur la langue Yiddish, in *Préparatifs de noces à la campagne*, Paris: Gallimard, 478-483
Kanyalika K. Z. (1975) 'Duniani kuna watu', *Mulika* 7: 17-23
Kanyarukiga E. (1981) Littérature nationale de langue africaine. Euphrase Kezilahabi, romancier tanzanien contemporain, Université Paris III, Paris, unpublished dissertation
Kezilahabi E. (1973) 'The Development of Swahili poetry: 18th-20th Century', *Kiswahili* 42/43, 62-67
____(1975b) 'Riwaya za upepelezi katika fasihi ya kiswahili', *Kiswahili* 45: 36-40
____(1976) *Shaaban Robert: Mwandishi wa riwaya*, University of Dar es Salaam, Dar es Salaam
____(1980) 'The Swahili Novel and the Common Man in East Africa', in Ulla Schild (ed.), *The East African Experience: Essays on English and Swahili Literature*. Berlin: Reimer, 75-84
____(1985) *African Philosophy and the Problem of Literary Interpretation*, Madison: The University of Wisconsin
____(1988) 'Ideological and Material Problems in the Production of Swahili Literary Works', *Kiswahili* 55: 36-44
Khamis S. A. M. (2001a) 'Classicism in Shaaban Robert's Utopian Novel *Kusadikika*', *Research in African Literatures* 32: 47-6
____(2001b) 'Fabulation and Politics in the '90s in Kezilahabi's Novel *Nagona*', in Charles Bodunde (ed.), *African Languages Literature in the Political Context of the 1990s*. Bayreuth: Breitinger, 119-133
Kimura E. (1991) Mabadaliko ya kijamii na riwaya ya upelelezi Tanzania. Dar es Salaam: Chuo Kikuu cha Dar es Salaam
Kitsao J. (1982) *An Investigation of Themes in Swahili Literature and an Application of Stylostatistics to Chosen Texts*, University of Nairobi: Nairobi
Lugano R. S. (1989) *Mwanamke katika Riwaya za Kezilahabi*, Nairobi: Chuo Kikuu cha Nairobi
Madumulla J. S. (1986) 'The Development of the Modern Kiswahili Novel in Tanzania with Special Attention to that of the Seventies'. Unpublished dissertation, Leipzig: Karl-Marx Universität
____(1987) 'Maendeleo ya wahusika katika riwaya ya Kiswahili Tanzania', *Kiswahili* 54: 66-76
____(1988) 'Riwaya ya Kiswahili (Tanzania) katika Miaka ya Themanini', *Mulika* 20: 9-25
Maganga M. 'A. Maisha ya Shaaban Robert na mawazo yake', in Farouk M. Topan, ed., *Uchambuzi ya maandishi wa Kiswahili: kitabu cha Kwanza*, Dar es Salaam: Oxford University Press, 1971
Mattew M. L. (1976) 'Fani ya hadithi: riwaya', *Kioo cha Lugha* 6: 7-13

Mazrui A. M. (1984) 'Dunia Mti Mkavu', *Kiswahili* 51, 198-208
Mbatiah A. M. (1997) 'Commitment in the Swahili Novel: An Appraisal of the Works of Said Ahmed Mohamed', *Kiswahili* 59: 13-20
____(1998) 'Mienendo Mipya katika Uandishi ya Kezilahabi: *Nagona* na *Mzingile*', *Mulika* 24: 1-13
____(1999) 'The origin and development of the swahili thesis novel in Tanzania', unpublished thesis, University of Nairobi, Nairobi
Mbughuni P. (1978a) *The politicization of Kiswahili literature*. Ohio ID: Indiana University Press
____(1978b) 'The Theme of a New Society in the Kiswahili Prose Tradition', *Kiswahili* 48, 17-37
Mhina G. (1967) 'Style in swahili', *Swahili* 37: 189-191
Mlacha S. A. K. (1984) 'Riwaya za visiwani (1970-1980) na ujenzi wa jamii mpya', *Mulika* 16: 4-31
____(1985) 'Wahusika katika riwaya za Kiswahili Tanzania (1970-1982)', *Mulika* 17: 29-45
____(1986) 'Uprooting the Traditional Culture in Kiswahili Prose Fiction', *Africana Marbugensia* 19: 95-106
____(1987) *The portrayal of cultural conflict in Kiswahili prose fiction: a structural study of the novels of Euphrase Kezilahabi*, London: SOAS
____(1988) 'The Imagery of Conflict on the Three Novels of Kezilahabi', *AAP* 16: 149-157
____(1989) 'The Use of Metaphors in Kezilahabi's Novel: *Rosa Mistika*', *Kiswahili* 56: 25-31
Mlacha S. A. K. and Madumulla J. S. (1991) *Riwaya ya Kiswahili*, Dar es Salaam: Dar es Salaam University Press
Mmahani A. P. W. (1976) 'Uhuru wa Watumwa – J. Mbotela', *Kioo cha Lugha* 6: 32-36
Mohamed S. A. (1973) 'Mzimu wa watu wa kale. Bwana Musa si "Jini"', *Mulika* 3: 42-47
____(1997) 'Learning from Mwenda Mbatia: the Literary Critic', *Kiswahili* 60: 87-96
Mulokozi M. M. (1976) 'Fasihi na Mapinduzi', *Kioo cha Lugha* 4/5: 84-94
Musau P. M. (1985) 'Euphrase Kezilahabi: Mwandishi aliyekataa Tamaa', unpublished dissertation, University of Nairobi
Ndalu A. and King'ei K. G. (1989) *Kamusi ya methali za kiswahili*, Nairobi: Heinemann Kenya
Njogu K. (1997) *Uhakiki wa Riwaya za Visiwani Zanzibar*, Nairobi: Nairobi University Press
Ohly R. (1973) 'Historical approach to Swahili literature: as heretofore an open question', *Kiswahili* 43: 79-87

_____(1981) *Aggressive prose*, Dar es Salaam: Institute of Kiswahili Research

Omari C. K. (1972) 'Uandishi kwa Jamii', *Kioo cha Lugha* 2: 4-8

Ramadhani J. A. (1972) 'Fasihi ya kiswahili', *Mulika* 2: 6-11

Rettová A. (2011), 'L'existentialisme et la littérature swahili', in V. Coulon and X. Garnier (eds), *Les littératures africaines. Textes et terrains*, Paris: Karthala: 427-442

Robert M. (1977) *Roman des origines et origines du roman*, Paris: Gallimard

Rosset C. (1976) *Le réel et son double*, Paris: Gallimard

Sacleux Ch. (1939) *Dictionnaire swahili-français*, Paris: Travaux et mémoires de l'Institut d'ethnologie.

Saffari A. J. (1993) Uchawi katika riwaya za kiswahili. *Fasihi, Uandishi na Uchapishaji. Makala ya semina ya umoja wa waandishi wa vitabu Tanzania.* Uwavita: Dar es Salaam University Press

Sengo T. S. Y. (1973a) 'Dhima ya fasihi kwa maendeleo ya jamii', *Kiswahili* 43: 76-78

_____(1973b) 'Uwanja wa Tahakiki', *Kioo cha Lugha* 3: 10-12

Senkoro F.E.M.K. (1972) 'Nionavyo *Mzishi wa Baba ana Radhi*', *Kioo cha Lugha* 2: 9-13

_____(1973) 'Ndimi na hisi za wahakiki', *Kio cha Lugha* 3: 4-6

_____(1976) 'Utamaduni katika riwaya ya Kiswahili', *Kiswahili* 46: 74-97

_____(1987) *Fasihi na jamii*, Dar es Salaam: Press and Publicity Centre

Shariff I. N. (1991) 'Islam and Secularity in Swahili Literature: an Overview', in Kenneth W. Harrow, ed., *Faces of Islam in African Literature*. Portsmouth/London: Heinemann/James Currey, 1991. 37-57

Shija A. N. (1971) Wahusika wa Shaaban Robert, in Farouk M. Topan (ed.), *Uchambuzi ya maandishi wa Kiswahili*, Dar es Salaam: Oxford University Press

Swaleh A (1997) 'The Image of Woman in S.A. Mohamed's *Tata za Asumini*', *Kiswahili* 60: 25-30

Van Dine S.S. (1928) 'Twenty rules for writing detective stories', *The American Magazine*.

Wamitila K. W. (1991) 'Nagona and Mzingile: Kezilahabi's Metaphysics', *Kiswahili* 58: 62-68

_____(1997) 'The Kiswahili Writers and the Critic: a Response to Mwenda Mbatia's Polemics', *Kiswahili* 60: 97-106

_____(1998a) 'A philosophical labyrinth: tracing two critical motifs in Kezilahabi's prose works', *Swahili Forum V*, 79-91

_____(1998b) 'Toward unlocking Kamata Kangi's *Walenisi*: a case of parabolic narrative?' *Kiswahili* 61: 83-93

____(2001) *Kamusi ya methali*, Nairobi: Longhorn Publishers
Whiteley W. H. (1969) *Swahili. The Rise of a National Language*, London: Methuen
Williams J. C. (1973) 'Mzimu wa watu wa kale', *Mulika* 3: 33-36

Index

Abdulla M. S. 17, 65, 72, 73, 142, 143, 144, 146, 147, 148, 150, 151, 152, 153, 154, 155, 156, 157, 158, 159, 161, 162, 179, 182, 188
Abdul-Wahab Z. B. 129, 182
Aiello F. 187
Akwilombe R. 17, 182
Allen J. W. T. 19, 20
Anduru A. 28, 182
Arnold R. 1, 187

Baalawy S. O. S. 24, 182
Baka A. 63, 182
Balisidya N. 76, 182
Banzi A. 30, 182
Barthes R. 147, 188
Bayard P. 145, 147, 148, 149, 161, 162, 188
Beckerleg S. E. 16, 188
Bernander L. 86, 188
Bertoncini E. 44, 101, 188
Berwouts K. 188
Binali P. S. 142, 188
Block H P. 182
Blommaert J. 17, 95, 188
Brommfield G. W. 5, 6, 188
Burhani Z. 70, 182
Büttner C. 182
Buyu J. 26, 30, 39, 183

Chachage C. S. 131, 132, 133, 134, 135, 183
Charo (Kateta Mwana) 23, 183
Chimerah R. 183
Chiume M. W. K. 105, 183

Dar es Salaam 3, 10, 103, 130, 131, 133, 142, 160
Deleuze G. and Guattari F. 2, 8, 13, 14, 179, 188
Dumila F. 63,183

East African Swahili Committee 5, 6, 7, 8, 9
Eastman C. M. 65, 188

Farsy M. S. 43, 44, 45, 183

Ganzel E. 128, 183
Gatare J. K. 188
Geranija P. C. 72, 183
Gibbe A. G. N. M. 10, 188

Habwe J. 70, 74, 183
Haj M. 64, 183
Harries L. 7, 8, 9, 19, 183
Hasani b. I. 143, 183
Hussein E. N. 142, 143, 188

initiation 15, 16, 24, 73, 76, 78, 79, 81, 83, 85

Kafka F. 2, 5, 8, 14, 179, 180, 188, 189
Kalindimya J. E. 128, 129, 183
Kamugisha T. A. 137-138, 183
Kanyalika K. Z. 143, 189
Kanyarukiga E. 189
Kareithi P. M. 105, 183
Katalambulla F. H. H. 144, 154, 155, 160, 183
Kenya 25, 63, 99, 102, 105, 137
Kezilahabi E. 1, 6, 9, 12-16, 39, 64, 68, 72, 74, 75-76, 78-94, 138, 140,

193

194 Index

142, 143, 179, 181, 183, 188, 189, 190, 191
Khamis S. A. 189
Kharusi N. S. 44-45, 184
Kiango S. D. 72, 184
Kibao S. A. 184
Kiimbila J. K. 104, 184
Kimura E. 143, 189
King'ala Y. M. 73, 74, 184
King'ei K. G. 63, 190
Kirumbi P . S. 72, 184
Kitereza A. 25, 26, 27, 30, 33-39, 184
Kitsao J. 6, 189
Kitogo S. 128, 184
Komba S. M. 72, 184
Kondo I. G. 64, 184
Kuboja N. J. 143, 144, 184

Levi G. 127, 128, 184
Lienhardt P. 143
Liwenga G. 135, 184
Lugano R. S. 189

Madumulla J. S. 1, 104, 189, 190
Maganga M. A. 189
Mambo Leo 5
Mattew M. L. 190
Mau Mau 105
Mazrui A. M. 11, 190
Mbatia(h) A. M. 9, 11, 12, 72, 184, 190, 191
Mbega O. 73, 184
Mbelwa H. C. M. 76, 129, 184
Mbogo E. 137, 184
Mbotela J. 2, 22, 99, 184, 190
Mbughuni P. 14, 95, 190
Mcharo P. A. 67, 184
Merinyo C. 72, 184
Mfaume B. 129, 184
Mhina G. 6, 7, 9, 10, 65, 67, 71, 185, 190
Mkangi K. 68, 69, 99-102, 185, 188
Mkufya W. E. 140, 185
Mlacha S. A. K. 3, 104, 190
Mmahani A. P. W. 190
Mnyampala M. 9

Mohamed S. A. 10, 11, 12, 16, 64, 68, 142, 161, 163-177
Moyo S. B. 127, 185
Mtobwa B. R. 99, 107, 108, 110-113, 128-131, 155, 178, 181, 185
Mukajanga K. D 68, 74, 185
Mulokozi M. M. 190
Mung'ong'o C. G. 10, 31, 32, 77, 135, 185
Muridhania K. 30, 66, 67, 185
Musau P. M. 190
Mushi J. S. 67, 185
Musiba A. E. 107, 108, 185
Muwanga A. S. 72, 183
Mvungi M. 129, 185
Mwaduma S. Z. 67, 186

Nairobi 77
National Swahili Council (BAKITA/ *Baraza la Kiswahili la Taifa*) 9
Ndalu A. 63, 190
Ndibalema C. 6, 186
Ndumbu A. C. 64, 186
Ngare P. 106, 186
Ngomoi J. 103, 186
Njama A. H. 72, 74, 186
Njogu K. 11, 190
Nkussa H. 129, 186
Nkwera F. V. 26, 30, 186
Nshiko T. 104, 186
Nurru S. M. 28, 186
Nyandindi M. Y. 64, 186
Nyaruba S. M. 129, 186
Nyasulu G. 129, 186
Nyerere J. K. 12, 95, 102, 103, 106, 113, 135, 186

Ohly R. 1, 17, 191
Ole Kulet H. R. 129, 186
Omari C. K. 12, 27, 129, 186, 191

proverb 23-25, 41, 42, 63

Ramadhani J. A. 4, 191
realism 4, 15, 24, 78, 104,
Rettová 120, 191

Riwa N. L. 24, 186
Robert (Marthe) 66, 67, 191
Robert (Shaaban) 1, 6, 7, 9, 23, 42, 46, 47-62, 63, 64, 98, 104, 144, 179, 186, 189,
Rosset C. 115, 126, 191
Ruhumbika G. 6, 33, 39, 135, 136, 186

Saffari A. J. 143, 186, 191
Sengo T. S. Y. 191
Senkoro F. E. M. K. 10, 26, 191
Shafi S. A. 11, 96-99, 105, 170, 186
Shariff I. N. 5, 191
Shija A. N. 56, 191
Simani E. M. 63, 187
Simbamwene J. M. 71, 73, 129, 187
socialism 102
Somba J. N. 76, 187
Suleiman M. 11, 23, 114, 115-126, 127, 187
Swaleh A. 191

tale 15, 22-25, 29, 40-47, 50, 58, 59, 65, 101, 103, 104
Tanzania 1, 9, 12, 14, 15, 16, 26, 27, 73, 95, 102, 104, 106, 107, 110, 112, 113, 135, 138, 142, 143, 154, 155
tradition 1, 5, 15, 19, 29, 33, 39-42, 47, 57-60, 64, 65, 67, 95, 103, 104, 143

Ugula P. 103, 187
Ujamaa 11, 15, 66, 81, 82, 90, 95, 102-104, 106, 107, 135, 136, 142, 186, 188
Ukerewe Islands 21, 25, 33, 34, 38, 39, 79, 89
Utopia 55, 60, 63, 91, 102-104, 189

Velten C. 19-21, 40, 45, 187

Walibora K. 139, 187
Wambura S. K. 64, 187
Wambura S. P. 66, 187
Wamitila K. W. 11, 63, 68, 72, 102, 140, 141, 187, 191
Whiteley W. H. 5, 187, 191
Williams J. C. 161, 192

Zanzibar 4, 11, 17, 44, 45, 96, 97, 123, 143, 144, 146, 147, 149, 59, 173, 174, 185, 187, 190